SHAKESPEARE:

a hidden life sung

in a hidden song

Ian Steere

For Anni

With thanks, too,

to Amy, Anna & John

And a salute to that small spirit of park

who none see go

Matador
5 Weir Road
Kibworth Beauchamp-
Leicester LE8 0LQ, UK
Tel: (+44) 116 279 2299
Fax: (+44) 116 279 2277
Email: books@troubador.co.uk
Web: www.troubador.co.uk/matador

British Library Cataloguing in Publication Data.
A catalogue record for this book is available from the British Library.

9781848765115

Printed in Great Britain by the MPG Books Group, Bodmin and King's Lynn

CONTENTS

PREFACE   iv

THE TRUTH OF THE SONNETS   1
Introduction   1
Shakespeare's Sonnets   1
Sonnet Theories   3
The Pembroke Theory   3
The Southampton Theory   6
Other Theories   9
The Thomas Nashe Evidence   11
The Case Developed   13
Timing of the Sonnets   17
Comparison with History   19
Possession of the Sonnets   22
Publication of the Sonnets   23
The Fair Friend   27
The Dark Lady   27
The Story of the Rival Poet   31
Rowse's Case for the Rival   36
The Case against Marlowe   38
The Clinching Evidence   40
Conclusions   45
Experiencing the Sonnets   52

A HIDDEN SONG RESUNG   55

Appendix A   Published by whose Will?   366
Appendix B   Crossing Paths with Thomas Nashe   383
Appendix C   A Search for Rosaline   400
Appendix D   Rival or Collaborator?   407
Appendix E   Hues in all their Hews   418
Appendix F   Who Threw Hate Away?   421
Appendix G   A Closer Look at Mr. WH   423

SOURCES & BIBLIOGRAPHY   426

PREFACE

Shakespeare's Sonnets: most enigmatic of his works, with their pervasive hints of underlying biography and riddles of publication. Fact or fiction? His or another's? Authorized or not? Arguments abound - unabated after more than two hundred years.

This book draws on substantive new evidence to reveal the truth. It serves serious students, but will also appeal to readers who are intrigued by mystery, entertaining history or just a wish to understand the poems.

Part I, *The Truth of the Sonnets*, starts with an overview of their story and the theories. It develops the evidence to resolve all but one of the main puzzles. It substantiates – for the first time beyond reasonable doubt - their revelations of the entangled affairs of a licentious young lord and three of his lovers. A compelling new explanation emerges for the strange death of Christopher Marlowe.

In Part II, *A Hidden Song Resung*, the primary evidence is supplemented and supported by further discovery within the Sonnets. Each of the 154 poems is accompanied by commentary and a modernized rendition, to allow easy assimilation of the medium and its layers of meaning. Bawdy subtext is explained and corroborated with usage within Shakespeare's plays (in some cases for the first time). History emerges in the voice of William Shakespeare, telling his own extraordinary story across the ages.

PART I

THE TRUTH OF THE SONNETS

Introduction

England's most famous author stands blurred in the shimmer of history. Some even challenge his authorship, so hazy is the detail of his life.

Consequently, although Shakespeare left us nearly one million words and a horde of characters, his own character and most of his activities have remained elusive.

Such mystery extends seemingly to his sonnets. These poems were, on contemporary observation, intended for private consumption[1]. Their language is often archaic and it is easy for us, living over four centuries later, to miss the subtleties and double meanings designed to stimulate their original audience, who had the advantage of context and background.

Nevertheless, with the many insights afforded by generations of analysts and a number of discoveries outlined below, the Sonnets shed startling light on the Stratfordian, his complicated love-life and several of his contemporaries.

Similar assertions have been made before. Each has lacked sufficient evidence and has failed to win general acceptance. Yet, in the following outline I expect to persuade anyone of an open mind that here survives part of the record of an extraordinary private life!

Shakespeare's Sonnets

In 1609 a collection of one hundred and fifty four poems, entitled *Shake-speares Sonnets*, was published by one, Thomas Thorpe, who provided an enigmatic dedication of these poems to their "only begetter", a Master "WH". Given its association with

---

[1]   In 1598 Francis Meres wrote in his *Palladis Tamia* that "the sweet witty soul of Ovid lives in mellifluous and honey-tongued Shakespeare, witness his *Venus & Adonis*, his *Lucrece*, his sugared sonnets among his private friends".

1

so popular an author at the summit of his career, this work was incongruous. It carried no acknowledgement from the poet. Its themes were often offensive to contemporary culture, yet sometimes boringly mundane. It attracted hostile comment[2]. And it sank into obscurity until interest arose some two centuries later, centred largely on what the work might reveal of the author.

The poems are presented in a structured order. Sonnets 1-126 (all of which lack any absolute indicator of a female subject) appear to be addressed to or for the benefit of a young man; Sonnets 127-154 appear largely to concern a dark-haired woman, whom the poet describes as his mistress. Observers have long recognized that the poems suggest an underlying story:

- Initially the poet urges an anonymous, effeminate-looking young aristocrat to secure his lineage through the fathering of a son in marriage.
- However, he becomes taken with the young lord. The urgings to marry cease and an intimate relationship develops between the two.
- The aristocrat then betrays the poet, being seduced by the latter's unidentified mistress, of dark hair and eyes, who has plagued the smitten poet in a dysfunctional, one-sided relationship.
- The distraught poet contrives to forgive the aristocrat, but is then superseded in the latter's esteem by a rival, who is preeminent among poets competing for the young lord's benefits.
- The poems continue with some bitterness and recriminations at this development until suddenly the rival disappears, with no explanation.
- The poet attempts to patch things up with the aristocrat, but is unsuccessful. And he loses his mistress.

For some two centuries, commentators have been divided on whether the sonnets contain biography, and, if so, who were their characters.

---

[2]   An original Quarto printing in the Rosenbach Library, Philadelphia, is annotated by its irate reader: "What a heap of wretched Infidel Stuff"

Sonnet Theories

There are three widely held orthodox theories. The first asserts that there is little to be read into the Sonnets but their artistry[3]. The appearance of an underlying story is regarded as coincidence, as part of their fiction or as contrived by editorial ordering of the poems. However, the odds are long that so many of the sonnets contribute by chance to the unusual, coherent and fictionally unattractive themes outlined above. Nor does such scepticism adequately explain the many highly prescriptive messages encountered in the collection[4]. The theory is essentially a default position, reliant on the absence of better explanations.

The Pembroke Theory

The second popular theory is based on the presumptions that Shakespeare controlled the publication of the Sonnets and that he dictated their dedication by Thorpe to Master WH. The latter is taken to be William Herbert, who became third earl of Pembroke in 1601. As the "only begetter" of the dedication, Pembroke is cast as their inspirer and hence as the young aristocrat of the sonnets[5].

There is a superficial plausibility to this notion, first aired by James Boaden in 1837. Pembroke resisted marriage in his youth[6] (as implied of the young aristocrat in the early sonnets) and, with his brother, he was a dedicatee of the First Folio of Shakespeare's plays, produced by the playwright's colleagues in 1623, several years after his death. That dedication is expressed in terms which suggest that the brothers had been enthusiastic supporters of Shakespeare and his plays.

---

[3]   This was the preferred position of Edmondson and Wells in their *Shakespeare's Sonnets* of 2004. Elsewhere, Professor Honan has dismissed the notion that the Sonnets are a reliable sketch of real characters, scenes or experiences.

[4]   For example in Sonnets 1-17, 26, 77, 82, 122 and 152.

[5]   As most recently championed by Professor Duncan-Jones in her *Shakespeare's Sonnets* of 1997 and 2006.

[6]   Though not from any antipathy to women; he was described as a charming, handsome womanizer and he had illegitimate issue by at least two different women, not his wife.

However, at the time Pembroke was Lord Chamberlain and hence responsible for the control of publications (a position in which he was succeeded by his brother). He would have been a natural choice as dedicatee for such a high profile work, particularly if he had enjoyed the drama presented therein[7]. Apart from this inference that, like many playgoers of the time, the Herberts were fans of the playwright, there is nothing to connect Pembroke closely to Shakespeare: no relevant dedications by the latter, no documented crossings of path, no contemporaneous gossip, anecdotes or plausible satirical allusions even.

In addition, on even a cursory inspection, the case is racked with strain and weaknesses. Thorpe's use of the title, "Master", indicates that his dedicatee had the social rank of Gentleman: an honorific applicable to only a small fraction of the male populace[8]. However, the use of such title in a public address of the Earl of Pembroke (or even a lesser aristocrat – any of whom would be socially superior to an ordinary Gentleman) would have been an unacceptable faux pas, which cannot be explained by ignorance or a misguided sense of familiarity. Thorpe and Shakespeare knew the form, as each had shown in other dedications to the aristocracy[9]. Nor, under the necessary interpretation of "begetter" as "inspirer" could Pembroke be regarded as the begetter of those sonnets concerning the Dark Mistress.

With its reliance on Shakespeare's proactivity in publication of the Sonnets, the theory is undermined by a number of indicators to the contrary, including the unusually terse title[10], disreputable

---

[7] In his *A Life of William Shakespeare* Sidney Lee comments: "To the two earls in partnership nearly every work of any literary pretension was dedicated at the period".

[8] It included lawyers, doctors, university dons, senior military officers, knights of the realm and persons of sufficient wealth to dress, live, spend and behave as a gentleman.

[9] Thorpe was aware of the publication in 1609 of a respectful dedication to Pembroke by John Healey. In his own dedication of 1610 to Pembroke (of another work by Healey), Thorpe followed this lead, addressing the earl as "the honorablest patron of the Muses and good minds, Lord William, Earl of Pembroke, Knight of the Honorable Order of the Garter" and so on. Dedications by Shakespeare are shown elsewhere in this book.

[10] Implying the same involvement of author in publication as Aesop of his Fables or Solomon of his Song

contents[11], the inclusion of some mediocre poetry, the absence of personal endorsement and a precedent for unauthorized poetry publications in Shakespeare's name[12]. In her *Shakespeare's Sonnets* of 1997, Professor Duncan-Jones seeks to counteract such indicators with a number of propositions put forward from time to time by supporters of the complicit author presumption:

- numerical correspondences in the sequencing of the Sonnets are perceived to suggest that their author must have been involved in an editorial process with publication in mind;
- a scenario depicting Shakespeare as publisher (which was postulated in 1612 by the poet, Thomas Heywood) is taken to relate to the Sonnets;
- an undated reference to Shakespeare having "lately published" his "works" (attributed to the poet, William Drummond) is taken to relate to the Sonnets;
- a dedication in 1616 by the author, Ben Jonson, which includes comments on change of Pembroke's title and the use of a cipher, is speculated to be a reference to a dedication of cryptic Sonnet messages to Master WH, with the inference that this was at the instigation of Shakespeare.

However, there is little or no basis for these surmises. An examination of the facts, described at Appendix A, shows that:

- there has been no systematic correlation of numbers in the sequencing of the Sonnets; correspondences which would have been expected do not appear; other alignments occur at a frequency well within the incidence expectable by chance;
- the publishing reference by Heywood clearly relates, not to the Sonnets, but to a third edition of *The Passionate Pilgrime*, published in 1612 under Shakespeare's name, without his consent;
- his own records suggest that Drummond never encountered the Sonnets and that Shakespeare's "works" was a reference

---

[11] With themes of masturbation, homo-eroticism, infidelity and heresies to orthodox Christianity – as brought out in Part II

[12] Seen in three editions of *The Passionate Pilgrime*, as discussed in Appendix A

to *The Passionate Pilgrime* - moreover, it is unlikely that he had knowledge of author involvement in any of the publications in Shakespeare's name;

- Jonson had an affectation for referring to titles in his correspondence - the whole of his lengthy dedication is perfectly explained by a wish to receive the Lord Chamberlain's protection against the reaction of those who might misconstrue the meanings of the barbed and seemingly cryptic epigrams being dedicated.

There are other weaknesses in the case for Pembroke[13], but it is unnecessary to go into these. Without better supporting evidence the theory is inadequate to sustain the concept that the Sonnets were, at least in part, biography.

The Southampton Theory

The third of the popular theories is based on an identification first mooted in 1817 by Nathan Drake. He suggested that the young aristocrat of the Sonnets was Henry Wriothesley, who, at the age of seven in 1581, became the third earl of Southampton.

Southampton is the only aristocrat for whom there is any evidence of a personal relationship with Shakespeare. In the preface to his 1709 edition of Shakespeare's works, Nicholas Rowe remarked anecdotally of the poet: "He had the honour to meet with many great and uncommon Marks of Favour and Friendship from the Earl of Southampton". The Stratford schoolmaster and historian, Joseph Greene, who discovered Shakespeare's executed will, wrote of the poet in 1759[14] that "the unanimous tradition of the neighbourhood where he lived is that by the uncommon bounty of the then Earl of Southampton he was enabled to purchase houses and land at Stratford". And the Earl was the sole addressee of Shakespeare's only known dedications: those of his long poems, *Venus & Adonis* and *The Rape of Lucrece*, published in 1593 and 1594, respectively.

Like Pembroke, he resisted marriage in his youth. Based on surviving portraits and descriptions, he well fits the Sonnet

---

[13] Including strains of timing and location

[14] In *The Gentleman's Magazine*

template of a beautiful, effeminate-looking noble[15]. One of Southampton's portraits as a youth was for many years believed to depict a long-haired woman: Lady Norton. Although he had a successful marriage to the woman he impregnated, there were strong contemporary inferences that he was bisexual.

The theory evolved over the years, reaching its most prominent development to date at the hands of the historian, Professor A.L. Rowse.

As depicted by Rowse in his *Shakespeare's Sonnets* of 1984, the sonnets, carrying strong echoes of the contemporaneous *Venus & Adonis* and *Love's Labours Lost*, were patronage poems provided to Southampton over the period 1592-5. Shakespeare loved or paid homage to the young aristocrat in platonic fashion, but was obsessed by the dark lady. Rowse identified her as Emilia Lanier (née Bassano), the former mistress of Henry Carey, Lord Hunsdon, later a patron of Shakespeare's stage company[16]. The Dark Mistress sonnets were composed in parallel to those addressed to Southampton (in particular Sonnets 40-42, whose theme they mirror) and were copied to him under the unusual circumstances of his patronage and the triangular relationship[17]. The preeminent rival poet was Christopher Marlowe, reportedly homosexual, whose death on 30 May 1593 brought to an end his competition for Southampton's patronage[18].

Based on a proposal by Gerald Massey in 1867, as later developed by Charlotte Stopes, Rowse asserts that the Master WH of Thorpe's dedication was Sir William Hervey, the widower of Southampton's mother. Rowse reminds us of the then common practice of addressing knights (but not the aristocracy)

---

[15]   After his attendance at the Queen's court in September 1592 he was praised along the following lines in Stringer's Latin verse: *No youth there present was more comely or more brilliant in the learned arts than this young prince of Hampshire, though his face was scarcely adorned by a tender down.*

[16]   Rowse discovered the lady and her relationship with Hunsdon in the diaries of Simon Forman.

[17]   Some of these were apparently aired elsewhere, as suggested by Meres, since two of the sonnets in this category, 138 and 144, were included, in slightly different form, in a pirate publication of 1599, *The Passionate Pilgrime.*

[18]   The casting of Marlowe as the Rival Poet was first publicly proposed by Robert Cartwright in 1859.

with the honorific, "Master"[19]. And he points out that, on the basis of his wife's preserved last will and testament, Hervey would have inherited all those possessions not specifically bequeathed to another, following her death in 1607[20].

Rowse tacitly assumes that the Sonnets in manuscript were filed broadly in chronological order of receipt within the two categories subsequently preserved by Thorpe. He further assumes that these were accompanied by a long poem published with the Sonnets, entitled therein: *A Lover's Complaint by William Shakespeare* (the hero of which is a youth apparently similar in looks to the fair youth of the Sonnets). All of these he has passing to Southampton's mother and then, after her death, to Thorpe via Hervey.

No element of this theory is unsustainable. The Sonnets can be interpreted, with only occasional strain, to fit the theory well and there is nothing in the poems or in the generally recognised histories of Shakespeare, Southampton, Marlowe and Hervey which firmly disqualifies their identification with the characters.

However, Rowse produced little evidence outside of the Sonnets to support the relationships suggested by the theory. And there are some potential contra-indicators or gaps which he does not address.

For example, there is an indication of Marlowe's association at the time with a patron other than Southampton. There remains no collection of his poems which corresponds with that imputed to the Rival Poet of the Sonnets. And Rowse does not assess why Shakespeare's *Venus* dedication of 1593 appears so distant in tone, given the contemporary intimate friendship with Southampton depicted in the Sonnets; nor does he explain why the poems might reasonably have passed to Southampton's

---

[19] The Dowager Countess of Southampton applied the title "Master", rather than "Sir", to each of her second and third husbands, both knights. Sir Francis Bacon was referred to as Master Bacon. Rowse discovered that this common social practice was also applied in the House of Commons (where Hervey was a Member of Parliament).

[20] The will survives in the National Archives. A letter of 17 November 1607 from her son-in-law, the Earl of Arundel, remarks that the Dowager Countess "had left the best of her stuff to her son and the greatest part to her husband".

mother or why Hervey would have the Sonnets published against the likely wishes of his aristocratic stepson.

As presented by Rowse, therefore, the theory is persuasive in part, but is inconclusive.

Other Theories

Other Sonnet theories have abounded in the last two hundred years. These include the notions that the sonnets encode prophesies or secret messages, and that their author was really Christopher Marlowe, Sir Francis Bacon, Edward de Vere (the 17th Earl of Oxford) or someone else.

Those who doubt Shakespeare's authorship of the works attributed to him (including the Sonnets) point to Shakespeare's lack of a university education, the patchy detail of his history and the supposed lack of hard evidence either that he wrote these works or that he had the means to write as he did of aristocratic or foreign settings.

The doubters go on to postulate a cover-up conspiracy to discount the strong evidence of his authorship emanating from literate people who knew Shakespeare well. Such persons included Richard Field, his fellow Stratfordian (who printed his *Venus & Adonis* and his *Lucrece*), Heminges and Condell, his stage company colleagues (who published the First Folio of plays in his name after his death, with affectionate remembrances) and the eminent poet-playwright, Ben Jonson, who was both critic and eulogizer of his works (and who also did not go to university)[21].

To this hypothesis held in common, individual anti-Stratfordian groups add tailored arguments which promote their particular candidate for Author. Read in isolation, some of these arguments appear persuasive. However, none withstands close probing. Marlovians who doubt this assessment should read on. Baconians and Oxfordians may be interested in my website, www.realshakespeare.com. Here, subjected to new evidence, their

---

[21] These witnesses by no means represent the complete case for Shakespeare. There are other witnesses, such as Thomas Heywood (Appendix A), and further powerful evidence for his authorship, as, for example, pointed out by Jonathan Bate in his *The Genius of Shakespeare*, or as summarized by Reedy and Kathman on the website http://shakespeareauthorship.com

key "proofs" fall down – though their underlying discoveries deserve respect for the light they shed on Shakespeare's life.

Some anti-Stratfordians seek additional support in messages supposedly hidden in anagrams, acrostics or other forms of code within the Shakespearean collection - a form of "proof" that is both exceptionally unreliable and susceptible to providing the result that the seeker wishes to see[22]. This becomes very evident when different sets of supporters are able to derive supposedly encoded messages supporting their candidate, sometimes from the same source.

And the awkward question remains: why, if there is such risk to the author that his identity must be kept secret, would he provide clues to undermine his own machinations? The chance of unwanted discovery arising therefrom in his lifetime would be far greater than that of any desired enlightenment of the world which he might hope for beyond his death.

In summary, each alternative author case has serious weaknesses and relies on assumptions more numerous and much more far-fetched than any which allow Shakespeare the ability to have written his works. Some have attempted to remedy these weaknesses with a postulated cabal or committee of authorship, comprised of varying permutations of the many candidates, including Shakespeare, himself. However, fatal additional shortcomings of this theory arise on consideration of motive, practicality, logistics and the chance of secrets surviving as the numbers of participants multiply.

The Sonnets, themselves, point strongly to Shakespeare as author. They are the only known manifestation of Meres' reference to "his sugared sonnets"[23]. The poet appears to pun on his own name in a number of the poems where the word "will" is

---

[22] This subject was dealt with exhaustively and impartially by two professional cryptologists, William and Elizabeth Friedman in their 1957 publication, *The Shakespearean Ciphers Examined*. They concluded that no one had managed to demonstrate a cipher in Shakespeare. More importantly, they established a standard for assessment of potential codes which is now often forgotten or ignored. In Appendices A and D, in relation to the so-called Bible Code and the Stratford Monument wording, respectively, I provide examples of this phenomenon.

[23] Footnote 1

represented in Thorpe's original publication with an initial capital letter and (in some cases) italics (Sonnets **57, 135, 136** and **143**). He portrays himself as unwealthy (**29, 37, 80**), unaristocratic (**25, 26**), with common manners (**89, 111**) and lacking university education (**78**). These themes are strongly hinted at in many others of the sonnets. Conversely, nowhere is he depicted with a different name or as rich, aristocratic or learned (ie university-educated). As is brought out in Part II, following, the detail of the Sonnets is wholly consistent with autobiography and patronage poetry by an author with the name and status of the Stratfordian.

For all these reasons the credibility of alternative author theories is low. I shall return to the specific case for Marlowe later. However, let us first look at some further evidence for Shakespeare's authorship and his relationship with Southampton, based on associations with another author of the time.

The Thomas Nashe Evidence

The Sonnet theme of an aristocratic young man becoming lover to both his poet and that poet's mistress is extraordinary, if not unique. Yet, at a time strikingly consistent with the Southampton theory - June 1593 - the satirical author, Thomas Nashe, evoked this very theme with the following words addressed to the Earl, himself: *A dear lover and cherisher you are, as well of the lovers of Poets, as of Poets themselves.*

Nashe made this remark within a peculiar, extended mimicry of Shakespeare's dedication of *Venus & Adonis*, as applied to his own work, *The Unfortunate Traveller*. His dedication of the latter to Southampton has been assessed by many commentators as an obsequious imitation, made in the hope of obtaining patronage. Most of these interpreters regard his comments on cherishing poets and their lovers as praise for the Earl's love and support of the arts – perhaps exaggerated by Nashe in the interests of flattery.

However, on closer inspection of the language of the dedication and Nashe's history and writing style, such assessments become unsustainable. Much of the address is double-edged in its meaning and the sarcastic tone suggests that Nashe cared not a whit for Southampton's patronage. Some of the phraseology is frankly insulting. In a second edition of the book, produced a few months later, the "dedication" is absent and there is no evidence that Nashe ever received any significant support from Southampton.

His references to "poets", within a lampoon of the *Venus* dedication, also point to Shakespeare. The Sonnets apart, there is no evidence that Southampton had a personal relationship with any other recognized poet, prior to 1603[24]. In 1589 the waspish Nashe had denigrated playwrights who did not attend university and who provided unwanted competition for "better pens". And in 1592 he was suspected by contemporaries of instigating a similar attack (for imitation or plagiarism of one's betters) on an unqualified playwright. In short, it looks as though, by June 1593, Nashe was disaffected with both Southampton and his patronage of Shakespeare.

This notion is in line with the implications of a satirical in-house play, *The Returne from Parnassus* (Part 1) which was produced c.1600 by an anonymous writer and acted by students at St. John's, Cambridge. The play includes two characters, Ingenioso and Gullio, who are caricatures of the college's fellow alumni, Nashe and Southampton[25]. In the play Ingenioso is forced by his poverty to kowtow to his despised and niggardly patron, Gullio, a pompous, gullible popinjay of a Courtier, derided for his love of Shakespeare (both man and works). After Gullio's lascivious designs are thwarted by his own shortcomings, including his insistence on Shakespearean-style verse to entertain, he dismisses Ingenioso, who bids him good riddance with eloquent vilification.

But why would Nashe have fallen out with Southampton? The answer is provided in his work, *Pierce Pennilesse*, published around August 1592. Here, in a colourful closing address to his readers, Nashe rails at length against an anonymous, non-performing

---

[24] In 1593 Barnabe Barnes wrote a commendatory sonnet to Southampton (as the fourth of seven dedicatees of his *Parthenophil and Parthenophe*). So did Gervase Markham in 1595 (when Southampton was the third of four dedicatees of his poem on Sir Richard Grenville). In each case the Earl's low positioning in the order of dedicatees and the lack of any repetition suggests that the dedication was both speculative and unrewarded.

[25] The caricature of Southampton as Gullio was discerned by Dr Gregor Sarrazin in 1895.

patron, a Courtier who is avoiding him and who, he implies with a Latin maxim, has failed to deliver on promises of payment, because "at this time he is not provided for him". He urges scholars to be more careful in their dedications and not to cast away so many months' labour on a "clown" that knows not how to treat them: "for what reason have I to bestow any wit on him, that will bestow none of his wealth on me".

In Appendix B I set out the evidence in greater detail and I show that, contrary to previous interpretations, Nashe continues his diatribe with sarcastic praise and veiled insults of this niggardly patron, whom he now addresses as a *Ganymede* and an *Amyntas*. Each of these names had homoerotic associations and there are other indications, including the words of Gabriel Harvey, that the unnamed butt of Nashe's extended irony must have been Southampton.

The evidence from several sources shows that Nashe's sarcastic attacks on "Amyntas" were continued when he was goaded into his equally sarcastic dedication of *Traveller* some months later. And all the circumstances of that address point to Shakespeare as a poet he says was loved by Southampton. In their complete context, those words on the Earl's love of poets and their lovers resound with mockery of a real and embarrassing triangular relationship, which mirrors that depicted in the Sonnets[26].

The Case Developed

With such mirroring of so rare a theme, and its associations with both Southampton and Shakespeare, the Nashe evidence provides powerful support for the position that (i) the Sonnets were written by Shakespeare, (ii) they were addressed at least in part to Southampton and (iii) they contain intimate biography from earlier than June 1593. Let us now consider other pointers towards Southampton, described below and in immediately following sub-sections.

---

[26] This situation is also consistent with hints by Gabriel Harvey of a scandal involving Shakespeare and Southampton – see Appendix B.

In Sonnet 1 the addressee is identified with "beauty's *Rose*". In its original printing the opening letter of *Rose* is upper case, consistent with the publication's convention for flower names. Unusually, however, the whole word is depicted in italics, suggesting that there is a special attribute or significance to the word[27]. The rose association continues to appear as an intermittent theme throughout Sonnets 1-126, and conspicuously so in Sonnets 54, 95 and 109. In the latter the poet actually hails the addressee as "my Rose". For whatever reason, therefore, it appears that the word was used as a nickname of endearment.

Some commentators have considered that here is a clue to the identity of the young aristocrat. The historian, Dr. G.P.V. Akrigg, was ambivalent to this notion. In his *Shakespeare & the Earl of Southampton*, he observes that the pronunciation of Southampton's surname, Wriothesley, in informal practice seemed almost invariably to have been contracted to three syllables at most[28]. Indeed, he says the "io" was usually reduced to a single vowel with most people, apparently, saying "Risely"[29] but with a few possibly saying "Rosely"[30]. However, this latter, lukewarm assessment seems understated, given other indicators. Thomas Nashe once dedicated a poem to a "Lord S", whom he described as a "sweet flower" and "fairest bud the red rose ever bare" (Appendix B). And Jonathan Bate has pointed out that Southampton's home at Titchfield was emblazoned with a heraldic representation of roses.

Further down in Sonnet 1, the poet refers to his addressee as "only herald to the gaudy spring". The Wriothesley family's rise

---

[27] This highlighting, by way of opening capital letter and overall italicization, occurs for only some twenty five words in the Sonnets. Some of the highlighting is in line with convention at the time for classical character names (such as *Cupid* or *Philomel*) or technical terms imported from Latin (such as *Audite and Quietus*). The convention is extended to *Will*, where clearly a pun on the author's name is intended (Sonnets 135, 136, 143).

[28] A notice in the Titchfield parish register of the burial on 28 December 1624 of the third earl's son records him as Lord James Wryosley.

[29] In the registration of the marriage of Southampton's sister to Thomas Arundel, at St Andrew's Church in June 1585, her name is spelt Wrisley.

[30] The author of *A Shakespeare Glossary* (1911), C. T. Onions, reported that "the name is pronounced Rosely by persons now living", though Akrigg was unable to verify this with a search in the 1960s.

began with a dynastic profession as heralds. The first Earl's grandfather was a Garter King-of-Arms, succeeded in this post by the first Earl's uncle[31]; his father was the York herald and his cousin was the Windsor herald. In the early 1590s Southampton was the sole surviving male in his family (and as such the only potential wellspring of that aristocratic house). I suggest, therefore, that the words are a clever play on a combination of circumstances unique to Southampton.

Sonnets 1-17 are themed on the need for the unmarried addressee to provide an heir. The implication is that he needs to be persuaded to marry. There is documentary evidence (which we will touch on later) of Southampton's reluctance to marry during the period 1590-94.

In Sonnet 13 the poet, urging the young aristocrat to marry and get a son, says "You had a father; let your son say so". The reference in the past tense to the young man's father would jar if that father were alive at the time of writing. Southampton's father had died in 1581, when the son was only seven.

The hero of *Venus & Adonis*, dedicated by Shakespeare to Southampton in 1593, has attributes similar to those of both Southampton and the Fair Youth of the Sonnets. Adonis, an effeminate looking, beautiful youth, is lusted after but resistant to the seductions of the love goddess, Venus. In verses 28, 29 and 127 she urges Adonis to beget offspring, in terms which resonate with those within Sonnets 1-17: a strange tactic for a sexual predator, unless the works shared a common theme and model.

In each of Sonnets 103 and 105 the poet claims that all his songs, verse and praises are directed to one person, the addressee of the sonnet. There is probably some licence taken in this declaration: however, after May 1593 it would have been impossible for Shakespeare to have directed the claim credibly towards anyone other than Southampton, to whom he had dedicated *Venus & Adonis* then *Lucrece*. The claim is echoed in Shakespeare's dedication to Southampton of *Lucrece*: "What I

---

[31] It was this uncle, Sir Thomas Writh, who adapted the family name to Wriothesley. His herald son wrote *Wriothesley's Chronicle*, a history preserved only through a transcription instigated by our third Earl.

have done is yours, what I have to do is yours, being part in all I have, devoted yours".

Sonnet 107, following, has been analysed more than most, because of the clues it offers to the time of its writing:

> *Not mine own fears, nor the prophetic soul*
> *Of the wide world dreaming on things to come,*
> *Can yet the lease of my true love control,*
> *Supposed as forfeit to a confined doom.*
> *The mortal Moon hath her eclipse endured,*
> *And the sad augurs mock their own presage;*
> *Incertainties now crown themselves assured,*
> *And peace proclaims olives of endless age,*
> *Now with the drops of this most balmy time*
> *My love looks fresh, and Death to me subscribes,*
> *Since, spite of him, I'll live in this poor rhyme,*
> *While he insults o'er dull and speechless tribes.*
> *And thou in this shalt find thy monument,*
> *When tyrants' crests and tombs of brass are spent.*

Like most commentators, Rowse interprets "the mortal Moon" of line 5 as Elizabeth Tudor[32]. He sees the enduring of her eclipse as an indication that Elizabeth had come through a crisis, suggested to be the Dr Lopez events of 1593-4 (when her doctor was accused and convicted of plotting to poison her on behalf of Spain). He regards the "peace" and "balmy time" of lines 8 and 9 as references to the ending in 1594 of the religious civil war within France, which enabled a small English army to be recalled.

However, others have put forward a powerful case for the eclipse being permanent, being the death the "mortal" Elizabeth in 1603, followed by the peaceful transition to the monarchy of her successor, James I, and his immediate moves to eliminate the long ongoing hostilities between England and

---

[32] Elizabeth was generally characterized in poems of the time as Diana or Cynthia, the Moon goddess.

Spain[33]. This interpretation is more persuasive. Rowse's equating of an eclipse with what was actually only an alleged and unsuccessful plot seems strained by comparison. And the interpretation of eclipse as a death fits well with the inference of a tyrant's passing in the final line of the sonnet (Elizabeth Tudor would have been regarded by Southampton as a tyrant, for reasons explained below).

Line 4 is haunting. With its reference to a "confined doom", it appears to suggest exactly such a circumstance. Both Southampton and Pembroke underwent brief confinements in prison for impregnating a Queen's maid of attendance (in 1598 and 1601 respectively) – hardly confined "dooms". However, in 1601 Southampton was condemned to death (for his part in the Essex plot to overthrow Elizabeth), which sentence was commuted to life imprisonment in the Tower of London. He was freed only on the accession of James I to the throne, after Elizabeth's death. The poem's affinity with both Southampton and the year 1603 is thereby strengthened.

Timing of the Sonnets

What are we to make of the Sonnet 107 associations, which cast doubt on Rowse's assessment that all the Sonnets were written between 1592 and 1595? The answer, I propose, is to be found in the interpretation of Sonnets 97-104.

These sonnets point to periods of separation of poet from addressee. Sonnets 97 and 98 allude to a separation during a spring and summer: at least six months (though there may well be an allegory here for a longer, bountiful period in the poet's life). The language and themes of Sonnets 100-103 all point to further significant periods of separation. Sonnet 103 sounds jaded and its words imply that there will be no more verse written to the addressee. Then appears the following, beautiful Sonnet 104, completely different in tone and energy, thereby suggesting that there had been yet another period of separation:

---

[33] This assignment to 1603 was first made by an unidentified "J.R." in 1848. Various other commentators have since supported this dating, including Sidney Lee, H. C. Beeching and Dover Wilson.

To me, fair friend, you never can be old,
For as you were when first your eye I eyed,
Such seems your beauty still: three winters cold
Have from the forests shook three summers' pride,
Three beauteous springs to yellow autumn turned
In process of the seasons have I seen,
Three April perfumes in three hot Junes burned,
Since first I saw you fresh, which yet are green.
Ah, yet doth beauty like a dial-hand
Steal from his figure, and no pace perceived;
So your sweet hue, which methinks still doth stand,
Hath motion, and mine eye may be deceived:
For fear of which, hear this, thou age unbred:
Ere you were born was beauty's summer dead.

Rowse (and many others) have taken literally the above seasonal references to the period of friendship. This is why he limits the periods of separation inferred from Sonnets 97-104 to no more than a year or so, and puts a maximum period of three or four years on the overall time span of the sonnets. Other commentators warn that there may be artificiality here, following conceits of the time. Sidney Lee, for example, points out that three years was the conventional period which sonneteers allotted to the development of their passion.

However, on reflection, one has to wonder why, under either interpretation, anyone would comment on a lack of ageing after only three years. A normal young man is not going to deteriorate in appearance in that time and such a notion would undermine even a conceit of the sort envisaged by Lee.

I suggest, therefore, that here is a different form of conceit, applied to a situation which is far from artificial. In real life one tends to comment on a lack of physical deterioration only after a period of separation or privation commensurate with normally perceptible ageing. And then, if one is suitably impressed, or in flattery or reassurance mode, one says "You look as good as ever!" or "You've hardly changed at all!" Or, if one were a poet, one might take ageing periods of around, say, twelve years and in flowery language present them as being only three.

Consequently, we may see the three season-cycles referred to in Sonnet 104 as a form of flattery or reassurance after a time of separation within a period of acquaintanceship substantially longer than three years. The key is line 6, which, I suggest, can be rendered as "In that amount of seasoning (ie process of ageing) I have seen [in you]". On this basis the information in Sonnet 104 is consistent with a resumption in composition of the sonnets after Southampton's emergence in 1603 from his "confined doom".

The only serious objection to identifying the, then, thirty year old Southampton as the friend of Sonnet 104 might be his address as a sweet or lovely boy in Sonnets 108 and 126. However, the use of a word associated with youthfulness in an address was, and is, common in a long-standing relationship, whether used in affection or flattery. The poet admits as much in Sonnet 108, where he goes on to say *"eternal love, in love's fresh case, weighs not the dust and injury of age"*[34].

With this modification of the Rowse theory, the story underlying the Sonnets starts in or around 1592 and ends in or around 1604, albeit with some sizeable gaps of time in which no sonnets were composed, suggesting long periods of separation[35].

Comparison with History

Such a scenario is consistent with history: Shakespeare and Southampton, both readily available in 1592-4 for the situations depicted in Sonnets 1-96 (and for Shakespeare's contemporaneous compositions and dedications to Southampton of *Venus* and *Lucrece*), were busy on very different activities for most of the post-*Lucrece* period from late 1594 until 1603.

---

[34] Indeed, as brought out in Part II, the sonnet as a whole (and those following) can be construed as reaction to the friend's cynicism on reception of the preceding sonnets 104-107, which proclaim his freshness and beauty and the poet's constant love. Sonnet 126, uniquely structured, looks like an envoi and a sentimental farewell after their final break, signaled by Sonnet 125.

[35] This timing is also consistent with conclusions reached by MacDonald P Jackson in his *Rhymes in Shakespeare's Sonnets: Evidence of Date of Composition*, based on vocabulary in Shakespeare's plays.

After the plague-enforced closures of the London playhouses for much of 1592-4 Shakespeare was back in show business working hard as actor, playwright and company stakeholder. As his wealth mounted he was also increasingly involved from 1596 in family-elevation, commercial and investment matters.

The Earl had to manage significant issues in relation to his debt-laden family estate, for which he assumed responsibility on his majority in October 1594. He embarked on an affair with a Queen's maid of attendance, Elizabeth Vernon[36] in 1595, culminating in her pregnancy in 1598 and a clandestine marriage unapproved by the Queen, bringing a consequent brief imprisonment.

In 1596, 1597, 1599 and 1600 he was involved in the planning and execution of overseas military campaigns, including voyages under the command of the Earl of Essex to the Azores and to Ireland. In 1598 he was part of a lengthy embassy to Paris.

It was from the 1599 campaign in Ireland, where he distinguished himself in a number of courageous actions, that there arose one documented indication of his bisexuality. According to one, William Reynolds, Southampton showered unusual attention on his Corporal General of the Horse, Piers Edmunds, who "ate and drank at his table and lay in his tent....the earle Sowthamton would cole [embrace] and hug him in his armes and play wantonly w[ith] him".

Although this report in the Cecil papers[37] arose from a potentially inimical source in relation to a subsequent trial, it is unlikely that such comments would have been made frivolously, given the number of available witnesses.

In late 1599, after his return from Ireland, the Earl became temporarily re-occupied with the world of the stage, as, according to one report, he killed time with daily visits to watch plays. It seems highly probable that the paths of poet and erstwhile patron again crossed at this point.

---

36 She was the cousin of his role model and close friend, Robert Devereux, Earl of Essex, who had secured her position with the Queen.

37 As recorded by Akrigg, BL, MS M/485/41

In late 1600 Southampton returned from military forays to Ireland and the Low Countries to become embroiled in the plot led by Essex to depose Elizabeth Tudor. The plot failed and he was sentenced to death in February 1601.

In the event, pleas by his mother and his wife, his own repentance and the support of Sir Robert Cecil secured a commutation of sentence to one of life imprisonment in the Tower. Here, stripped of his earldom, he languished for two years, sometimes seriously ill, until Elizabeth's death in March 1603.

On his release and restoration to his earldom by James I in April 1603, Southampton must have had much to deal with, as he resumed control of his life and the family estate. The latter, in depleted form, had been managed by his trustees and mother and now was considerably enhanced by gifts from the King.

Nevertheless, he appears to have resurrected an interest in drama within months. In a letter[38] sent to Sir Robert Cecil in 1604 there is report of the Earl organizing a private performance of *Love's Labour's Lost* by Shakespeare's company for the new queen. In any event, it is not unreasonable to suppose that the poet would have contacted his old patron, to congratulate him for his escape from his confined doom.

In fact, with his new wealth and enhanced status, there is evidence that the Earl was courted by many authors. These attentions, quite absent in the preceding few years, must have aroused some cynicism, even when they were accepted.

A further coincidence, which may not have gone unremarked by the Earl, was the closure of London playhouses for some thirteen months after May 1603, following a new outbreak of plague. As in 1592-4, this would have severely dented Shakespeare's earning capacity. All these factors fit well with the addressee's cynical reception of Sonnets 104-126, as suggested in those poems.

---

[38] Salisbury MSS., XVI, 415 per Akrigg

Possession of the Sonnets

With the above history and a little more background, there emerge several feasible or actual circumstances involving the Earl's mother. In turn, these suggest a number of ways in which she might reasonably have come into possession of the Sonnets, as required by the Rowse/Stopes theory.

A compliment to his mother, in Sonnet 3, and the son's initial reluctance to marry have led some observers to theorise that the first seventeen sonnets were composed with her knowledge and approval. She would, on this basis, have been familiar with the existence and provenance of the poems.

On or after the Earl's marriage in 1598 he may not have wanted the Sonnets in his possession, since these conveyed information of a sort that few husbands would wish their wives to see. In this scenario his mother, nostalgic and appreciative of their artistry, asks or is asked to keep them.

Alternatively, a similar outcome could have been triggered by either of her son's two imprisonments.

The first of these occasions was in 1598, when both the Earl and his new wife were confined (albeit in reasonable comfort) for several weeks at Fleet prison, in punishment for their unauthorized marriage. During this time his mother may have been the natural informal trustee of access to his personal papers, though there was then some strain between her and her son in relation to her own re-marriage plans.

However, by far the most likely cause of transfer would have been the Earl's second and solo incarceration for treason in 1601. On this occasion all his possessions (apart from certain land and buildings transferred several years before to a trust) were subject to confiscation by the State. An inventory of his possessions forfeit was made under the direction of the Queen's Solicitor-General, Sir Thomas Fleming in April 1601[39]. Although only a scrap of this record survives today, it shows vividly the thoroughness of the exercise, with its references to articles such as carpets and stools as well as "old mappes".

---

[39]   As described by Akrigg in *Shakespeare and the Earl of Southampton.*

To avoid loss of privacy and possession who more likely than his mother (who had her own separate households) to safeguard items such as personal papers? Certainly, based on the fact of her visits to him at the Tower in the company of his advisors, she appears to have had more involvement in the management of his remaining possessions than did his loving but less worldly wife[40]. And the Earl's closest friends, whom he might otherwise have entrusted, were dead or imprisoned, having been implicated in the same treasonable activities.

In my above interpretation of the later sonnets, 104-126 (taken to have been written in 1603/4), Shakespeare's efforts to renew his friendship with Southampton are rebuffed and they are estranged[41]. In this scenario it is not difficult to imagine the Earl complaining to his mother and threatening to destroy these latest and, if not already passed on, earlier poems. She, probably already in possession of the latter, asks to keep them all, and is indulged by him.

Some might contend that the intimate details of their content would inhibit the Earl from allowing the Sonnets into the hands of his mother. However, this process was probably involuntary in its initiation, as suggested above. In any case she, like most mothers, presumably knew her son's nature and would have loved him none the less: and he would have known this.

Publication of the Sonnets

Southampton's mother died in 1607. The Sonnets were published by Thomas Thorpe in 1609. To complete our test of the Stopes/Rowse theory of publication, let us analyse the circumstances.

Thorpe was an experienced publisher, who included Chapman and Jonson in his repertoire. He might reasonably have expected

---

[40] A letter of authorization from the Queen's Privy Council to the Lieutenant of the Tower accedes to Southampton's request "to have the favour to see his mother, and to conferre with her and some others that were putt in trust with his estate". It permits a visit by the Dowager Countess and "any two of those persons whom he shall desire, that have been dealers in his estate".

[41] This estrangement, incidentally, suggests a further reason for the dedication of the first Folio of Shakespeare's plays by Heminges and Condell to the Herbert brothers.

the aristocratic subject of the Sonnets to resent their publication and to bring his considerable resources to bear uncomfortably on a publisher suspected of piracy. Consequently, we may infer that Thorpe sought to protect both his reputation and his person with a reference to a legitimate source in his following, now enigmatic dedication:

To the only begetter of these ensuing sonnets Mr WH all happiness and that eternity promised by our ever-living poet wisheth the well-wishing adventurer in setting forth. TT.

With its succinct references to an only begetter and "our" poet, the wording cleverly invokes legitimacy but obfuscates its source. Since clarity would have been easy to achieve, presumably Thorpe felt uncomfortable or defensive about aspects of the publication, including, perhaps, the wish to defend its "fair friend" with anonymity as best he could. In short, the dedication looks like a compromise.

Allowing time for probate and other distractions (such as William Hervey's rapid moves to re-marry), the publication in 1609 fits well with the notion that it was initiated by Hervey. Stopes envisaged the latter as a loyal family friend, who, on inheriting the Sonnets, thought they were too good to be lost.

However, this characterisation does not fit. First, in such circumstances a loyal family friend would have consulted his stepson, Southampton, who was hardly likely to have given his approval. Second, in the unlikely event that he did approve, the Earl would then surely have been openly included by Thorpe in his dedication of a probably abridged version of the Sonnets.

But is there any evidence that Hervey was on sufficiently bad terms with his stepson to proceed with a sale of the Sonnets against the Earl's likely wishes, or that he was sufficiently self-confident or opportunistic to do so?

Hervey's history certainly indicates courage, self-confidence and opportunism. From relatively humble beginnings he rose to become a wealthy landowner and grandee of the realm, being knighted for bravery and military prowess on the way[42] and serving as a Member of Parliament[43] and rear-admiral in the navy[44].

Further, there is evidence that Southampton did not approve of Hervey. According to information in the Cecil papers[45] the Earl's feelings of "discomfort and discontentment" with the prospects of his mother's marriage to Hervey and his "scorn" for the latter's attitude were conveyed to her in November 1598 from Fleet prison by Southampton's mentor and friend, the Earl of Essex.

The latter also warned Hervey that his marriage to the Dowager Countess would carry the risk of making an enemy of Essex as well as being regarded as a "mischief" to Southampton. Hervey, however, was undaunted by the opposition of two aristocrats. He defended himself firmly and made it clear to Essex that he would not be deflected by what he regarded as unfounded opposition.

It seems that Southampton was obliged to accept the union. However, his antipathy must have been revived or heightened by the spectacle of his step-father attending to the well-being of the much younger Cordell Annesley in 1603 and 1604[46], followed by an engagement to that wealthy lady some three years later, within weeks of the death of Southampton's mother.

Indeed, in these circumstances it is easy to imagine the Earl treating Hervey with contempt, as the latter benefited simultaneously from the Dowager Countess's will[47] and the

---

[42] He distinguished himself in the defeat of the Spanish Armada in 1588 and as a ship commander in the Cadiz and Azores expeditions of 1596 and 1597, led by Essex.

[43] He was MP for Petersfield from 1604 until 1611.

[44] He also served in many high councils or committees. Ultimately he rose to the peerage, as Baron Hervey of Kidbrooke.

[45] Salisbury MSS., XIV, 79-81, as recorded by Akrigg in his *Shakespeare & the Earl of Southampton*

[46] Hervey was the executor of her father's will in 1604, of which she was the main beneficiary. Her older married sisters attempted in 1603 to take control of their father's substantial assets on grounds of his dementia. They also attempted to contest the will on his death. Neither action was successful.

[47] She was independently wealthy through her second marriage to Sir Thomas Heneage, who died in 1595. Heneage disliked the husband of his only child and took steps in his will

largesse of the Annesley estate. Developing this scenario, we can also readily envisage the offended and strong-willed Member of Parliament taking a golden opportunity for both retaliation and profit through publication of the Sonnets[48].

In all respects, then, Hervey provides a match to the template of Thorpe's provider. His social status and initials fit those of Thorpe's addressee. His legitimate ownership of the poems in manuscript is highly plausible. He appears to have been on uneasy if not hostile terms with his stepson. He was bold and opportunistic; and he had the status and character to take on the risk of retribution from the Earl.

In such a scenario, Southampton would, as intended by Thorpe, immediately have understood the publisher's dedication and source – obscure to anyone not in the know. To complete the picture, I suggest that here is how that dedication might have looked in modern terms, without any defensive disguise:

To that gentleman of standing, William Hervey, who - bestowed with these sonnets - is their one rightful bestower, I wish, as we set out in our respective ventures, all happiness and that endless lineage sung by our famous poet, whose name will never die.[49]

As we can now see, this explanation of how the Sonnets came to be published is based on reasonable assumptions and it fits to perfection all the facts of a complex set of circumstances: the powerful pointers to their main character, the disreputable contents, the absence of author endorsement, legitimate possession of the poems, Thorpe's position, the timing of events and the enigmatic dedication.

---

to ensure that much of his estate passed to his second wife, the Dowager Countess of Southampton.

[48] He may also have been settling a score with Shakespeare, if Hervey's new wife had been upset by the playwright's apparent reminders of her father's senility in *King Lear* – see Appendix G.

[49] This interpretation equates *begetter* with *propagator* or *genitor* - one who passes on life which he was given (in this case Shakespeare's eternal lines). It suggests some wit in Thorpe, given the circumstances described and the parallel associations with the recently wed Hervey's prospective family line.

The Fair Friend

Let us now consider a summary of the pointers established, so far, for Southampton as principal addressee and subject of the Sonnets.

His name gives a deeper sense to the highlighting and/or frequent allusions to *Rose*, flowers and buds (as in Sonnets **1, 54, 95, 109** and many others). He was the only male in an aristocratic family (as in Sonnets **1, 26** etc). He came from a dynasty of heralds (**1**). He was an effeminate-looking, fair-complexioned youth (**20** etc). He was reportedly bisexual (**20, 52, 110**). His father was dead (**13**). In his youth he was reluctant to marry (**1-17**). He was the dedicatee of a best-selling poem by Shakespeare, which resonates with the early sonnets (**1-17**). He and Shakespeare are strongly linked to Nashe's mocking commentary that he was a lover to poets and their lovers (**40-42**). He was Shakespeare's only known personal patron and the only one who could, within reasonable licence, be designated the sole recipient of verse from the poet (**103, 105**). Anecdotally he bestowed many favours on Shakespeare (**117**). He suffered a true "confined doom" (**107**). His history and connections are consistent with the portrayal in the poems and explain perfectly the complex and unusual circumstances associated with their publication.

There is no other candidate for Fair Friend who can come remotely close to this level of correspondence. Nor is there anything in the Sonnets to contradict the identification[50]. On any reasonable assessment, therefore, the case for Southampton is overwhelming. And there is more to come.

The Dark Lady

Given Southampton as Shakespeare's fair friend of the Sonnets, what then is the evidence for the existence of their

---

[50] In his *Shakespeare*, Bill Bryson suggests that the Fair Youth had "golden tresses", unlike Southampton, who had auburn hair. Here he is evidently referring to Sonnet 68 and he is wrong, since that sonnet makes it clear that the golden tresses are those of wigs worn by the youth's companions of Sonnet 67.

mutual mistress of the poems, who had black hair and eyes and a dark nature[51]?

The theme of the Dark Mistress is not attractive. After worshipful praise at the beginning of the story, she is castigated by the poet. She is depicted as moody, unfaithful and promiscuous. The relationship is one-sided, traumatic and unhappy, and there is no resolution or comeuppance. In short, there is the gritty feel of reality and a lack of the ingredients of poetic tradition or popular fiction.

As earlier explained, the Nashe evidence, including hints from Gabriel Harvey, gives powerful support to the occurrence of a triangular relationship between Southampton, Shakespeare and the latter's lover, as depicted in the Sonnets. It also points to its likely timing: in months before Nashe's mocking address to Southampton of June 1593.

Rowse's identification of Emilia Bassano-Lanier has been analysed by numerous researchers. She was an accomplished poet from a family of Italian musicians, who, for a time, was mistress to Lord Hunsdon (the subsequent patron of Shakespeare's stage company). She was younger than Shakespeare, in accordance with a suggestion of the Sonnets. Most of our knowledge of her has come from an analysis of her poems and the papers of the astrologer, Simon Forman, whom she consulted over a period of years.

It is evident that she moved in circles which overlapped with those of Shakespeare at a time appropriate to the theory. Her complexion is unproven, though two cousins reportedly had distinctively black hair. Supporters point to Italian backdrops and potentially connected names in Shakespeare's plays. Some see associated puns in the Sonnets. More persuasively, Martin Green points out that her maiden surname, Bassano, had connotations of darkness (in French and Italian)[52] – something unlikely to be

---

[51] Her skin tone is conditionally described as "dun" in Sonnet 130, but this is in the context of an ironical definition of whiteness, set at the luminosity of snow, against which benchmark any skin tone is darker. Consequently, the shade of her skin could be anything within the range of albino to swarthy.

[52] In his treatise, *Emilia Lanier IS the Dark Lady of the Sonnets*, English Studies – Amsterdam: Vol 87, No. 5, October 2006, PP 544-576, British Library

lost on a poet fond of wordplay. There is also a documented link with Southampton, who was the originating sponsor of a strange monetary award to her husband in 1604[53].

However, the evidence to date, though cumulatively impressive, remains circumstantial. And there is a potential snag: Emilia's pregnancy, around that time, would presumably for some months have been a deterrent to the physical intimacies indicated in Sonnets 40-42. Forman tells us that "being with child she was for colour married to a minstrel [Alphonso Lanier]". This marriage was registered in October 1592, on which basis most observers project a birth date to early in 1593 (under modern dating). However, although the Bassanos and Laniers were practising Christians, I have been unable to substantiate this projection with any birth or baptismal record for Emilia's son, Henry. Forman's words are vague enough that Henry could have been born as early as, say, July 1592 (which would remove the snag) or as late as April 1593 (which would reinforce it).

In Appendix C I provide more detail, including informed speculation on Emilia's whereabouts in the summer of 1592 and the reason for the absence of registration relevant to the birth of her son, Henry. Without further evidence, however, all we can reasonably conclude is that she is, to date, the only realistic candidate to be the shared dark girlfriend of Shakespeare and Southampton.

Without a firm identification the existence of this adventuress is substantiated mainly by the Nashe evidence, considered above. However, there are also suggestive parallels between the Dark Mistress of the Sonnets and two Shakespearean characters from different plays, who share the same name: *Rosaline* (whose pronunciation in Shakespeare rhymes with "mine").

---

[53] In August 1604, as recorded in the National Archives, Alphonso Lanier was granted the valuable monopoly of excising London hay and straw imports for twenty years – on the face of it an odd award, given his status as a minor musician and no record of any outstanding services to the Crown. However, in a contemporaneous letter to Robert Cecil, Bishop Bancroft promotes the award, saying Lanier "was put in good hope of your favour by the Earl of Southampton". Evidently the Earl was supporting Lanier's case and Bancroft had been co-opted by Southampton to add his own endorsement of the grant.

The first of these characters appears at some length within *Love's Labour's Lost*. She has shading similar to that of the Dark Mistress: black eyes, eyebrows and hair, and is described as the "worst" in a group of four women, as "a whitely wanton with a velvet brow" and as having a "light [also meaning easy or wanton] condition in a beauty dark". She is feisty, quick-witted and tantalizing, determined to make life a misery for her besotted suitor, Berowne, and she stays out of his reach indefinitely. She says of Berowne: *"The blood of youth burns not with such excess as gravity's revolt to wantonness"*, conjuring up echoes of an older man plagued by his passion for a woman who does not reciprocate his feelings.

The second Rosaline appears by reference only, as Romeo's first love in *Romeo and Juliet*. She is described as being rich in beauty, witty, pale, hard-hearted, resistant to love, unobtainable: a "white wench" with black eyes and scarlet lips (as evoked in Sonnet 142) who had bewitched and tormented Romeo.

The two plays were, on most current interpretations of the evidence, composed in their first form and originally performed during the period 1593-95. As pointed out by Frank Harris some hundred years ago, the physical characteristics of each Rosaline are more described than those of nearly all other characters in all of Shakepeare's plays. We know nothing, for example, of how Juliet looked, or Romeo or Hamlet. Harris and other commentators have seized on this distinction to suggest that the Rosalines are based on a real person who was known to Shakespeare.

Certainly, the sharing of name and attributes by characters in plays so different in setting and themes, but composed so closely together in time, seems significant – particularly as the attributes also match those of our Dark Mistress in sonnets composed (as we have seen above) around 1592-4.

If the *Rosalines* were a projection or echo of the Dark Mistress it is highly unlikely, for several reasons, that Shakespeare would have used her real name. However, I fell to wondering whether, nevertheless, there was some significance to the name used in the plays.

Most sources suggest that *Rosaline* was a variant of *Rosalind*, a Germano-Scandinavian name which had come to England via the Normans. However, I could find no indication that the name *Rosaline* existed prior to these character creations by Shakespeare. Perhaps, therefore, the name was coined or adapted by him for a specific reason, and, with this in mind, I looked at potential source-words.

The first, obvious such source is *Rosa*, Latin for Rose. What word might then have triggered "line"? To my surprise and fascination, I found that *line* is one expression of the Latin verb, *lino, linere*, meaning to smear, cover or befoul. On this basis *Rosaline* would equate in meaning to something like *Rose Besmircher*. Such a name would be powerfully apt and evocative in the context of a Rose seduced by the Dark Mistress, as complained of in the Sonnets. And it would also carry the beautiful disguise, which is such a hallmark of Shakespeare's wit.

On their own these circumstances might be dismissed as strange coincidence. Within this framework, however, they reinforce the evidence as to the existence of the Dark Mistress and the chronology of the relevant sonnets.

The Story of the Rival Poet

At this point the case for underlying biography within the Sonnets is powerful. Two of its four principal characters – the Sonneteer and the aristocrat he loved – have, on an overwhelming balance of probability, been identified as Shakespeare and Southampton. Their triangular relationship with a third, the dark haired woman by whom the poet felt betrayed, is in line with cohering, persuasive evidence. And the reasons for, and route to publication of such private and intimate biography are comprehensively explained.

What then, might we ask, was the nature of the "love" between the Sonneteer and his aristocratic patron? Although Rowse was adamant that it was platonic, there are too many persuasive indications to the contrary. For example, in Sonnet 20, the poet hails his friend as the "master-mistress of my passion". He goes on to refer to the youth's penis and, though he rules out its use for himself, does not exclude the opposite scenario. In

Sonnet 52 a "blessed key" takes on a distinctly phallic shape as it brings the poet to "sweet up-locked" treasure and the youth is "had"[54]. In Sonnet 110 the poet promises not to "grind" his "appetite" elsewhere, his friend being "a god in love". And all this is against the background of a ready sexual intimacy, portrayed throughout the sonnets and starting in the early procreation poems with their several jocular references to masturbation[55].

Interestingly, however, there are indications that the youth felt that there was not enough of this love. For example, Sonnet 23 pleads rather implausible reasons for the poet's lack of attention. And he, in effect, excuses the infrequent operation of his "key" in Sonnet 52 by citing the increased pleasure brought with rarity. Such references contrast strongly with the lust and passion displayed in Sonnets 40-42 and the parallel Mistress sonnets. A sense emerges of a Sonneteer who is sufficiently flexible, sexually, to do what is needed for patronage, but whose stronger urges are heterosexual.

Against this background, let us now turn to the story which appears to unfold within Sonnets 56 through 94, starting with the anxious-sounding Sonnet 56:

> *Sweet love, renew thy force: be it not said*
> *Thy edge should blunter be than appetite,*
> *Which but today by feeding is allayed,*
> *Tomorrow sharpened in his former might.*
> *So, love, be thou: although today thou fill*
> *Thy hungry eyes even till they wink with fullness,*
> *Tomorrow see again, and do not kill*
> *The spirit of love with a perpetual dullness.*
> *Let this sad interim like the ocean be*
> *Which parts the shore, where two contracted new*
> *Come daily to the banks, that when they see*
> *Return of love, more blest may be the view.*

---

[54] Similar imagery is evoked in Scene 19 of Marlowe's *The Massacre at Paris*, when Mugeroun is accused of cuckolding the Duke of Guise by using his key to access the "privy chamber" of the Duchess.

[55] As brought out in Part II of this book.

> *As call it winter, which, being full of care,*
> *Makes summer's welcome thrice more wished, more rare.*

Here disquiet is suggested in the relationship between poet and youth. Love is apparently dwindling and unable to match "appetite". It seems, too, that one of the pair has absented himself from the other in a "sad interim".

The reference in the third quatrain to lovers parted by a stretch of water evokes the ancient Greek myth of Hero and Leander, in which Leander, a fair youth, swims the waters of the Hellespont which separate him from his love, Hero, a virgin priestess of Venus.

In the immediately following sonnets, 57 and 58, it becomes apparent that it is the youth who is absenting himself with others, much to the chagrin of the poet. The sonnets smack of the poet's jealousy and irritation at the youth's egoism, reinforcing the sense of a close relationship between the pair, albeit that their difference in social station is also emphasised. In the closing couplet of reproach in Sonnet 57, the word "will" (which had the secondary meanings in Elizabethan English of sex, sexual organ or sexual desire) is given an initial capital letter in the original, apparently to emphasise the pun on the poet's name. The triple pun reinforces the sense that the jealousy is partly sexual in its nature and that the sonnet is autobiography:

> *So true a fool is love that in your Will,*
> *Though you do anything, he thinks no ill.*

The sonnets continue on a range of subjects, generally contriving to praise the youth or to affirm the constancy of the poet's love, but the theme of jealousy (and hence competition) never disappears for long. In Sonnet 61 he complains of being far off from the youth while others are "all too near". In Sonnet 66 he rails at various injustices concluding with "Simple truth miscalled simplicity and captive good attending Captain ill"[56]. In Sonnet 67 there is a diatribe aimed at the youth's companions(s).

---

[56] Rowse points out an echo here of Marlowe's "And all his captains bound in captive chains" (*Tamburlaine*, Part I, III, iii, 115)

In Sonnet 69, he accuses the youth of making himself "common" with his behaviour, to give his reputation "the rank smell of weeds". This would have been taken as bitter insult by any aristocratic addressee and would surely have triggered hostility and resentment.

Correspondingly, the poet's tone shifts and becomes placatory. In Sonnets 71-74 the poems become self-deprecating and contemplate his death, metaphoric or otherwise[57] (with some beautiful poetry, competition perhaps forcing Shakespeare to his best efforts). They reek of pathos and invitations to consider life without the poet (and thus to regret his displacement). Finally in Sonnet 76 he admits that his poems are insufficiently inventive and in Sonnet 78 he acknowledges openly that he is in competition with more learned poets for the youth's favours.

The first quatrain of Sonnet 78 is interesting in its wider implications:

> *So oft have I invoked thee for my Muse,*
> *And found such fair assistance in my verse,*
> *As every **Alien** pen hath got my use*
> *And under thee their poesy disperse.*

Originally distinguished in italics and with opening capital letter, the meaning of the word "Alien" in line 3 is apparently stretched beyond the standard (like the "Rose" of Sonnet 1 – discussed earlier). The clue may lie in the accompanying word, "pen", used here primarily as a synonym for "writer", but carrying a phallic overtone[58].

On this basis, perhaps the stressing of "*Alien*" is indicative here of an outsider who is also sexually unconventional - hinted at, too, in the conclusion to the line, "hath got my use [of you]". I suggest that a similar overtone appears in *As You Like It*, where two cousins, Rosalind and Celia, banishing themselves to the

---

[57]　In Part II, I explore the interpretations of the death theme in the context of these sonnets, including the likelihood that it is, in effect, a reference to the death of the friendship.

[58]　Similar usage can be seen in *The Merchant of Venice*, where Gratiano (whose wife has just threatened to cuckold him with a doctor's clerk) responds: "I'll mar the young clerk's pen" (V, i, 237).

forest, take disguises. Rosalind dresses as a boy and chooses to call herself *Ganymede*, a name then heavily associated with homoeroticism. Celia, who has seemed to be in love with Rosalind, responds by saying she will be called "something that hath a reference to my state: *Aliena*" (I, ii).

In Sonnet 79 our poet reminds the youth that he was the latter's original protégé. Now he is in danger of displacement. He debunks the verse of his main rival. He acknowledges with another phallic overtone, however, that the youth, his "sweet love", "deserves the travail of a worthier pen".

Sonnet 80, on the pre-eminent rival, is revealing:

> *O, how I faint when I of you do write,*
> *Knowing a better spirit doth use your name,*
> *And in the praise thereof spends all his might,*
> *To make me tongue-tied, speaking of your fame.*
> *But since your worth, wide as the ocean is,*
> *The humble as the proudest sail doth bear,*
> *My saucy bark, inferior far to his,*
> *On your broad main doth wilfully appear.*
> *Your shallowest help will hold me up afloat,*
> *Whilst he upon your soundless deep doth ride;*
> *Or, being wracked, I am a worthless boat,*
> *He, of tall building and of goodly pride.*
> *Then if he thrive and I be cast away,*
> *The worst was this: my love was my decay.*

Dr. G.R. Ledger points out sexual innuendo in this sonnet, which he suggests may allude to the physical characteristics of the rival. The probability of this and other sexual innuendo[59] is, I propose, strengthened by the reference to the rival riding on the youth's soundless deep (a similar maritime metaphor also being used with sexual overtones in Sonnet 137, where our poet's mistress is likened to a bay where all men ride).

The sonnets continue with efforts to compete poetically, as well as to cast his rival as guilty of exaggerated praise, which cannot capture the youth's true beauty and essence. But in Sonnet

---

[59] Described in the commentary to Sonnet 80 in Part II

84 our poet's patience snaps and he again insults the youth, accusing him of being "fond on praise". He is losing the competition.

Then suddenly, in Sonnet 86, the subject of the rival poet is couched largely in the past tense. The rival is mentioned in no more sonnets. He is gone:

> *Was it the proud full sail of his great verse,*
> *Bound for the prize of all too precious you,*
> *That did my ripe thoughts in my brain inhearse,*
> *Making their tomb the womb wherein they grew?*
> *Was it his spirit, by spirits taught to write*
> *Above a mortal pitch, that struck me dead?*
> *No, neither he, nor his compeers by night*
> *Giving him aid, my verse astonish-ed.*
> *He, nor that affable familiar ghost*
> *Which nightly gulls him with intelligence,*
> *As victors of my silence cannot boast;*
> *I was not sick of any fear from thence;*
> *But when your countenance filled up his line,*
> *Then lacked I matter: that enfeebled mine.*

Sonnets 87-94 go on to depict the aftermath of the truncated rivalry. The poet appears to pay the price for offences given in his efforts to avoid displacement. He struggles to recover the goodwill of the young aristocrat and he remains uncertain of his standing. The high point of their relationship is clearly long gone.

Rowse's Case for the Rival

Rowse's case for Marlowe as the rival poet is based on: (i) the likely dating of composition of the Sonnets; (ii) Marlowe's known pre-eminence as a poet and playwright in 1592-3; and (iii) a number of pointers within the above story.

As we have already seen, there is powerful evidence to place Sonnets 1-96 in the period 1592-4, as claimed by Rowse. Line 1 of the valedictory sonnet 86 suggests unconditional respect for the rival, in contrast to the preceding sonnets where all apparent deference is qualified by implied or stated shortcomings[60]. Marlowe was reported killed unexpectedly on 30 May 1593 and, as Rowse points out, the respect and finality of tone in this poem point strongly at this permanent departure.

The references to spirits and their aid have provoked much debate and various theories over the years. Rowse suggests that Marlowe's highly successful play, *Dr Faustus*, was being staged around the time of his death. He proposes that the hero, Faustus, who contracted to sell his soul in exchange for supernatural aid from demons, was regarded as a dramatic projection of Marlowe, himself: hence the current tense, artfully used in line 10, "nightly gulls him with intelligence".

Rowse makes further connections through the echo of Hero and Leander in Sonnet 56. Around 1592/3 Marlowe was working on his long poem, *Hero & Leander*, which Rowse theorises was designed to secure the patronage of Southampton in competition with Shakespeare's *Venus & Adonis*. He points to parallels in phrasing within the two poems, which, he claims, show that each poet was aware of the other's work[61]. In his poem, Marlowe describes Leander in sensuous terms corresponding with Southampton's then effeminate appearance, smooth white skin and long "dangling tresses". The poem becomes positively erotic in its depiction of Leander's swim, during which the sea-god, Neptune, takes his opportunity to caress various parts of the youth's body. However, it was not formally published before Marlowe's death and he made no dedication; consequently, such evidence remains subjective.

Rowse, regarding Shakespeare's love as platonic, speculates in passing that Marlowe's homosexuality might have favoured him in the competition for the bisexual Earl's favours. Although Rowse flew in the face of the evidence regarding the nature of Shakespeare's love, and he showed no recognition of the overtones of a sexual dimension to the rivalry (suggested above in relation to Sonnets 56-86), it appears from these and the pointers

---

[60] As brought out more fully in commentary on the poems in Part II

[61] Set out in his *Christopher Marlowe*, within the chapter *The Rival Poets*

to Marlowe's homosexuality[62] that he was right about this aspect of the rivalry.

The Case against Marlowe

There is no separate evidence that Southampton had a personal relationship with Marlowe[63], though they did overlap in their spells of education at Cambridge. But is there any evidence which rules out such a relationship?

As with most persons of the time, our knowledge of Marlowe's activities and movements is slight. Nevertheless, such information as we have suggests some unusual conduct and events in the years and weeks leading up to his disappearance in May 1593[64].

Though then facing grave charges before the Queen's privy council, Marlowe was allowed out on bail (in contrast to his unfortunate friend, the poet, Thomas Kyd, who, in the same matter, was imprisoned and tortured without trial). He was then purportedly killed by accident, while in the exclusive company of three men, Frizer, Skeres and Poley, all of whom had connections to the Queen's security services. The inquest into his death by the Coroner of the Queen's Household, the exoneration of his killer and the report of his burial occurred with uncommon haste and few of these facts became common knowledge.

The circumstances suggest that Marlowe was the victim or tool of political machination, which was probably triggered by a fear of unwelcome information that might come to light under questioning at his impending trial. This might well have related to Kyd's assertion, among others, that Marlowe had been guilty of treason in his promotion of James of Scotland (a pretender to Elizabeth's throne).

---

[62] Described in Appendix D

[63] Nor is there such for any other recognized poet before 1603, except Shakespeare and Nashe (who qualify on the basis of evidence put forward in this outline). As previously noted, the unrepeated one-of-a-multitude dedications of Barnabe Barnes and Gervase Markham show all the signs of speculative appeals for a patronage which was never realized.

[64] For an intriguing and persuasive analysis of Marlowe's life and connections with the Queen's intelligence services see *The Reckoning* by Charles Nicholls.

Whatever the underlying reason, if political machination was involved, the prime candidate for architect of Marlowe's disposition is William Cecil, Lord Burghley: Lord Treasurer and chief advisor to the Queen, a member of her Privy Council and *de facto* controller of her security service. Burghley had been involved with some previous unusual activities by Marlowe[65]. With his son, Sir Robert Cecil (by then also on the Privy Council, and his successor as controller of the security service), he was uniquely in a position to pull the strings necessary to keep Marlowe out of jail (but isolated) and to bring about an appropriate disposal prior to trial.

Some commentators build from this base a hypothesis that Marlowe's death was faked and that he adopted secret identities as an intelligence agent, who continued to write as a sideline under the umbrella of the Shakespeare name. As with all the other alternative author theories, it relies on further assumptions (some of which are tenuous) and cherry-picked evidence, which is either contradicted by other evidence, or is capable of different interpretation.

I discount this version of an alternate author theory, for the solid general reasons already given. However, in order to provide a more specific assessment, I attach at Appendix D a summarized biography of Marlowe and an analysis of the nature of the reasoning offered by speculators that he wrote Shakespeare's works.

Arising from this assessment, the only matter which might militate against Marlowe being the rival of the Sonnets is the suggestion that, at the time of his death, Marlowe already had a patron (who was not Southampton) and that he was thought to have been living at the household of that patron, Thomas Walsingham.

---

[65]   Including (i) an intervention in 1587 to allow him to receive his Masters degree, in which it was confirmed that Marlowe had been absent from university on unusual business for the Queen and (ii) adjudication in 1592 on accusations against Marlowe by one, Richard Baines, of counterfeiting, treason and papacy in the Dutch port of Flushing.

However, the facts are very sparse on the nature of Marlowe's relationship with Walsingham[66]. There is little evidence of literary sponsorship and there are solid pointers that Walsingham would not have been his only benefactor in this respect. Moreover, it is unlikely that Walsingham was then a man with cash to spare[67]. Nor is there more to be read in the association of Marlowe with Walsingham's residence than that this was where someone said or thought he would be during the last two weeks of May.

I shall return to these points later, but, in short, there is nothing in the facts to preclude the proposition that, during the months up to May 1593, Marlowe, like Thomas Nashe before him, attempted to win benefits from his fellow Cambridge alumnus, the third Earl of Southampton.

The Clinching Evidence

The demonstrations of biography elsewhere in the Sonnets, and the comfortable fit between Marlowe's history and the story of the rival poet in Sonnets 56-86, together suggest strongly that those poems also contain biography. The case would be proven beyond reasonable doubt if we could: (i) tighten the dating of composition of Sonnets 56-85 to a period ending just before Marlowe's reported death at the end of May 1593, and (ii) find corroboration for the reality of the story depicted in those sonnets.

---

[66] Although Charles Nicholls is persuasive in his presentation (in *The Reckoning*) of circumstantial evidence that Walsingham had been linked with Marlowe through activities for the security services prior to 1590.

[67] He had been imprisoned for default of debt, prior to his inheritance in 1590 of a family manor with all its maintenance requirements. It seems that for a while thereafter he needed to resort to con-tricks in order to supplement his income. He was involved, with Frizer and Skeres, in a scheme of early 1593 to fleece the inheritance of a young man named Woodleff (as described in David Riggs' *The World of Christopher Marlowe*). His wealth and his knighthood came later, through activities perhaps facilitated by his wife's connections with the Queen or services to Burghley.

I propose that the key to such clinching evidence lies in Shakespeare's following dedication to Southampton of his poem, *Venus & Adonis*, first published before early June 1593[68]:

To the Right Honourable Henry Wriothesley,
Earl of Southampton, and Baron of Titchfield.

Right Honourable,

I know not how I shall offend in dedicating my unpolished lines to your Lordship, nor how the world will censure me for choosing so strong a prop to support so weak a burden, only if your Honour seem but pleased, I account myself highly praised, and vow to take advantage of all idle hours, till I have honoured you with some graver labour. But if the first heir of my invention prove deformed, I shall be sorry it had so noble a godfather: and never after ear [cultivate] *so barren a land, for fear it yield me still so bad a harvest. I leave it to your Honourable survey, and your Honour to your heart's content, which I wish may always answer your own wish, and the world's hopeful expectation.*

Your Honour's in all duty,

William Shakespeare.

This first of Shakespeare's only two public dedications looks distant and obsequious, albeit with an undertone of familiarity in its ending: largely appropriate if the poet and earl had been strangers to each other, but strangely diffident for a pair who had shared the intimacies portrayed in Sonnets 20, 22, 31 and 52. With such intimacy one would expect a tone more akin to that of the affectionate *Lucrece* dedication made to Southampton a year later (and reproduced here towards the end of Appendix A).

However, if Sonnets 56-85 do indeed include biography for the period immediately prior to news of Marlowe's death, then the *Venus* dedication would have been written at a time when Shakespeare was suffering from fear, anger, jealousy and injured pride at his displacement in patronage and friendship.

---

[68] It was registered at the Stationers Company on 28 April 1593 and a copy was purchased on 12 June 1593, according to the diary (now held at the Folger Shakespeare Library) of one, Richard Stonley.

This would not only explain its tone. With the background provided by the Sonnets, one can go further and discern a double edge to the following sentiments expressed by Shakespeare within the dedication: *"But if the first heir of my invention prove deformed, I shall be sorry it had so noble a godfather: and never after ear so barren a land, for fear it yield me still so bad a harvest"*.

These words, taken at face value, as they would by persons unaware of the underlying situation, suggest humility by the poet regarding the first work published in his name and self-deprecation in his association with the Earl. However, on closer inspection there are oddities.

First, the words seem superfluous. The dedication flows well – and arguably better - if they are deleted. Second, the words "heir" and "deformed" are not the most natural to accord with the theme. One would expect words like "offered fruit" and "stunted" instead, given the analogy therein of farming and harvests.

The word "heir" is and was more commonly used to describe a human. Further, though often used as a synonym for offspring, its meaning is, and was, one who inherits or receives as a result of a gifting.

As for "deformed", its root word of "form" then had much stronger connotations of an original or perfect version, in line with classical philosophies (alluded to, for example, in Sonnet 43).

In summary, the extract highlighted above looks like an addition to an already sensible and internally consistent dedication and it appears designed to carry alternative meanings, appropriate to a human who is to receive something and who seems adversely changed from a better version of himself.

Accordingly, the words can be construed as: "But if the first dedicatee of any of my compositions [Southampton] proves to be debased from what he was, I shall be sorry, as the man who originally encouraged my poetry was such a noble patron: and I will never again devote my efforts to such an undiscerning ingrate for fear of the same poor return".

When the underlying mood of the writer is assessed in this light, other nuances suggest themselves. For example, he concludes the dedication with the words *"I leave .... your Honour to your heart's content ...* ". There is nothing untoward in these, perhaps. Nevertheless, they are strangely intimate words: ones which would well fit the sentiments of a former pet, who has been spurned for another; ones which may even be questioning the integrity of the dedicatee.

Deliciously, on further inspection, the parallel meanings extend throughout the piece. Here is an open rendition thereof, covering the full body of the dedication:

I know not how you will discern insult in this dedication of my unpolished lines to your Lordship. Nor do I know how the world will censure me for choosing what is relatively so substantial a work to honour such a lightweight.

If my only reward is your Honour's apparent pleasure I will, nevertheless, be flattered and promise to work as hard as I can to provide you with something more serious in theme.

On the other hand, if the first dedicatee of any of my compositions proves to be debased from what he was, I shall be sorry, as the man who originally encouraged my poetry was such a noble patron: and I will never again devote my efforts to such an undiscerning ingrate for fear of the same poor return.

I leave it for your honourable scrutiny and I leave your honour to the one who currently contents you. I hope he will be the constant slave of your self-centred whims in that manner which all look forward to behold.

The complexity and coherence of the hidden theme, and its perfect congruence with that of the relevant sonnets, rule out any significant possibility of a fluke[69]. The parallel theme was clearly intentional and we can imagine the satisfaction taken by the disgruntled poet in cocking a snoot at his fickle friend, in a way which was so open and yet so skilfully disguised. We can also imagine his chagrin when, on learning of Marlowe's death (between the composition of Sonnets 85 and 86) he realizes that he has taken the risks of further offending unnecessarily!

---

[69] Some might wonder whether the hidden theme points, instead, to Shakespeare's displeasure with the situation depicted in Sonnets 40-42, where Southampton beds the dark mistress. However, there is no real congruence with these sonnets, where Shakespeare contrives forgiveness of the young earl and there is none of the insult and bitterness towards him which emerges from the rival poet sonnets, nor any suggestion that Shakespeare's compositions for the Earl are under-appreciated.

This concept can be extended with a second take on the Latin inscription which immediately precedes Shakespeare's dedicatory address to Southampton in its original printing:

> *Vilia miretur vulgus; mihi flavus Apollo*
> *Pocula Castalia plena ministret aqua.*

The inscription, taken from Elegy 15 of Book 1 of Ovid's love poems translates as "Let the common man admire trash or vile things; may golden Apollo serve me full cups of Castalian waters [being the fountain created by Apollo, which provided poetic genius or inspiration]".

Since the theme of *Venus & Adonis* was taken from Ovid's *Metamorphoses* the quotation can be interpreted at its face value of an intention to provide the reader with poetry of an Ovidian stamp and class, albeit thereby suggesting a degree of pomposity in the author.

However, the quote could also be associated with Marlowe, who had composed a celebrated rendition of Ovid's Elegies in English of rhyming iambic pentameter[70].

Seen in this light and that of the story in the Sonnets, the inscription instead looks like a dig at Southampton, suggesting that he was common or vulgar (as first mooted in Sonnet 69) for his admiration of Marlowe's offerings, be they the trash of exaggerated praises, referred to in Sonnets 82-85, or the sexual benefits hinted at in Sonnets 78 and 80.

The young Earl's perception of any of these unflattering pieces of wit, which resonate with Shakespeare's more direct insult within the privacy of Sonnet 84, would further explain his subsequent coldness and the poet's attempts to placate and justify, as portrayed in Sonnets 87-91.

In turn, the beautiful, multi-dovetailed fit of three completely independent sources of information – Marlowe's history, the *Venus* dedication of 1593 and the Sonnets – reinforces, to a point beyond reasonable doubt, all three Sonnet character identifications: Shakespeare, Southampton, and Marlowe. Anyone

---

70   Marlowe had rendered these two lines poetically as: *Let base-conceited wits admire vile things, Fair Phoebus lead me to the Muses' springs.*

inclined to dismiss as accident the extensive double-meanings within the *Venus* dedication should look at the subsequent *Lucrece* dedication (towards the end of Appendix A) to appreciate just how remote is this possibility. The correlation of the Sonnets with every aspect of the double-layered complex of messages discernible in the *Venus* dedication shows that the poems sing of real events in the personal history of their author.

Conclusions

We now have assurance beyond reasonable doubt that: (i) the author of the Sonnets was William Shakespeare of Stratford; (ii) most of the sonnets were printed in sequences reflecting their chronology; and (iii) the Sonnets contain biography, mainly concerning Shakespeare and the third Earl of Southampton, but also dealing with their shared mistress and Christopher Marlowe.

The above explanation of Shakespeare's dedication to Southampton of *Venus & Adonis* – so long misunderstood - also removes any reasonable doubt that he was the author of that work. The dedication, itself, is a gem of wit.

The contents of both the Sonnets and *Venus & Adonis* show that Shakespeare was familiar with classical works and philosophies. Though, like Ben Jonson, he never attended university, he had, by May 1593, as he claimed in Sonnet 78, advanced his "rude ignorance" and reached the heights of the learned.

Thomas Nashe, that satirical author and outspoken critic, had a much closer and more vitriolic relationship with Southampton and Shakespeare than has previously been discerned. On the cohering evidence of his own writings, and those of Gabriel Harvey and the author of the *Parnassus* plays, he had regarded Shakespeare as a serious literary competitor and a wooer of Southampton, from 1592 at latest. Shakespeare, able to engage the highly educated Southampton over a long period, must have had well developed social skills. He thereby gained access to an aristocratic grapevine and modus operandi, as well as those of the rural and working class environment from which he sprang.

All the above circumstances reinforce the orthodox position, already powerfully supported, that Shakespeare was a well-read, resourced and skilled author. In combination, they bury beyond recovery one of the fundamental arguments used by all champions of Shakespearean authorship surrogacy: that Shakespeare did not have the wherewithal to compose his plays.

With the assurance of biography, and more background, we can also make reasonable extrapolations in relation to Marlowe's termination as the Rival of the Sonnets.

We have already seen of persuasive arguments that Marlowe's strange disappearance was engineered and that, if so, the most likely puppet-master was Lord Burghley. However, with the revelation of Marlowe's contemporaneous affair with Southampton, a compelling new dimension emerges - because Burghley was also closely connected with the Earl. He was, at the time, the young lord's legal guardian and the man who had been responsible to the Queen for his upbringing and education since the age of eight.

The Privy Councillor had been pressing Southampton to wed and, in his capacity as guardian, had contracted him to marriage with Burghley's own grand-daughter. Southampton was resisting this arrangement, but Burghley must have been hopeful that, with his influence and the prospect of a heavy financial penalty should Southampton default, the marriage would go ahead[71].

At the time the Earl's prospects looked rosy. A few months earlier he had impressed Stringer and others at the Queen's reception in Oxford. By May 1593 a rumour was circulating that he was to be created a Knight of the Garter[72]. However, Burghley would surely have known of his young ward's close relationship with Marlowe in the weeks leading up to that fateful May. It is unlikely that he would have approved, knowing both Marlowe and his reputation, summarised later by the author of the Parnassus plays:

---

[71] Burghley had been keen to match Southampton with Elizabeth Vere from around 1590. Southampton had asked for a year's delay, and then continued to prevaricate. Burghley eventually contracted her to William Stanley, the new Earl of Derby, whom she wed in January 1595, three months after Southampton had reached his majority. Under the rules of wardship and in his own capacity as Master of the Wards, he proceeded to levy the huge fine of £5000 on his former ward.

[72] As recorded by Akrigg and Stopes in their biographies of Southampton

> *"Marlowe was unhappy in his buskined muse,*
> *Alas unhappy in his life and end.*
> *Pity it is that wit so ill should dwell,*
> *Wit lent from heaven, but vices sent from hell."*

Then, through his connections with the state security services, Burghley would have learned, before did the Privy Council as a whole, of the nature of Kyd's accusations against Marlowe, including treason, propagation of heresy in relation to the Queen's Church of England, and associations with sodomy. He would surely have foreseen the risk of Southampton being dragged into the case, either by a prosecution seeking further evidence, or through the poet desperately pointing to his high ranking friends: not an attractive outlook for the bisexual earl, whose parents were Catholics. Nor would this have been enjoyable for Burghley, who, as the earl's guardian, would doubtless have been held accountable to some degree for his protégé's activities and friendships.

Whether looking out for his own skin, or to protect the reputation and prospects of his ward (and grand-daughter), or, most probably, for all these reasons, Burghley would have required Southampton to abandon Marlowe as soon as Kyd had pointed his finger. He would also have taken steps to get the man from Canterbury away from the young aristocrat. He could readily have achieved this by arranging an offer of harbour from Marlowe's ostensible benefactor, the self-serving Thomas Walsingham, who was also connected to the security services. Southampton (and Marlowe) would have needed little persuasion to cooperate, when confronted with the accusations against Marlowe.

It may be that Burghley had hoped to be able to defuse the situation quietly and peaceably, while Marlowe was safely quarantined by Walsingham. Nevertheless, the case against Marlowe progressed, with further accusations emerging of past improprieties[73]. In these circumstances both Burghley and

---

[73] Baines, Marlowe's accuser of the previous year at Flushing, was quick to support and expand upon Kyd's assertions, as shown by the surviving note of his own testimony. Here

Southampton would have been concerned to minimise any evidence of Marlowe's close association with the Earl, including the destruction of any incriminating letters or poems. They would also have preferred the poet to disappear before the completion of his trial and to remain incommunicado permanently[74].

All this extrapolation is consistent with history and the reality of the poet's death, as reported by the coroner. Marlowe duly disappeared from the scene, as did any direct evidence of a previous association with Southampton[75]. He also vanished from subsequent sonnets, addressed in private by Shakespeare to the Earl, and composed at intervals until their cessation around 1603/4.[76] In May 1593 one of the brightest minds of the day was snuffed out like a candle: to end a wick which had dipped in just the wrong place and time.

As for Shakespeare, further analysis gives rise to an astonishing suspicion: that it was he who instigated events leading to the untimely deaths of both Marlowe and Thomas Kyd! Consider the evidence of history and as established above:

---

he referred ominously to other available witnesses, described as "some great men who in convenient time shall be named".

[74] Burghley had a reputation for Machiavellian ruthlessness. When Ferdinando Stanley, fifth earl of Derby with a Catholic background and a potential claim to the succession, died mysteriously in April 1594, one of his allies was convinced that he had been poisoned on Burghley's orders. Ferdinando's demise allowed his brother, William Stanley – described by George Carey as a "nidicock" [nincompoop] – to become Earl of Derby, whereupon he wed Burghley's grand-daughter. Both events helped to insure the Cecils against unattractive contingencies on the Queen's death. The full account is given in Ian Wilson's *Shakespeare; the Evidence*.

[75] *Hero & Leander*, which did not threaten Southampton, survived, probably because Marlowe had taken it to work on while in Walsingham's custody. It was published five years later by Edward Blount, with a peculiarly phrased dedication to Walsingham, who was almost certainly the source of the publisher's material.

[76] However, Southampton's promotion to the Garter never materialized in the Queen's lifetime. It seems that the "rank smell of weeds", discerned initially by Shakespeare, seeped up into loftier air and, with continuing peccadilloes, kept her doubtful of him. It seems probable that Shakespeare learned some of the detail of Marlowe's demise from Southampton, given *Touchstone's* reference in *As You Like It* to striking "a man more dead than a great reckoning in a little room". The phrase echoes the circumstances of Marlowe's death, as well as the word "reckoning" [meaning also a "bill"] used in the coroner's report.

- In the weeks leading up to May 1593 Shakespeare's enjoyment of indulgences from Southampton was threatened by a more successful rival, Marlowe.

- During this time Shakespeare was completing his long poem, *Venus & Adonis*, to be dedicated to the first heir of his invention, Southampton.

- It is likely that Marlowe was then also working on his long poem, *Hero & Leander*. There are hints in each of these works that its author was aware of the other and was adapting content accordingly. The male subject in each poem is an idealized version of the Earl of Southampton as he was in 1592/3.

- The publication of *Venus* appears to have been completed in haste. It was registered in the Stationers Register on 18 April 1593, under the aegis of a man of influence, the Archbishop of Canterbury. It was on the street within weeks.

- As is borne out by his rise from provincial grammar school boy to wealthy stage company co-owner, Shakespeare was a streetwise man of resourcefulness and determination. He was bold and, when offended, he hit back – both qualities being shown in his double-layered *Venus* dedication and in the insults of Sonnets 69 and 84.

- He was probably prepared to fight dirty. In November 1596 he, together with one, Francis Langley, was the target of a restraining writ, implying an association with the skulduggery of a business feud[77]. Not long after this, he apparently resorted to bribery in order to acquire a family coat of arms[78].

- In April 1593 there had appeared on the streets of London some inflammatory anti-immigrant material which had led the Privy Council to instigate a search for the culprits. Then, on 5 May 1593 there emerged a threatening, anonymous poem in the same vein, which conveyed a suggestion that

---

[77] The writ was issued on behalf of William Gardiner. Langley was an entrepreneur with a record of violence and extortion and Gardiner was a corrupt magistrate, previously petitioned against by Langley – both sides apparently squabbling in relation to the business of theatre houses.

[78] As described by Duncan-Jones in her *Ungentle Shakespeare*

Marlowe was involved[79]. It was this document which led to Marlowe becoming implicated in more serious charges, arising during the subsequent investigation. In turn these led to his death.

With these facts, it is easy to envisage Shakespeare's hand in the events of May 1593. However, let me fill in the gaps with some assumptions.

It is reasonable to suppose that the Stratfordian would have been anxious to get his *Venus & Adonis* out well before Marlowe could formally publish *Hero & Leander* (probably to be accompanied by an effusive and witty dedication to Southampton). Marlowe's poem was formidable and likely further to overshadow Shakespeare's efforts to impress, at a time when he wanted whatever reward was available from a young aristocrat of limited resources[80].

It would have been easy to persuade the vain earl to use his contacts to help with an expedited publication of *Venus*[81]. However, it would also help Shakespeare's cause if he could put a spanner in his rival's works and, perhaps, cause delay in those very works. Even if delay was unforthcoming, how pleasant to discomfort a rival who had come on to his patch and was threatening both his privileged friendship and his livelihood!

What better way to distract Marlowe, and to distance him from Southampton, than by forcing him to fight off charges of impropriety?[82] Marlowe was no stranger to brushes with

---

[79] The poem, now known as the Dutch Church Libel, was posted on a church wall. Rediscovered by Arthur Freeman in the Bodleian Library, it is constructed in rhyming iambic pentameter and runs to over fifty lines – clearly the work of an author with ability. It is signed "per Tamberlaine", evoking Marlowe's popular play, and has references discernible in others of his plays.

[80] As a minor, Southampton was property-rich but relatively cash-poor, his estate affairs being under the control of his guardian, Lord Burghley.

[81] Whether or not expedition was a factor, Shakespeare may anyway have sought the offices of a reliable registrant, if he was away from London during April. Interestingly, the Archbishop, John Whitgift, had been a sometime employer and patron of Thomas Nashe during the three years ending late 1592, when this association ceased for no obvious reason. It is now reasonable to speculate that Whitgift chose Southampton above Nashe, following the latter's insults of the earl, as described in Appendix B.

[82] Sonnets 33-39 can be interpreted to suggest that this strategy would have occurred naturally to Shakespeare, given his own experience. Sonnets 33-35 hint that the triangular

authority, and any mud that could be flung at him was likely to be sticky. Easy for Shakespeare (though not for most) to concoct an inflammatory poem that pointed to Marlowe, even if few would believe that the latter would so obviously hint at his own perpetration. However, with luck, he would be inconvenienced and minds would be jogged on his colourful history. If necessary, a few more red herrings could be scattered around as and when necessary.

As it happened, further intervention was apparently unnecessary. Probably through cruel mis-chance, the poem and the resultant interrogation of the poet, Kyd, re-kindled different unsavoury matters concerning Marlowe. This development allowed others, hostile to the poet, the chance to fan the flames. A likely candidate is Baines, who had fallen out with Marlowe at Flushing and who would probably have been delighted to provide elaboration on Kyd's assertions[83]. At some point it became evident to Burghley that Southampton would be drawn into the wider proceedings, at considerable detriment to both guardian and ward. From then on Marlowe's fate was sealed[84].

Would Shakespeare have foreseen all this? Unlikely, I suggest. But, on the facts, he is a prime suspect of being the spark for Marlowe's death.

Putting aside such suspicions, we can, nevertheless, now perceive the Stratfordian in a more penetrating light. Here he is - a grandmaster of his language, unveiled through his own words: the son of a provincial burgher, who rose to fame and fortune in London; a family man and bi-sexual adventurer, embroiled in two extraordinary and traumatic triangular affairs, whose patron and lover was an earl, who sought to bring down a queen, and whose brilliant rival was an agent for that queen and was killed for that earl.

---

affair involving the Dark Lady had started. Sonnet 36 suggests that Southampton had been warned off too close an association with an upstart actor of liberal tendencies, leading to a separation of the pair, depicted in Sonnets 37-39.

[83]   The involvements of Kyd and Baines in Marlowe's downfall are described briefly in Appendix C.

[84]   As, by mis-chance, was that of Kyd, who never recovered from the torture and loss of patronage occasioned by his being dragged into the proceedings. He died the next year.

Here is a private man in a public arena, whose own story is as strange and eventful as that of any of his creations!

Experiencing the Sonnets

A newcomer in search of an uplifting poetic experience may be disappointed in Shakespeare's Sonnets. Though some of the poetry is glorious, there is, on first perception, much mundane content and limited aural beauty.

There are two main reasons for this. First, as we have seen, most of the sonnets were, in effect, private correspondence with Henry Wriothesley on matters relevant to the pair. Second, Shakespeare would often have been obliged to sacrifice aural elegance in order to express the witticisms and parallel meanings of which he was so fond. It is the combination of resonance and linguistic subtlety which puts the Sonnets into a class of their own. Reading a Shakespearean sonnet can be like staring at one of those pictures with hidden patterns. A change of perspective abruptly transforms a bland, shallow scene into a startling, three dimensional tapestry.

With this understanding of their background, we are partially equipped to experience the Sonnets in the manner intended by Shakespeare. In other respects, however, we remain at a severe disadvantage - due to evolutions in meanings and pronunciations within the English language. Nevertheless, we can seek at least an approximation of that experience and, in the process, obtain further clues to the underlying biography.

Set out in Part II, following, is each of the one hundred and fifty four poems, accompanied by commentary which builds upon the above discoveries. Here also is a modernized rendition of each sonnet, which - one way or another – is sure to enhance appreciation of the original, represented above in each case.

Portrait of Henry Wriothesley, 3rd Earl of Southampton, reproduced under copyright from a private collection. The portrait has been dated to the period 1590-3, close to that of the early sonnets

PART II

A HIDDEN SONG RESUNG:

SHAKESPEARE'S SONNETS

SONNET 1: The story begins with this first of seventeen poems urging procreation (implicitly to produce a male heir) on one who, in progressive descriptions, emerges as an aristocratic youth of feminine beauty. As established beyond reasonable doubt in the preceding Part I, the addressee of this and most of the other sonnets was Henry Wriothesley, third Earl of Southampton.

In what becomes a hallmark of the Sonnets, there are subtle overtones and parallel meanings as well as occasional poetic distortions of grammar (as in line 14), all of which can provide difficulties in interpretation.

In its original publication, the word *"Rose"* in line 2 is distinguished by italic printing, probably denoting an unusual significance or extension of meaning. In this case it suggests a nickname, arising from elisions of Southampton's name to its easier and more intimate form of expression: "Rosely".

The phrase *"only herald to the gaudy spring"* in line 10 appears mildly peculiar until its full context is discerned. As the only surviving male of an aristocratic family, which had sprung from a dynasty of heralds, Southampton was its only potential propagator. The *"gaudy spring"* suggests a burgeoning of that aristocratic house and carries – given other hints - an overtone of ejaculate.

The jocular hints of unproductive solo sex are subtle enough that they might be dismissed, were it not for their continuation in a number of the ensuing sonnets.

SONNET 1

From fairest creatures we desire increase
That thereby beauty's **Rose** *might never die,*
But as the riper should by time decease
His tender heir might bear his memory:
But thou, contracted to thine own bright eyes,
Feed'st thy light's flame with self-substantial fuel,
Making a famine where abundance lies.
Thyself thy foe, to thy sweet self too cruel.
Thou that art now the world's fresh ornament
And only herald to the gaudy spring,
Within thine own bud buriest thy content
And, tender churl, mak'st waste in niggarding.
Pity the world, or else this glutton be:
To eat the world's due, by the grave and thee.

We want life's fairest all to multiply
So beauty's *Rose* might live eternally
And as the older ones in time should die
Their young offspring may bear their memory.
But you, a moth drawn to your own bright flame,
Feed your life's fire with your own fount's resource,
To turn abundance into sterile shame,
Yourself your foe, to your sweet self too coarse.
Thus you, who are the world's new bright young thing,
Sole herald of the life-spring, Nature's gift,
Inhume your own seed in self-pleasuring,
A dear fool, wasting wealth through too much thrift.
Grant us our due or else you'll come to be
Buried with a glutton's progeny.

SONNET 2: At the time of these early sonnets Southampton was about eighteen years of age and Shakespeare around twenty eight. The poet had a wife and three children, who remained in the family home in Stratford, at least two days' journey away from his working environment in London.

The Earl was the only son of staunchly Catholic parents, whose marriage had become strained within four years of his birth, and who had become estranged when he was six.

Following the death of his father, shortly before his eighth birthday, the young earl had become a ward of the Queen's chief advisor, Lord Burghley.

After early schooling at Cecil House in London, Southampton had gone on to become, at twelve, an undergraduate of Burghley's old college, St John's, Cambridge. By the age of sixteen he had received his MA degree and had been admitted to Grey's Inn, in London, for the finishing education popular with wealthy young men of the time. Such experience promoted familiarity with high society, art and the stage, as much as the workings of the law.

In lines 5 and 6 of this sonnet, Shakespeare uses the words "*beauty*" and "*treasure*". In context, such words have sexual connotations, signified here by their close proximity to the words "*use*" (in line 9) and "*lusty*", respectively. "*Count*" in line 11 was then pronounced "cunt", its summing suggesting a pun on the outcome of suggested endeavours in the realm of such pleasure (see commentary at Sonnet 109 for an illustration of similar punning by Shakespeare on the word "*country*").

SONNET 2

When forty winters shall besiege thy brow
And dig deep trenches in thy beauty's field,
Thy youth's proud livery, so gazed on now,
Will be a tattered weed of small worth held:
Then, being asked where all thy beauty lies,
Where all the treasure of thy lusty days,
To say within thine own deep-sunken eyes
Were an all-eating shame and thriftless praise.
How much more praise deserved thy beauty's use
If thou couldst answer "This fair child of mine
Shall sum my count and make my old excuse",
Proving his beauty by succession thine.
This were to be new-made when thou art old
And see thy blood warm when thou feel'st it cold.

When forty winters have besieged your brow
And dug deep trenches in your beauty's earth,
The proud robe of your youth, so gazed on now,
Will seem a tattered rag of little worth.
And then when asked where all your beauty lies,
Where all the treasure of your lusty youth,
To answer in the spent of hollow eyes
Would give such travesty its shameful truth.
How much more fit were beauty's use assuaged
With your response that "This fair child of mine
Is product of my grind and why I've aged",
His beauty yours, the fruit of your green vine.
Thus would you be renewed when you are old,
And see your blood glow warm when it feels cold.

SONNET 3: Around 1590, when Southampton was sixteen, Burghley had decided to commit his ward to marriage. Such a contract was within his powers as guardian and an early marriage made sense, given the precarious position of the Southampton line, whose succession was dependent on a son from its only surviving male. Burghley had chosen for bride his own granddaughter, Elizabeth Vere (daughter of the 17th Earl of Oxford), then some fifteen years of age.

Such a marriage made good sense. The bride-elect came from a noble family, superior to the Wriothesleys in both prestige and longevity. They were established Protestants and their association would have helped to diminish the taint of Catholicism attaching to the young earl's family. However, the prospective groom had been reluctant to commit and had procrastinated for months, much to the frustration of Burghley, who was supported in his aims by the young lord's mother and his maternal grandfather.

In lines 9 and 10, Shakespeare slips in a compliment to the Earl's mother. This, together with the relentless urgings to procreate in the first 17 sonnets, has led some to suggest that these sonnets were sponsored or, at least, encouraged by this would-be grandmother.

The *"die single"* of line 14 supplements the hint of masturbation in the *"self-love"* of line 8. The word *"die"* had the secondary meaning of experiencing orgasm.

SONNET 3

Look in thy glass and tell the face thou viewest
Now is the time that face should form another,
Whose fresh repair if now thou not renewest
Thou dost beguile the world, unbless some mother.
For where is she so fair whose uneared womb
Disdains the tillage of thy husbandry?
Or who is he so fond will be the tomb
Of his self-love to stop posterity?
Thou art thy mother's glass and she in thee
Calls back the lovely April of her prime,
So thou through windows of thine age shall see,
Despite of wrinkles, this thy golden time.
But if thou live remembered not to be,
Die single and thine image dies with thee.

Reflect upon yourself, lest you forget
The one seen in your glass would be betrayed,
As would the world, if he does not beget:
Renew himself, make mother of some maid.
For where is she so fair, whose untilled womb
Would not desire your plough and husbandry?
Or who's that fool, so self-loved to entomb
Himself, unmated with no progeny?
You are your mother's glass, and in you she
Calls back the lovely April of her prime:
So you, in images elsewhen, will see,
Through age and wrinkles, this your golden time.
If you live life forgotten to world's view,
Expend alone, your image dies with you.

SONNET 4: An image of the Earl in his teens has been identified in a surviving portrait. For many years it was thought to have been that of a long-haired woman wearing lipstick and rouge (see plate at end of Part I). Details of clothing and jewellery date the portrait to the period 1590-3.

Later-drawn portraits, including a Hilliard miniature when he was around twenty, show that that the Earl kept his tresses at an unfashionable shoulder-length well into his thirties[85].

In this sonnet, Shakespeare continues a secondary theme of wasteful masturbation, with words and phrases like *"spend upon thyself"*, *"abuse"* and *"having traffic with thyself alone"* - which follow the *"treasure of thy lusty days"* and *"beauty's use"* of Sonnet 2, and *"die single"* of Sonnet 3. Such allusions were presumably for the amusement of the young earl and, perhaps, his friends, but were sufficiently subtle to be missed, or ignored, by other readers (including perhaps his mother).

---

[85] Such depictions may be readily inspected online, by googling "earl Southampton portraits"

SONNET 4

Unthrifty loveliness, why dost thou spend
Upon thyself thy beauty's legacy?
Nature's bequest gives nothing but doth lend,
And, being frank, she lends to those are free.
Then, beauteous niggard, why dost thou abuse
Thy bounteous largesse given thee to give?
Profitless usurer, why dost thou use
So great a sum of sums yet canst not live?
For, having traffic with thyself alone,
Thou of thyself thy sweet self dost deceive.
Then how, when Nature calls thee to be gone,
What acceptable audit canst thou leave?
Thy unused beauty must be tombed with thee,
Which, used, lives the executor to be.

O wasteful loveliness why do you spend
Upon yourself your beauty's legacy?
For Nature makes bequest, but just to lend,
And, open, lends for sharing openly.
So beauteous skinflint why do you abuse
The bounteous plenty given you for giving?
O gainless usurer why do you use
Such treasure if you can't make life worth living?
For, playing only with yourself alone,
You then deprive yourself and your sweet heir:
When Nature calls you in to pay her loan
How can your life's account show true and fair?
Your beauty tossed away will die with you,
But used would live in those you pass it to.

SONNET 5: Towards the end of 1591 there had emerged another indicator of the Earl's demeanour and Burghley's irritation with his ward's resistance to marriage. One of the politician's secretaries, John Clapham, had produced a small book in Latin verse, entitled *Narcissus*, which he dedicated to Southampton.

Clapham's story of Narcissus is based on the classical Greek myth of a beautiful young man who falls so much in love with his own image that he pines to death. However, pointedly, Clapham's Narcissus dwells in a "blessed" island ruled by a Virgin Queen – transparently the England of Elizabeth Tudor. In his Latin dedication to Southampton, Clapham wishes him an increase in manliness. With these touches, it would have been apparent to all that Southampton was being portrayed as effeminate, narcissistic and sterile: stinging insults, which must have been approved by Burghley.

It is clear from the Sonnets that Shakespeare also recognised the Earl's absorption with his looks, and his fondness for praise. The poet plays to these themes consistently, albeit for the most part in terms of affection.

In this sonnet, the *"flowers distilled"* for scent would have included roses, evoking the *Rose* of Sonnet 1 and its potentially deeper meaning, suggested in the commentary to Sonnet 1.

SONNET 5

Those hours that with gentle work did frame
The lovely gaze where every eye doth dwell
Will play the tyrants to the very same
And that unfair which fairly doth excel.
For never-resting time leads summer on
To hideous winter and confounds him there;
Sap checked with frost and lusty leaves quite gone,
Beauty o'ersnowed and bareness everywhere.
Then, were not summer's distillation left,
A liquid prisoner pent in walls of glass,
Beauty's effect with beauty were bereft,
Nor it, nor no remembrance what it was.
But flowers distilled, though they with winter meet,
Leese but their show; their substance still lives sweet.

Those gentle hours which framed their craft to make
The lovely view which all now gaze upon
Will turn on it and tyrant-like will take
Away that fairness nothing has outshone.
For never-resting Time leads summer to
The ugliness of winter, cold and bare;
Leaves dead and gone and sap all frozen through
With oversnow of beauty everywhere.
Then, were not summer's distillation pent,
A liquid heir, a scent in bottled thrall,
Then beauty's air would go where beauty went,
And none recall how it had been at all.
But flowers distilled, though they with winter meet,
Lose but their bloom; their essence lives on, sweet.

SONNET 6: Though they pursue the same agenda of family succession, the seventeen procreation sonnets seem to represent a counter to the offensiveness of *Narcissus*. The bluntness of Clapham's message is replaced with affection, praise, ribald humour, intimacy, wit and common sense.

The same air of calculated contrast pervades the poet's contemporaneous *Venus & Adonis*, the more so for elements shared with *Narcissus*: their common source (Ovid's *Metamorphoses*), their hero - a beautiful youth interacting with both the goddess Venus and a sexually rampant stallion - and his ultimate transformation into a flower[86].

Nevertheless, the agenda of procreation reflects the ambitions of his guardian and his mother, rather than those of Southampton. This suggests that one, or both, of these persons was the stimulus here for Shakespeare, perhaps building on the latter's initial acquaintanceship with the Earl, through a shared interest in the stage.

In his dedication of *Venus* (reproduced and discussed in the preceding Part I), Shakespeare refers to the young aristocrat as the "godfather" of his poetry. Apparently, Southampton had, in his turn, encouraged and enabled the playwright to apply his hand seriously to the composition of verse.

This sonnet continues and binds together the overt and parallel themes developed in the preceding two. In line 13, the term *"self-willed"* carries a double meaning, difficult to replicate in modern English, since the word "will" could then allude to sexual desire or activity.

---

[86]   As discerned by Akrigg in his *Shakespeare & the Earl of Southampton.*

SONNET 6

Then let not winter's ragged hand deface
In thee thy summer ere thou be distilled:
Make sweet some vial; treasure thou some place
With beauty's treasure, ere it be self-killed.
That use is not forbidden usury
Which happies those that pay the willing loan;
That's for thyself to breed another thee,
Or, ten times happier, be it ten for one.
Ten times thyself were happier than thou art
If ten of thine ten times refigured thee:
Then what could death do, if thou shouldst depart,
Leaving thee living in posterity?
Be not self-willed, for thou art much too fair
To be death's conquest and make worms thine heir.

So don't let winter's worn-out hand debase
Your summer's flow before you've been distilled:
Enrich some vessel, come into that place
With beauty's treasure, else it die self-spilled.
This would not be forbidden usury
Since it would help those willing to repay
By giving back to you your progeny
Or, ten times better, ten of you one day.
And you'd be ten times better off than now
If ten of yours made tenfold imagery:
Then what could death do if you took your bow
And left whilst living in posterity?
Don't be self-loving; you are much too fair
To die and let mere worms become your heir.

SONNET 7: The sonnet structure in English – three quatrains, each with its internal rhyme, and a final rhyming couplet, generally all expressed in rhythmic sentences of ten syllables – had evolved relatively recently. Shakespeare's use of the structure reflects a craze of the time, triggered by the publication in 1591 of Sir Philip Sydney's sonnet cycle, *Astrophel & Stella*, which had appeared to depict his love from afar of Penelope Devereux[87]. The imagination of the literary classes had been fired and, within months, other sonnet cycles were being composed by many accomplished poets, including Thomas Watson, Henry Constable, Barnabe Barnes, Samuel Daniel and Michael Drayton.

In the final line of this sonnet, Shakespeare makes a pun on the sun/son echo used elsewhere in his works (eg *King John, II, i*). In fact, the intent to apply this pun appears to have driven the whole structure of the poem, though there is also a first hinting at the social status of the youth, with terms like "*gracious*", "*homage*" and "*majesty*".

With its play on Elizabethan sexual euphemisms - "*noon*" and "*die*" - the concluding couplet transforms what, at first sight, seems a rather staid poem into a witty continuation of the dual themes of the preceding sonnets.

---

[87] She was the sister of Southampton's great friend and role model, Robert Devereux, the 2nd Earl of Essex. She had been prospectively linked in marriage to Sydney but had ended up marrying Lord Rich.

SONNET 7

*Lo, in the orient when the gracious light
Lifts up his burning head, each under eye
Doth homage to his new-appearing sight,
Serving with looks his sacred majesty.
And having climbed the steep-up heavenly hill,
Resembling strong youth in his middle age,
Yet mortal looks adore his beauty still,
Attending on his golden pilgrimage.
But when from highmost pitch with weary car,
Like feeble age, he reeleth from the day,
The eyes, 'fore duteous, now converted are
From his low tract and look another way:
So thou, thyself out-going in thy noon,
Unlooked-on diest unless thou gettest a son.*

When first from east appears the source of light
Uplifting fiery face towards the sky
All those around revere this new-born sight,
In awe of that majestic gaze on high.
And when it's climbed the way to noon's steep height,
Just as a vigorous youth will scale a hill,
We mortals keep heed of its golden might,
And are enamoured with its splendour still.
But when it plunges, worn from its attack,
And, like enfeebled age, limps from the day,
Those eyes which had been following its track
Ignore its fall and look another way.
So you will, on your climaxing, subside,
Expend alone, if son-rise is denied.

SONNET 8: English, as it was spoken in Elizabethan England, differed in pronunciation from most current renditions. Some believe that its best approximation, today, lies in the dialect of certain isolated communities on the East coast of the USA, which retain language affinities with the early days of English colonisation.

From the perspective of most current English speakers, there has been a significant degree of vowel shift, as well as a differing of emphasis in certain combinations of vowels. As a result, some combinations no longer sound or rhyme as they did for Shakespeare.

For example, "room" and "Rome" sounded the same to Shakespeare, as did "reason" and "raisin". "Convert" and "desert" rhymed with "part". "Die" was pronounced "di-ee" and therefore rhymed with "memory" but "sea" rhymed with "say".

In this sonnet, lines 6 and 8 would have rhymed in Shakespeare's pronunciation, probably aided by a rolling and emphasis of the final "r", as is still the practice in many modern English dialects.

SONNET 8

Music to hear, why hear'st thou music sadly?
Sweets with sweets war not, joy delights in joy:
Why lov'st thou that which thou receiv'st not gladly,
Or else receiv'st with pleasure thine annoy?
If the true concord of well-tun-ed sounds,
By unions married, do offend thine ear,
They do but sweetly chide thee who confounds
In singleness the parts that thou shouldst bear.
Mark how one string, sweet husband to another,
Strikes each in each by mutual ordering,
Resembling sire and child and happy mother
Who, all in one, one pleasing note do sing:
Whose speechless song, being many, seeming one,
Sings this to thee: "Thou single will prove none".

Why are you sad from music, Music Speaker?
Life's pleasures don't conflict, joy goes with joy.
Why do you love what makes your feelings bleaker,
Or welcome things which hurt you to enjoy?
If such true concord of harmonic sounds
In married unions distress your ear,
They do but sweetly chide you, who confounds
In solitude what need to share and rear.
See how each string, in sweet tune with another,
Combines to give a joyous rendering,
Resembling father, child and happy mother
Who, all as one, one pleasing note thus sing.
Their wordless tunes, together sounding one,
Sing this to you: "Alone you're good as none".

SONNET 9: The procreation sonnets show great skill in their balancing of unwanted advice with the techniques of seduction:- affection, flattery, humour and wit. It is probably no coincidence that, in 1592, with enforced closures of the London playhouses, the young Earl would have represented a golden opportunity to a playwright seeking alternative support and social advancement.

The word *"makeless"*, in line 4, is commonly defined as "mateless", ie lacking a husband. I suggest, however, that a wife's "make" is her offspring, and that the concept of lacking a child fits better with the remainder of the sonnet.

The overt theme is one of the youth wasting his attributes, if he doesn't pass these on through marriage and offspring. However, the innuendo of waste through masturbation continues, with phrases like *"consum'st thyself"*, in line 2, and *"beauty's waste"*, in line 11 (which can be interpreted as semen, wittily killed in line 14 through a shame committed on himself).

SONNET 9

Is it for fear to wet a widow's eye
That thou consum'st thyself in single life?
Ah, if thou issueless shalt hap to die
The world will wail thee like a makeless wife.
The world will be thy widow and still weep
That thou no form of thee hast left behind,
When every private widow well may keep,
By children's eyes, her husband's shape in mind.
Look what an unthrift in the world doth spend
Shifts but his place, for still the world enjoys it;
But beauty's waste hath in the world an end
And, kept unused, the user so destroys it.
No love towards others in that bosom sits
That on himself such murd'rous shame commits.

Is it for fear you'd make a widow cry
That you consume yourself in solo life?
Yet if you, issueless, should chance to die
The world would mourn, as if your childless wife.
The world would widowed be and ever weep
That you had left no part of you behind,
Unlike a widowed mother who would keep,
Through sight of offspring, husband's cast in mind.
No matter what a profligate might spend,
His wealth but shifts, for still the world enjoys it;
But beauty's waste has only got one end
And, misapplied, its user so destroys it.
No love for others lives inside his frame,
Who on himself commits such murd'rous shame!

SONNET 10: Now Shakespeare talks about love of another, for the first time in the sonnet sequence. In addition, in line 13, he invokes Southampton's love for him. This gives rise to the perhaps stupid-sounding question, what does he mean by "*love*"?

In those days, "love" had a wider range of meaning than now. At one end of the spectrum, "loving" would mean "doing good for", and, in this sense, a "lover" would be no more than a supportive, good friend. Thus in *King Lear (I, i, 25)* the character Gloucester, meeting a friend's son for the first time, says "*I must love you*". There are many examples of the use of the word in this sense, both in plays and in surviving documentation and correspondence of the time.

However, at the other end of the spectrum, "love" could mean the physical act of love or passionate adoration, as it can today.

Some commentators believe that, in the context of the fair youth sonnets, the word was being used exclusively in a "good friends" sense. Others disagree.

My view evolved from an assessment of the contexts in the sonnets, taken as a whole. Based on this I think that the "*love*" expressed in the sonnets generally falls within the same range of meanings as the word evokes today, and usually I have not sought to interpret it differently.

The "murd'rous hate" of line 5 would be way over the top, were it not continuing the ribald teasing of the preceding sonnet's last line.

SONNET 10

For shame deny that thou bear'st love to any
Who for thyself art so unprovident.
Grant, if thou wilt, thou art beloved of many,
But that thou none lov'st is most evident:
For thou art so possessed with murd'rous hate
That 'gainst thyself thou stick'st not to conspire,
Seeking that beauteous roof to ruinate
Which to repair should be thy chief desire.
O, change thy thought, that I may change my mind!
Shall hate be fairer lodged than gentle love?
Be, as thy presence is, gracious and kind,
Or to thyself at least kind-hearted prove:
Make thee another self, for love of me,
That beauty still may live in thine or thee.

For shame deny that you bear love for any,
When of yourself you're so improvident.
I grant you that you are beloved of many,
But that you love none is most evident.
For you're so filled with murderous disdain
You cannot even stop self-injury
By wilfully refusing to maintain
That house which should be your priority.
O think again, so I may change my mind!
Should hate have fairer lodgings than sweet care?
Be, as you show yourself, gracious and kind,
Or to yourself, at least, be kind and fair:
For love of me produce another you,
So beauty lives on in you and yours too.

SONNET 11: More humorous double meanings in lines 1 to 4 of this sonnet. Southampton is being reassured that separation from both his young age and his youthful emissions[88] can be compensated by a pregnant wife and/or his offspring.

Interpretation of the Sonnets is complicated by vagaries of spelling and punctuation in the original edition.

The spelling of words in Elizabethan times was flexible, and there is a degree of variance within the Sonnets: for example the word "beauty" is spelt both in this way and as "beautie", sometimes even within the same sonnet.

Similarly, the convention for punctuation within the Sonnets is not entirely consistent. Analysis has suggested that there were two compositors involved in the original printing, each of whom applied a convention slightly differing from the other's.

It is possible, therefore, that such vagaries arose essentially during a printing of the Sonnets, which was not carefully checked by the author. However, it is equally probable that Shakespeare, himself, was careless of both spelling consistency and punctuation.

Either way, and in particular where the grammar has been compressed, it becomes more difficult to assess the exact meaning of a phrase and the extent to which nuances, distinctions or double-meanings may have been intended and indicated.

---

88   As pointed out by Duncan-Jones, inheritance was commonly seen as the transmission of blood. In context, the latter thereby became a synonym of semen.

SONNET 11

As fast as thou shalt wane so fast thou grow'st
In one of thine from that which thou departest,
And that fresh blood which youngly thou bestow'st
Thou mays't call thine when thou from youth covertest.
Herein lives wisdom, beauty and increase,
Without this, folly, age, and cold decay:
If all were minded so the times should cease
And threescore year would make the world away.
Let those whom nature hath not made for store,
Harsh, featureless and rude, barrenly perish:
Look whom she best endowed she gave the more,
Which bounteous gift thou shouldst in bounty cherish:
She carved thee for her seal, and meant thereby
Thou shouldst print more, not let that copy die.

No matter that you wane, you'll grow as fast
In one of yours, in whom you leave your youth;
And that fresh blood, a juice from youthful past,
You may call yours when you are long in tooth.
In such lies wisdom, beauty and increase;
Without this, folly, age and cold decay.
If all had views like you mankind would cease:
Just three score years for all to pass away.
Let those whom Nature would not wish to keep,
Coarse, ugly brutes, die without replication;
But those she best endowed did not come cheap,
And such great gifts deserve appreciation.
She made you as her cast, and meant thereby
You should make more, not let your pattern die.

SONNET 12: Shakespeare turns to a vivid countryside setting, to pursue the procreation theme.

As established in the preceding Part I, Sonnets 1-126 deal substantially, or wholly, with the fair friend – identified as Southampton. The remaining sonnets, 127-154, deal mainly with another character: a woman who has dark hair and eyes, and who is described by the poet as his mistress.

Several of the dark mistress sonnets appear to describe a situation also dealt with in parts of the Southampton sequence, albeit from another angle. Indeed, the parallel is so close that Rowse is adamant that the relevant sonnets are co-topical and concurrent.

This concept of chronological overlap is made persuasive by independent evidence of dating, brought out in Part I[89]. Such overlap is therefore, worth recalling at relevant points in a sequential reading of the fair friend sonnets and, from time to time, I shall suggest where the dark mistress sonnets might fall on that basis.

---

[89] Including the evidence associated with Thomas Nashe and the *Rosalines*

SONNET 12

When I do count the clock that tells the time
And see the brave day sunk in hideous night,
When I behold the violet past prime
And sable curls all silvered o'er with white,
When lofty trees I see barren of leaves,
Which erst from heat did canopy the herd,
And summer's green all girded up in sheaves
Borne on the bier with white and bristly beard:
Then of thy beauty I do question make
That thou among the wastes of time must go,
Since sweets and beauties do themselves forsake
And die as fast as they see others grow:
And nothing 'gainst Time's scythe can make defence
Save breed, to brave him when he takes thee hence.

When I can hear the clock which ticks the time
And see the bright of day turn into night;
When I behold the bluebell past its prime
And dark hair showing silver curls and white;
When lofty trees I see devoid of leaves,
Which lately shaded herds, as hot sun seared,
And summer's green corn girded up in sheaves
Borne on the bier with white and bristly beard:
Then I must of your beauty wonder why
Into the wastes of time you let this go,
Since all that's beautiful is going to die
And wane as fast as youngsters are to grow:
For nothing can against Time's scythe defend
But will, if bred, defy him at the end.

79

SONNET 13:   This marks the first occasion on which Shakespeare's own feelings for Southampton are aired overtly, with his salutations of "*love*" and "*dear my love*".

The past tense, used in the statement of line 14, "*You had a father*", recognises the death of Southampton's father some ten years before.

Most commentators emend the poet's originally separate words "*your self*", in the first line, to a modern day compression of "yourself". I suggest that such emendation detracts from its intended meaning.

The third quatrain carries a double meaning for "*house*", referring to both the young lord's body and his family line (echoing a similar metaphor in Sonnet 10). Again, "*husbandry*" evokes both a personal status of marriage and a more general status of maintenance of the family or House.

SONNET 13

O, that you were your self! But, love, you are
No longer yours than you yourself here live:
Against this coming end you should prepare
And your sweet semblance to some other give.
So, should that beauty which you hold in lease
Find no determination: then you were
Yourself again, after your self's decease,
When your sweet issue your sweet form should bear.
Who lets so fair a house fall to decay,
Which husbandry in honour might uphold
Against the stormy gusts of winter's day
And barren rage of death's eternal cold?
O, none but unthrifts: dear my love, you know
You had a father: let your son say so.

If only you stayed you without restriction!
But, love, you keep your self just till you're dead.
You should prepare for terminal eviction,
And in some other have your likeness bred,
So that the beauty which you hold on lease
Will have no end, but that you then will be
Seen in your own after your own decease,
When your child bears sweet similarity.
Who lets so fair a house fall in decay
When husbandry might cause it to uphold
Against the stormy gusts of winter's day
And barren night of death's eternal cold?
O, none but wastrels! My dear love, you know
You had a father: let your son say so.

SONNET 14: In line 2, Shakespeare uses the word "*astronomy*". I have rendered this as "astrology", since this is what is being envisaged here (in Elizabethan times there was no real distinction between the two disciplines). Though he makes many references in his plays to astrological concepts, he never uses the word "astrology" (nor for that matter "astronomy").

There are echoes here of sonnet number 26 of Sydney's *Astrophel & Stella*, where the poet muses on astrology, and also equates the eyes of the beloved with stars.

The original publication of *Shakespeare's Sonnets* in 1609 also included an undated long poem entitled *A Lover's Complaint by William Shakespeare*.

This poem describes the sorrows of a young maid, who has been seduced and abandoned by an effeminately beautiful, young man. The latter has "*browny locks*", which play against his lips in the wind, and he is described in other terms similar to those used in the Sonnets to depict Southampton.

However, there is no other correspondence with the Sonnets. The poem, a pleasant read, seems designed essentially as an exercise in flattery and entertainment.

SONNET 14

Not from the stars do I my judgement pluck,
And yet methinks I have astronomy,
But not to tell of good or evil luck,
Of plagues, of dearths, or season's quality.
Nor can I fortune to brief minutes tell,
Pointing to each his thunder, rain and wind,
Or say with princes if it shall go well,
By oft predict that I in heaven find.
But from thine eyes my knowledge I derive,
And, constant stars, in them I read such art
As – truth and beauty shall together thrive
If from thyself to store thou wouldst convert;
Or else of thee I this prognosticate:
Thy end is truth's and beauty's doom and date.

I do not pluck my judgements from the stars,
And yet I'd say I use astrology,
But not to tell of when luck helps or mars,
Of plagues, of dearths or meteorology.
Nor can I warn each what each moment brings,
To scry wind, thunder and precipitation,
Or give advice to princes and to kings,
Derived from frequent cosmic divination.
For I obtain my insight from your eyes,
Those constant stars, which help me such foresee
As faith and beauty's bloom without demise,
If you turn from yourself to progeny.
But if you don't I hereby prophesy:
Both faith and beauty go the day you die.

SONNET 15: On first reading, it seems that Shakespeare has finally given up his urgings of Southampton to marry and get a son. However, this sonnet is but part one of a brace, and therefore needs to be read in conjunction with Sonnet 16. This practice of coupling two sonnets is repeated a number of times during the sonnet sequence.

In the final line, the poet introduces what will become a recurring refrain: his ability to keep the Earl immortally young and fair, through verse.

The hero of *Venus & Adonis*, dedicated by Shakespeare to Southampton in 1593, also shares the Earl's attributes. Adonis, an effeminate looking, beautiful youth, is lusted after but resistant to the seductions of the love goddess, Venus.

She urges Adonis to procreate, in terms which resonate with those of the Sonnets, for example:

> *Things growing to themselves are growth's abuse:*
> *Seeds spring from seeds and beauty breedeth beauty;*
> *Thou wast begot; to get it is thy duty.* (Verse 28)

> *By law of nature thou art bound to breed,*
> *That thine may live when thou thyself art dead;*
> *And so, in spite of death, thou dost survive.*
> *In that thy likeness still is left alive.* (Verse 29)

> *What is thy body but a swallowing grave,*
> *Seeming to bury that posterity*
> *Which by the rights of time thou needs must have,*
> *If thou destroy them not in dark obscurity?*
> *If so, the world will hold you in disdain,*
> *Sith in thy pride so fair a hope is slain.* (Verse 127)

SONNET 15

When I consider every thing that grows
Holds in perfection just a little moment,
That this huge stage presenteth nought but shows
Whereon the stars in secret influence comment;
When I perceive that men as plants increase,
Cheered and checked even by the self-same sky,
Vaunt in their youthful sap, at height decrease,
And wear their brave state out of memory:
Then the conceit of this inconstant stay
Sets you most rich in youth before my sight,
Where wasteful Time debateth with Decay,
To change your day of youth to sullied night.
And all in war with Time for love of you,
As he takes from you, I engraft you new.

When I consider every thing that grows
Has but a tiny moment of perfection;
That this world's just a stage which puts on shows,
To which the stars give secretive direction;
When I perceive that men grow like a vine,
Both boosted and curtailed by that same sky,
Abound in youthful sap, at peak decline,
Their prime forgot in twinkling of an eye:
Then musing on this transitory stay
Calls you to mind, your youth still shining bright,
Where I can see Time scheming with Decay
To turn your youthful day to tarnished night.
And so I fight with Time for love of you;
As he destroys, I build your bud anew.

SONNET 16: This continues Sonnet 15, and plays on the word *"lines"*, to evoke the lines of a poem and the lines of a picture, as well as lineage of an ancestral sense.

The *"give away yourself"*, in line 13, suggests a giving away in marriage, as well as a giving away of the seed for planting in *"maiden gardens"*. The analogy, in line 7, of flowers to offspring, conjures up, again, the image of the *Rose* of Sonnet 1.

As an aside to any reader interested in the chronology of the dark mistress sonnets, it seems likely that Sonnets 127-129 would fall before, or during, these procreation sonnets. A reading of these three mistress sonnets at this stage does give an interesting perspective on what is to come, within the Southampton sequence.

SONNET 16

But wherefore do not you a mightier way
Make war upon this bloody tyrant, Time?
And fortify yourself in your decay
With means more bless-ed than my barren rhyme?
Now stand you on the top of happy hours,
And many maiden gardens, yet unset,
With virtuous wish would bear your living flowers,
Much likelier than your painted counterfeit:
So should the lines of life that life repair,
Which this time's pencil or my pupil pen,
Neither in inward worth nor outward fair,
Can make you live yourself in eyes of men.
To give away yourself keeps yourself still;
And you must live, drawn by your own sweet skill.

But why not use a much more potent way
To fight against the ravages of Time,
And so protect yourself from your decay
With means more fruitful than my barren rhyme?
You're standing at the peak of all your powers,
With many virgin soils to cultivate,
Which graciously would bear your living flowers,
Much more like you than pen or brush portrait.
So would Life's artistry preserve that line,
Which neither human painter nor my pen
Can match, that's in- and outwardly so fine,
And keep what's you alive in living men.
Just give yourself away to stay forever;
You'll live on, shown through your own sweet endeavour.

SONNET 17: With this sonnet comes transition. Shakespeare seems far more focused on praising Southampton's beauty, than on urging him to procreate. The previously relentless theme seems here to appear almost as an afterthought, in the final couplet. After this, there is no more hectoring on marriage and reproduction.

The sonnet also uses "*you*" and "*your*", instead of "thou" and "thy", contrary to Shakespeare's more usual practice when employing the second person singular.

In fact, he first does this in Sonnet 13, and then, again, in the Sonnet 15/16 brace, but, in both these cases, this choice has an impact on rhyming. Here, there is no such consideration. Is this of any relevance?

"Thou" was used as an intimate form of the singular "you", in a convention similar to current practice in French, where "tu" is used in an intimate sense, instead of the more formal "vous". In Shakespeare's day this convention was changing – at least in Southern England – so either form was acceptable for the second person singular generally, though poetically the older form remained popular.

In the Sonnets the use of "*you*" occasionally contributes to the rhyme, but more often it doesn't. In one sonnet (24), the two forms are mixed, and in this case "*you*" can plausibly be equated with "one", as in a third person generality. There appears to be no discernible pattern of usage.

SONNET 17

Who will believe my verse in time to come
If it were filled with your most high deserts?
Though yet heaven knows it is as a tomb
Which hides your life and shows not half your parts.
If I could write the beauty of your eyes
And in fresh numbers number all your graces,
The age to come would say "This poet lies:
Such heavenly touches ne'er touched earthly faces".
So should my papers, yellowed with their age,
Be scorned like old men of less truth than tongue,
And your true rights be termed a poet's rage
And stretch-ed metre of an antique song:
But were some child of yours alive that time,
You should live twice, in it and in my rhyme.

Who would believe my verse in times to come,
If it contained the praise which is your due?
For, heaven knows, it shows not half your sum:
It's like a tomb which hides the living you.
If I could catch the beauty of your eyes
And in my poems render all your graces,
The age to come would say "This poet lies:
Such heaven never shone from earthly faces".
Thus would my script, in yellowed disrepair,
Be scorned like old men babbling too long,
Your just praise deemed poetical hot air:
The outworn strains found in an antique song.
But if some child of yours lived in those times,
Then you'd live twice: in him, and in my rhymes.

SONNET 18: This is, perhaps, Shakespeare's best known and most-loved sonnet. Many people, unfamiliar with the Sonnets as a whole, remain unaware that it is evidently addressed to a young man, whom we now know was Henry Wriothesley. Such readers are, of course, influenced by the use of the words *"lovely"* and *"fair"*, which most of us tend to associate with a female subject. However, we have only to look at a few examples, such as Sonnet 13, which refers to the *"sweet semblance"*, *"beauty"* and *"fair"* body of the poet's clearly male love, to see that such adjectives are far from female-oriented in the Sonnets. Sonnet 19, clearly addressed to a male, continues the theme of this one. In later sonnets, the poet also applies *"lovely"* to a male subject with his *"lovely knights"* (Sonnet 106) and his *"lovely boy"* (Sonnet 126).

SONNET 18

Shall I compare thee to a summer's day?
Thou art more lovely and more temperate:
Rough winds do shake the darling buds of May,
And summer's lease hath all too short a date:
Sometime too hot the eye of heaven shines,
And often is his gold complexion dimmed:
And every fair from fair sometime declines,
By chance or nature's changing course untrimmed.
But thy eternal summer shall not fade,
Nor lose possession of that fair thou ow'st;
Nor shall death brag thou wander'st in his shade,
When in eternal lines to time thou grow'st:
So long as men can breathe, or eyes can see,
So long lives this, and this gives life to thee.

Shall I compare you to a summer's day?
You are more lovely and you're more forgiving;
Rough winds will shake the darling buds of May
And summertime is all too fleet, short-living.
Sometimes the sun in heaven burns too bright,
And oft its gold allure is dulled in cloud,
And all that's beautiful will meet its night,
Dimmed by bad luck or Nature's changing shroud.
But your eternal summer will not fade,
Nor lose its splendour, shrunk in aged defeat;
Nor will Death boast he keeps you in his shade
As you, in lasting verse, shine on complete.
So long as men can breathe, or eyes can see,
So long lives this, and this gives life to thee.

SONNET 19: This continues the closing theme of the preceding sonnet:- the defiance of time, through immortal verse. Although the poetry is not as inspired as that of its famous precursor, this sonnet does give the sense of a more intimate form of love.

The *"phoenix"*, referred to in line 4, was a long-lived bird of ancient myth, which consigned itself to flames every five hundred years, only to arise from its ashes, reborn and youthful.

SONNET 19

Devouring Time, blunt thou the lion's paws,
And make the earth devour her own sweet brood;
Pluck the keen teeth from the fierce tiger's jaws,
And burn the long-lived phoenix in her blood;
Make glad and sorry seasons as thou fleet'st,
And do what'er thou wilt, swift-footed Time,
To the wide world and all her fading sweets:
But I forbid thee one most heinous crime –
O, carve not with thy hours my love's fair brow,
Nor draw no lines there with thine antique pen:
Him in thy course untainted do allow
For beauty's pattern to succeeding men.
Yet do thy worst, old Time: despite thy wrong,
My love shall in my verse ever live young.

Corrosive Time, you blunt the lion's claws,
And make the earth a grave to creatures all;
Extract the slashing fangs from tiger's jaws,
And hold the phoenix in her ashen pall.
Bring bright and gloomy seasons with swift paces
And do that which you will, fleet-footed Time,
To all the world and all its fading graces,
But I forbid you one most grievous crime:
You shall not mark your hours on my love's brow,
Nor let your ageing pen draw lines careworn:
Him, who's Beauty's template, you'll allow
To pass unscathed for those yet to be born.
But if, old Time, you heed me not or worse,
My love will always live young in my verse.

SONNET 20: Here is a pivotal and much-quoted sonnet, which has triggered endless debate on the nature of Shakespeare's relationship with the young lord.

The phrase "*master-mistress of my passion*" suggests a far deeper emotion than the well-wishing form of love, discussed at Sonnet 10.

One has to wonder, as well, whether, behind the words, there was a physical dimension to the relationship. Rowse and many others are adamant that there was not, either at the time of writing or subsequently. Their principal argument is based on lines 11 and 12, in which the poet professes himself thwarted by the youth's possession of a thing, not to his purpose (it is quite clear what the thing is even in modern English, but, in Elizabethan English, "*thing*" was also slang for "penis", as was "prick").

However, the Rowse argument is, of course, inconclusive. First, Shakespeare is clearly expressing some sort of physical dimension to his love for, or attraction to, Southampton, merely by introducing the subject of the young lord's anatomy; second, there could be a physical relationship, even though the youth's "*thing*" might not be to the poet's usage or purpose; and, third, even if there were no physical aspect to the relationship at the time of writing, this would not rule out a subsequent change.

Line 7 has also triggered much discussion, including the theory that the youth's name was Hews or Hughes. The reasoning for my interpretation, and commentary on the sonnet structure, are set out in Appendix E.

The final couplet is beautifully crafted in its ambiguity (more apparent when one ignores the apostrophes inserted by later editors). Is the Earl inclined to take his pleasures like a woman? Is it the poet's prick which he loves? And is he "used" by his lovers?

SONNET 20

A woman's face with Nature's own hand painted
Hast thou, the master-mistress of my passion:
A woman's gentle heart, but not acquainted
With shifting change, as is false women's fashion;
An eye more bright than theirs, less false in rolling,
Gilding the object whereupon it gazeth;
A man in hue, all hues in his controlling,
Which steals men's eyes and women's souls amazeth.
And for a woman wert thou first created,
Till Nature, as she wrought thee, fell a-doting,
And by addition me of thee defeated,
By adding one thing to my purpose nothing;
But since she pricked thee out for womens pleasure,
Mine be thy love, and thy loves use their treasure.

On you a woman's face did Nature paint,
And you, the master-mistress of my heart,
Have woman's gentleness without the taint
Of changeability and female art.
With eyes more bright and gaze much more sincere,
A man in kind, all kinds in his control:
Enchanted all that come within his sphere,
Who draws men's eyes and stirs a woman's soul.
And first as woman she did you create,
Till Nature, as she carved you, lost her heart
And, adding somewhat more, did me frustrate:
No use to me your extra starring part.
But since you have a thing for female pleasure
Mine is your love and your loves use their treasure.

SONNET 21: This sonnet appears to mock the exaggerations, which were common in love sonnets of the time. Rowse points out that Sydney, in his pioneering *Astrophel & Stella*, calls upon sun, moon, stars and spring flowers in his praise of Stella[90].

The theme is very similar to that of Sonnet 130, and I wonder whether it might not have been intended originally for the dark mistress of that sonnet. Aspects of each sonnet are echoed in *Love's Labour's Lost*. Here Berowne (thought by Rowse and others to be a projection of Shakespeare, himself) falls in love with the dark lady, Rosaline, whom he praises in extravagant poetical language, before saying *"Fie, painted rhetoric! O, she needs it not: to things of sale a seller's praise belongs" (IV, iii, 240)*.

Such similarities suggest that here is a suitable chronological placing for Sonnet 130.

---

[90]   This, and subsequent attributions to Rowse within this section, relate to his commentary on the relevant sonnet, in his *Shakespeare's Sonnets* – see Bibliography

SONNET 21

So is it not with me as with that Muse,
Stirred by a painted beauty to his verse,
Who heaven itself for ornament doth use
And every fair with his fair doth rehearse,
Making a couplement of proud compare,
With sun and moon, with earth and sea's rich gems,
With April's first-born flowers, and all things rare
That heaven's air in this huge rondure hems.
O, let me, true in love, but truly write,
And then believe me, my love is as fair
As any mother's child, though not so bright
As those gold candles fixed in heaven's air:
Let them say more that like of hearsay well;
I will not praise that purpose not to sell.

O, I am quite unlike that sonneteer,
Stirred by a painted beauty to compose,
Who decks her out with heaven as veneer,
Invokes her name, wherever beauty shows,
To make a linkage in a proud compare
With sun and moon, with earth and gems in sea,
With April's flowering and all things rare
In this wide world beneath sky's canopy.
O let me, true in love, write only true,
And then believe me, my love is as fair
As any one who's lived, though to the view
Is less bright than gold stars in night's clear air.
Let them hype up, who love a story's telling;
I'll make no pitch on things which need no selling.

SONNET 22: Here, we have plays on the romantic notion (still reflected in today's language), that people in love exchange their hearts (through the "giving" of one's heart to a loved one). Thus, one lover's heart is portrayed as being in the breast of the other, and vice versa.

A couple of messages are suggested by the sonnet. The first is that Shakespeare is recognising the age difference between himself and Southampton, and that he looks much more mature than the beardless young lord.

The second is that a physical relationship has either begun or is being envisaged. There is clearly a love of high intensity being portrayed, and why would a platonic love be concerned with appearances of age?

SONNET 22

My glass shall not persuade me I am old,
So long as youth and thou are of one date:
But when in thee time's furrows I behold
Then look I death my days should expiate.
For all that beauty that doth cover thee
Is but the seemly raiment of my heart,
Which in thy breast doth live, as thine in me:
How can I then be older than thou art?
O therefore, love, be of thyself so wary
As I, not for myself, but for thee will,
Bearing thy heart, which I will keep so chary
As tender nurse her babe from faring ill.
Presume not on thy heart when mine is slain:
Thou gav'st me thine not to give back again.

My mirror's gaze will not make me feel old,
So long as you seem young and fair to eye.
But come the day you're wrinkled to behold
Then come the day I'll know I'm soon to die.
For all your beauty, glowing like sunshine,
Is but the comely garment round my heart,
Since this beats on in you, as yours is mine:
How can our ages then be split apart?
So of yourself, my love, you must take care
As I will me, not for myself, but you,
To keep your heart from dangers to beware
As mother frets on her sweet young issue.
Don't count upon your heart when mine is slain:
You gave me yours, not to have back again.

SONNET 23: This verse may be sincere, but it also sounds like an eloquent excuse for a lover, who is not showing enough affection to the loved one. And it gives a further suggestion that the relationship is now physical in some form. Who demands more constant attention than a new lover?

But it also raises some interesting possibilities. Is the poet merely a typical insensitive man, who has not been sufficiently demonstrative? Has his "love" cooled, because he has now got what he wanted? Or, were his wooing assurances of love somewhat over-stated in the first place, because he wanted Southampton's patronage?

SONNET 23

As an unperfect actor on the stage,
Who with his fear is put aside his part,
Or some fierce thing replete with too much rage,
Whose strength's abundance weakens his own heart:
So I, for fear of trust, forget to say
The perfect ceremony of love's rite,
And in mine own love's strength seem to decay,
O'ercharged with burden of mine own love's might.
O, let my books be then the eloquence
And dumb presagers of my speaking breast,
Who plead for love and look for recompense
More than that tongue that more hath more expressed.
O, learn to read what silent love hath writ:
To hear with eyes belongs to love's fine wit.

Just like an inept actor in a play,
Who in his fright forgets his lines and role,
Or shaking with emotion goes astray,
To overplay his part or lose control,
So I, for fear of failure, do not speak
The proper words to show my love for you,
And by my strength of feeling am made weak,
Overwhelmed with love that fills me through.
So let my written words now speak for me,
To make those silent speeches from my heart,
Which plea for love and seek validity
More than that silver tongue and speaker's art.
O, learn to read what silent love can write:
To hear with eyes is part of love's delight.

SONNET 24: The interplay between eye and heart was a common poetic theme of the time, also dealt with in Sonnets 46 and 47. Here, Shakespeare seems to be echoing the following quatrain by Henry Constable:

> *Thine eye the glass where I behold my heart,*
> *Mine eye the window through the which thine eye*
> *May see my heart, and there thyself espy*
> *In bloody colours how thou painted art.*

The above quatrain appeared in the ninth of twenty-one sonnets, printed in the 1592 edition of Constable's *Diana* sequence. Perhaps it had been a subject of recent discussion by Southampton and Shakespeare, triggering the latter's own take on the subject in this sonnet. In any event, in its concluding message there is a hint of doubt or reproach, suggesting that Southampton has not wholly accepted the reassurances of Shakespeare's preceding sonnet, or that a barrier has arisen between the pair for other reasons.

The "*steeled*" in line 1 is often emended to "stelled", an archaic word meaning "set" or "placed ", and used by Shakespeare in his poem, *The Rape of Lucrece* (verse 207).

SONNET 24

Mine eye hath played the painter and hath steeled
Thy beauty's form in table of my heart;
My body is the frame wherein 'tis held,
And perspective it is best painter's art.
For through the painter must you see his skill
To find where your true image pictured lies,
Which in my bosom's shop is hanging still
That hath his windows glaz-ed with thine eyes.
Now see what good turns eyes for eyes have done:
Mine eyes have drawn thy shape, and thine for me
Are windows to my breast, where-through the sun
Delights to peep, to gaze therein on thee:
Yet eyes this cunning want to grace their art
They draw but what they see, know not the heart.

My eye has played the painter to portray
Your beauty on the canvas of my heart;
My body is the frame for its display
In living form like best of painter's art.
For it's through skill of painter that you see
Your image truly caught without disguise,
And yours hangs in my heart, that gallery,
Whose windows are transparent to your eyes.
Now see what good turns eyes for eyes have done:
For mine have drawn your form, as yours see through
Into my heart to bring to it the sun,
And give it warmth which thus reflects on you.
Yet eyes still lack the techniques to impart
More than they see, and they don't know the heart.

SONNET 25: The first quatrain of this sonnet suggests that the poet is, at the time of writing, unsung and unwealthy. And this was almost certainly Shakespeare's situation in the early 1590s. By 1597, however, he was, by existing standards, a wealthy and established man, who had secured for his family the right to a coat of arms and to be regarded as of "gentle" status.

The third quatrain suggests the disgrace (after just one failing) of a worthy and accomplished warrior who had subjected himself to much effort in public service. Many commentators have enjoyed speculation on who this was and, therefore, when the sonnet might have been composed.

Rowse believed that the warrior was Sir Walter Raleigh, who was imprisoned in the Tower by Queen Elizabeth in August 1592, after discovery of his unauthorised marriage to one of her Maids of Attendance (following which he was out of favour for several years). The word, *"painful"* (line 9), meant "painstaking", an adjective appropriate to the meticulous Raleigh.

Line 9 ends in *"worth"*, which, because it does not rhyme, is often regarded as a misprint and emended to "fight".

SONNET 25

Let those who are in favour with their stars
Of public honour and proud titles boast,
Whilst I, whom fortune of such triumph bars,
Unlooked for joy in that I honour most.
Great princes' favourites their fair leaves spread
But as the marigold at the sun's eye,
And in themselves their pride lies buri-ed,
For at a frown they in their glory die.
The painful warrior famous-ed for worth,
After a thousand victories once foiled,
Is from the book of honour raz-ed quite,
And all the rest forgot for which he toiled:
Then happy I, that love and am beloved
Where I may not remove nor be removed.

Let those who are in favour with their stars
Of public honour and proud titles boast,
Whilst I, whom fortune from such triumph bars,
Take joy unseen in what I honour most.
Great favourites of monarchs flourish fair,
But, like the marigold which needs the sun,
With independence crushed beyond repair,
For at a frown they die, their glories done.
The tireless warrior of worth and fame
After countless wins but once falls short,
And sees from honour-rolls expunged his name,
Forgotten all his toils and wars he fought.
Then happy I, who loves and with love's kissed,
That I may not dismiss nor be dismissed.

SONNET 26: "*Lord*", in the opening line, reflects the Earl's status and title.

In line 3, "*ambassage*" is an archaic word, meaning a delegation of ambassadors. It suggests that this sonnet is, in effect, a covering letter sent, with a batch of other sonnets, to Southampton, who is not at hand for personal or individual delivery. Poet and earl have become separated by events.

The third quatrain carries a strong hint of material poverty (similar to that of the previous sonnet) and a hopeful suggestion, that some relief from a patron would be welcome.

SONNET 26

Lord of my love, to whom in vassalage
Thy merit hath my duty strongly knit,
To thee I send this written ambassage
To witness duty, not to show my wit:
Duty so great, which wit so poor as mine
May make seem bare, in wanting words to show it,
But that I hope some good conceit of thine
In thy soul's thought (all naked) will bestow it:
Till whatsoever star that guides my moving
Points on me graciously with fair aspect
And puts apparel on my tattered loving
To show me worthy of thy sweet respect:
Then may I dare to boast how I do love thee,
Till then not show my head where thou mayst prove me.

Lord of my bonded love, I strive to be
Most dutiful, as your great worth makes fit.
To you I send these works to speak for me,
To witness duty, not to show my wit:
Duty so great, which wit so poor as mine
May make seem bare through lack of words to show,
Though your kind heart may see through poor design
To my intent, and thereby worth bestow:
Until whatever star that guides my fate
Gives blessing on my path, with fair prospect,
And covers up my disadvantaged state
To show me worthy of your sweet respect.
Then I may dare to boast I love you so;
Till then avoid the test by lying low.

SONNET 27:   This sonnet, with those immediately following, appears to have been written in absence from the Earl. Probably, these poems are the *"ambassage"*, referred to in Sonnet 26.

"Travel", in the second line, is presented thus in most modern editions. However, the original 1609 Quarto edition presented it as *"travail"*, which, Duncan-Jones points out, was the spelling of both "travel" and "travail" – hard labour[91].

In Elizabethan English, *"intend"* (line 6) remained close in meaning to "stretch forth", in line with the Latin word, *"intendere"*, from which it was derived.

---

[91]   Unless otherwise referenced, all attributions in this section to Duncan-Jones relate to her commentary on the relevant sonnet, in her *Shakespeare's Sonnets* – see Bibliography

SONNET 27

Weary with toil, I haste me to my bed,
The dear repose for limbs with travel tired;
But then begins a journey in my head
To work my mind, when body's work's expired.
For then my thoughts, from far where I abide,
Intend a zealous pilgrimage to thee,
And keep my drooping eyelids open wide,
Looking on darkness which the blind do see:
Save that my soul's imaginary sight
Presents thy shadow to my sightless view,
Which, like a jewel hung in ghastly night,
Makes black night beauteous and her old face new.
Lo, thus, by day my limbs, by night my mind,
For thee and for myself no quiet find.

Weary from my toil I haste to bed,
The welcome rest for limbs all effort-worn;
But then begins a journey in my head,
With work for brain replacing that for brawn.
For then my thoughts, from where I am afar,
Will make to you each night incessantly
And keep my drooping eyelids wide ajar
Upon that dark that's all the blind can see:
Except that my imagination's sight
Displays your image to my sightless view,
To hang there like a jewel in fearsome night
And bring it beauty, melt its old taboo.
And so by day my limbs, by night my mind
For you and for myself no rest can find.

SONNET 28: This continues the theme of its predecessor sonnet, bewailing Shakespeare's separation from the young Earl.

With the outbreak of plague in London, it is likely that, during the autumn of 1592, Southampton would have removed to the country, perhaps to his family seat in Titchfield, Hampshire. Whether Shakespeare spent any time there, we do not know. But, wherever the Earl was then based, he must have been out and about on a number of personal and public affairs. He was probably involved in at least part of the mourning and funerary process for his mother's twin brother, who died in late June, and was buried at Midhurst, in early August. Southampton was in the Queen's retinue, for at least part of her provincial tour of that year, which had started in the summer. It was at her court in Oxford, in late September, where he, amongst others, attracted the praise of Stringer. And, he was surely occupied with at least part of the death proceedings for his maternal grandfather, Viscount Montagu, who died at his Surrey home, in mid-October, and was buried at Midhurst, in early December.

SONNET 28

How can I then return in happy plight
That am debarred the benefit of rest?
When day's oppression is not eased by night
But day by night, and night by day, oppressed?
And each, though enemies to either's reign,
Do in consent shake hands to torture me,
The one by toil, the other to complain
How far I toil, still farther off from thee.
I tell the day to please him thou art bright
And dost him grace when clouds do blot the heaven:
So flatter I the swart-complexioned night
When sparkling stars twire not thou gild'st the even.
But day doth daily draw my sorrows longer,
And night doth nightly make grief's length seem stronger.

How can I then return to good condition
When I'm denied the benefit of rest?
And night gives me no ease from day's attrition,
As day and night discord to steal my zest?
And both, though opposite in role and scope,
Unite to maximise my misery:
By one I toil, by other I then mope
On how more far from you my toil takes me.
By day I think how bright you make the day,
No matter if the sky is dimmed by cloud;
At night I also think of you this way,
Who lights the night though stars be lost in shroud.
But days still daily stretch my sorrows longer,
And nights still nightly make my grief the stronger.

SONNET 29: The tone of this sonnet suggests a period in Shakespeare's life when everything was going against him. During 1592, the London playhouses were closed for most of the time, following public disturbances and the outbreak of plague. This led to a substantial loss of livelihood for all those dependent on show business. Then, in early October, Shakespeare was publicly depicted as an upstart imitator (or plagiarist) of his betters, by Robert Greene, in his *Groatsworth of Wit* (as described in Appendix B).

It seems, also, that the poet was undergoing tribulations in other relationships. With this in mind, it seems not unreasonable to place Sonnets 131 and 132 around here in the chronological sequence.

SONNET 29

When in disgrace with fortune and men's eyes,
I all alone beweep my outcast state,
And trouble deaf heaven with my bootless cries,
And look upon myself and curse my fate:
Wishing me like to one more rich in hope,
Featured like him, like him with friends possessed,
Desiring this man's art and that man's scope,
With what I most enjoy contented least:
Yet in these thoughts myself almost despising,
Haply I think on thee, and then my state,
Like to the lark at break of day arising
From sullen earth, sings hymns at heaven's gate;
For thy sweet love remembered such wealth brings
That then I scorn to change my state with kings.

When out of luck and disdained in men's eyes
I, all alone, bemoan my outcast state,
Complain to heaven, heedless of my cries,
And dwell upon myself and curse my fate:
To envy one whose fortune's rich with hope,
His looks and friends and welcomes to the feast;
Desiring this man's skills and that man's scope,
With what I most enjoy contented least.
Yet in this mood of gloom and self-despise
I'll chance to think of you and then my state
Will, like the lark at break of day, arise
From sullen earth to sing at heaven's gate.
For your sweet love recalled's so rich a thing
I would not trade for fortune of a king.

113

SONNET 30:   The mood of depression continues, though expressed in beautiful language.

Duncan-Jones points out allusions to legal or commercial proceedings with words such as *"sessions"*, *"summon"*, *"expense"* and *"account"*.

Similar legalistic and commercial terms crop up in a number of other sonnets, leading some observers to theorise that Shakespeare must have had legal training. However, the use of legalistic expressions was a common conceit in popular Elizabethan works. For example, sonnet number 18, of Sydney's *Astrophel & Stella*, uses the terms *"audit"*, *"bankrupt"*, *"rent"* and *"lent"* in describing the poet's love[92]. And, Shakespeare would have become familiar with legal and commercial affairs in the running of stage-companies, which had numerous stakeholders, and were often embroiled in disputes with society and/or authority.

Ledger reminds us of a forebear to line 2, in the Apocrypha of the Old Testament (Wisdom of Solomon): *"For a double griefe came upon them, and a groaning for the remembrance of things past".*[93]

---

[92]   In his book, *The Shakespeare Claimants*, Gibson comments "Almost every other dramatist of the time, and other writers too, made as much use of legal phraseology as did Shakespeare, many a great deal more, and not a few handled it more adroitly, for Shakespeare's knowledge is far from being as impeccable as [claimed]".

[93]   All attributions to Ledger in this section relate to his commentary on the relevant sonnet, in his work on Shakespeare's Sonnets – see Bibliography

SONNET 30

When to the sessions of sweet silent thought
I summon up remembrance of things past,
I sigh the lack of many a thing I sought
And with old woes new wail my dear time's waste:
Then can I drown an eye, unused to flow,
For precious friends hid in death's dateless night,
And weep afresh love's long since cancelled woe,
And moan th'expense of many a vanished sight:
Then can I grieve at grievances foregone,
And heavily from woe to woe tell o'er
The sad account of fore-bemoan-ed moan,
Which I new pay as if not paid before.
But if the while I think on thee, dear friend,
All losses are restored and sorrows end.

When to the sessions of sweet silent thought
I summon up remembrance of things past
I sigh the lack of many things I sought
And rue time's waste on woes from dies long cast.
Then will I weep, from eyes which seldom flow,
For precious friends lost in that lasting night,
And mourn again old heartaches' bygone woe,
And miss too many things now passed from sight.
Then too I brood on grievances again,
Live through a blow by blow account once more,
And injustice and ills I suffered then,
I feel anew as if not felt before.
But if awhile I think on you, dear friend,
My losses are restored, my sorrows end.

SONNET 31:   Here, Shakespeare flatters and appreciates Southampton. "Others may have abandoned me, died or been left behind," he says, "but you are always there for me, and are as beloved by me as all of them."

In December 1592, Henry Chettle, the publisher of Greene's *Groatsworth of Wit*, had issued an apology in writing, apparently refuting the dead Greene's insult of Shakespeare. Chettle wrote of the target of Greene's attack: *"Divers of worship have reported his uprightness of dealings which argues his honesty, and his facetious grace in writing that approves his art"*. Such reference suggests an intervention, on Shakespeare's behalf, by a high ranking person or persons.

With its references to *"parts"*, there is, as Ledger points out, a faint hint of sexual double-entendre. However, the word, *"lover"* (line 10), in those days carried a much wider range of meaning than now (see commentary at Sonnet 10), and, in the context of this poem, probably covered friends, as well as sexual partners.

SONNET 31

Thy bosom is endear-ed with all hearts,
Which I, by lacking, have suppose-ed dead;
And there reigns Love, and all Love's loving parts,
And all those friends which I thought buri-ed.
How many a holy and obsequious tear
Hath dear religious love stol'n from mine eye,
As interest of the dead, which now appear
But things removed that hidden in thee lie:
Thou art the grave where buried love doth live,
Hung with the trophies of my lovers gone,
Who all their parts of me to thee did give –
That due of many now is thine alone:
Their images I loved I view in thee,
And thou (all they) hast all the all of me.

Your care for me brings back all those sweethearts,
Who, gone from me, I thought were ever fled,
And with them love, and all love's loving parts
And all those friends, supposed by me now dead.
How many a solemn and a mournful tear
Has faithful love drawn flowing from my eye,
As does befit those gone, who now appear
But absent friends, who hidden in you lie.
You are their end where bygone love lives on,
A keepsake holder for my loved ones flown,
Who have their share of me now all foregone:
That held by many is now yours alone.
I loved them all, whom in you now I see,
And you, their sum, have all the all of me.

SONNET 32: In line 4 the word "*lover*" is again used. However, as in the previous sonnet, the context suggests a wider meaning than is carried by the term in modern English.

Shakespeare, here, resorts to pathos, conjuring up the image of his death – perhaps hinting at the straits to which his poverty has brought him, and the relief which might be provided by a generous friend.

SONNET 32

If thou survive my well-contented day
When that churl death my bones with dust shall cover,
And shalt by fortune once more re-survey
These poor rude lines of thy deceas-ed lover,
Compare them with the bettering of the time,
And though they be outstripped by every pen,
Reserve them for my love, not for their rhyme,
Exceeded by the height of happier men.
O, then vouchsafe me but this loving thought:
"Had my friend's Muse grown with this growing age,
A dearer birth than this his love had brought,
To march in ranks of better equipage:
But since he died, and poets better prove,
Theirs for their style I'll read, his for his love."

If you're still here when I have had my day,
With life fulfilled, when I've met Death's blunt end,
And chance should lead you once more to survey
These poor crude works from your now dead dear friend,
Compare them with the progress since my peak
And, though they be outstripped by every pen,
Preserve them for my love, not their technique,
Surpassed by better skills from later men.
Then grant me only this one loving thought:
"Had he progressed with this progressive age,
Such pearls of verse would my friend's love have wrought,
As to rank proud with best on modern stage.
But, poets better in this interim,
Theirs I'll read for style, his for love from him."

SONNET 33:   A cloud has come over the relationship. It appears that the poet, having glamorised Southampton as his sun, the light of his days, is disappointed, though he continues to proclaim his love. The cause of the disquiet is not made clear at this stage.

Some have interpreted this sonnet as a requiem for Shakespeare's only son, Hamnet, who died aged 11 in 1596. Their starting point for this theory is the assumption that the poet is punning "sun" and "son", as he did in Sonnet 7. However, the context undermines this interpretation, since words like *"basest"*, *"ugly"*, *"disgrace"* and *"stain"* all suggest behaviour which one would not bring up in such a circumstance. And, this theme of disappointing behaviour continues in the following sonnets. Moreover, the spelling of sun as "Sunne" is consistent with the "Moone and Sunne" of Sonnet 35, and inconsistent with the "sonne" of Sonnet 7.

SONNET 33

Full many a glorious morning have I seen
Flatter the mountain-tops with sovereign eye,
Kissing with golden face the meadows green,
Gilding pale streams with heavenly alchemy,
Anon permit the basest clouds to ride
With ugly rack on his celestial face,
And from the forlorn world his visage hide,
Stealing unseen to west with this disgrace.
Even so my Sun one early morn did shine
With all-triumphant splendour on my brow;
But out, alack, he was but one hour mine,
The region cloud hath masked him from me now.
Yet him for this my love no whit disdaineth;
Suns of the world may stain when heaven's sun staineth.

Such glories of a dawn have I oft seen
Flatter mountain peaks, as heavenly eye
Drops kiss of gold upon the meadows green,
Delights pale streams with colours from the sky.
Yet then come brooding clouds to spoil the sight
With ugly veil across that warm bright face,
To turn the forlorn world back into night,
And hide the journey west in dark disgrace.
Just so, my sun one early morn did shine
With all-triumphant splendour on my brow;
Alas, but only brief was that light mine;
A dreary cloud has masked it from me now.
Yet this does not, by one bit, stunt my love;
Earth's suns may fail, as does the sun above.

SONNET 34: The tone of resentment at the young Earl's behaviour is strengthened. It appears that he has been responsible for a loss, painful to the poet. Nevertheless, Shakespeare again contrives words of forgiveness. Such magnanimity suggests either a deep and powerful love, or a constant awareness that here is a patron, or potential patron, to be kept cultivated. Perhaps both reasons apply.

The word "*loss*", at the end of line 12, is normally emended in modern editions to "cross", since otherwise the ending of line 10 is replicated.

SONNET 34

Why didst thou promise such a beauteous day
And make me travail forth without my cloak,
To let base clouds o'ertake me in my way,
Hiding thy brav'ry in their rotten smoke?
'Tis not enough that through the cloud thou break,
To dry the rain on my storm-beaten face,
For no man well of such a salve can speak
That heals the wound and cures not the disgrace:
Nor can thy shame give physic to my grief—
Though thou repent, yet I still have the loss:
Th' offender's sorrow lends but weak relief
To him that bears the strong offence's loss.
Ah, but those tears are pearl which thy love sheds,
And they are rich and ransom all ill deeds.

Why did you promise such a lovely day
And push me on without a coat or care,
Allowing clouds to blight me on my way
Which hid your charms from me in foul dark air?
It's not enough when you break through the cloud
To dry the rain on my storm-beaten face:
For no man nor his doctor can be proud
Of cures which heal the wound but leave ill trace.
Nor can your shame bring comfort to my grief,
Though you repent, for I still have my loss:
The sinner's sorrow brings but weak relief
To him who has to bear transgression's cross.
And yet your tears are pearls when shed in love,
So rich they pardon sins here and above.

SONNET 35:   More resentment from the poet and some clarification of Southampton's offence(s) emerge in this sonnet. It appears that he has a sensual or lustful flaw, and has stolen something of value to Shakespeare, although the latter continues to contrive forgiveness and excuses.

In line 4 ,"*canker*" is an abbreviation for "canker-worm", which meant caterpillar.

In line 8, I have followed Duncan-Jones' emendation of "their" to "*these*", based on her argument that the original printer misread "theis" as "their".

The references to defects of roses and buds (lines 2 and 4) will have carried a powerful, personal connotation, given Shakespeare's conceit of portraying the Earl as a young *Rose*.

SONNET 35

No more be grieved at that which thou hast done:
Roses have thorns, and silver fountains mud;
Clouds and eclipses stain both moon and sun,
And loathsome canker lives in sweetest bud.
All men make faults, and even I in this,
Authorising thy trespass with compare,
Myself corrupting, salving thy amiss,
Excusing these sins more than these sins are:
For to thy sensual fault I bring in sense;
Thy adverse party is thy advocate,
And 'gainst myself a lawful plea commence:
Such civil law is in my love and hate,
That I an accessory needs must be
To that sweet thief which sourly robs from me.

No longer feel remorse for what is done:
A rose has thorns; bright fountains stir up mud;
Clouds and eclipses haunt both moon and sun,
And creepy bugs lurk in the sweetest bud.
All men have faults, as I, in putting this
Condone your trespass with analogy,
To tell you wrongly sin is not amiss
And justify ill more than remedy.
For to your lustful flaw I give defence:
Your injured party is your advocate,
And so upon myself a suit commence.
Such civil war flares in my love and hate
As I must now become accessory
To that dear thief who harshly robs from me.

SONNET 36: This sonnet has a straightforward message - that the pair should not be seen together, albeit that Shakespeare's love for the young lord endures. But what are the *"blots"*, suddenly associated with the poet, which might blemish Southampton (whose flaws were the only ones being advertised in the preceding sonnets)?

The blots may have been the portrayals of plagiarism by Robert Greene (see commentary at Sonnet 29). More likely, they were the general associations with sexual and other aspects of the world of actors, which, in too close proximity, would have been unseemly to the reputation of an aristocrat. Perhaps these were thrown in the poet's face by an Earl, irked with the criticism of the unflattering analogies in the previous sonnets. However, in the light of clues described in Part I, it is equally plausible that Southampton had, in fact, been warned off the playwright by his guardian, Burghley, protective of the young lord's reputation.

SONNET 36

Let me confess that we two must be twain,
Although our undivided loves are one:
So shall those blots that do with me remain,
Without thy help, by me be borne alone.
In our two loves there is but one respect,
Though in our lives a separable spite,
Which though it alters not love's sole effect,
Yet doth it steal sweet hours from love's delight.
I may not evermore acknowledge thee,
Lest my bewail-ed guilt should do thee shame,
Nor thou with public kindness honour me,
Unless thou take that honour from thy name.
But do not so: I love thee in such sort
As, thou being mine, mine is thy good report.

Let me confess that we should separate,
Although our friendship keeps our loves as one,
So that those smears cast on to me by fate
Stay mine alone, and you are not undone.
Our mutual regard seeks joint welfare,
Though Fortune's spite may push our lives apart,
And while this cannot change that love we share,
It means less time for matters of the heart.
When we meet out I may not say hello
In case my scandals then attach to you,
And publicly you should not greet me so,
For fear your standing will diminish too.
So don't do this: my love is such to tell;
That, you being mine, your good name's mine as well.

SONNET 37: Here, Shakespeare appears self-sacrificing and magnanimous, while still contriving to draw attention to the disparity in their lots in life: a reminder perhaps that the young Earl (with all his abundance) has deprived the poor, "*despised*" poet of something. And, there is another strong hint that some tangible benefits would be welcomed.

Line 7 gives a further strong hint of Southampton's aristocratic status.

SONNET 37

As a decrepit father takes delight
To see his active child do deeds of youth,
So I, made lame by fortune's dearest spite,
Take all my comfort of thy worth and truth.
For whether beauty, birth, or wealth, or wit,
Or any of these all, or all, or more,
Entitled in thy parts do crown-ed sit,
I make my love engrafted to this store:
So then I am not lame, poor, nor despised
Whilst that this shadow doth such substance give
That I in thy abundance am sufficed
And by a part of all thy glory live.
Look what is best, that best I wish in thee:
This wish I have; then ten times happy me.

Just as an infirm father takes delight
To see his child cavort with energy,
So I, impeded by worst fortune's spite,
Take comfort from your worth and constancy.
For whether beauty, birth, wealth or fine brain,
Or some or all such attributes or more,
Ennobled in your provenance do reign,
I add my love to these, your fortune's store.
And then I am not handicapped or spent,
For love's reflection does such nurture give
That I, in your abundance, am content,
And through a part of your great glory live.
I wish whatever is the best for you;
Now ten times happy me, with wish come true.

SONNET 38: Shakespeare (apparently still barred from overt contact with Southampton, as suggested in Sonnet 36) continues his wooing of the young Earl. Here, he reverts to flattery, magnified by self-deflation.

In Greek mythology, the nine Muses were a sisterhood of goddesses, who promoted or inspired various forms of art, skill and knowledge. The meaning of the word, "Muse", was then extended to denote a source of inspiration or creativity, inspiration itself or creative output.

SONNET 38

How can my Muse want subject to invent
While thou dost breathe, that pour'st into my verse
Thine own sweet argument, too excellent
For every vulgar paper to rehearse?
O, give thyself the thanks, if aught in me
Worthy perusal stand against thy sight;
For who's so dumb that cannot write to thee,
When thou thyself dost give invention light?
Be thou the tenth Muse, ten times more in worth
Than those old nine which rhymers invocate;
And he that calls on thee, let him bring forth
Eternal numbers to outlive long date.
If my slight Muse do please these curious days,
The pain be mine, but thine shall be the praise.

How ever can my inspiration fail
While you are here, whose own sweet ways flow out
Into my verse, and thereby tell a tale
Too fine for common rhymes to tout about?
So give yourself the thanks if any thing
I write is worth the reading in your view;
For you, yourself, provide the themes to sing:
Then who's so dumb he cannot sing of you?
So be the tenth Muse, worth by ten times more
Than those old nine whom rhymesters call upon,
And he who invokes you may then be sure
Of timeless verse, alive when we're all gone.
If my small talents please these choosy days,
The toil is mine, but yours will be the praise.

SONNET 39: The sense continues of a clinging on by the poet, ostensibly accepting the separation, but anxious that their relationship should continue.

SONNET 39

O, how thy worth with manners may I sing,
When thou art all the better part of me?
What can mine own praise to mine own self bring?
And what is't but mine own when I praise thee?
Even for this let us divided live,
And our dear love lose name of single one,
That by this separation I may give
That due to thee which thou deserv'st alone.
O absence, what a torment thou would'st prove
Were it not thy sour leisure gave sweet leave
To entertain the time with thoughts of love,
Which time and thoughts so sweetly doth deceive,
And that thou teachest how to make one twain
By praising him here who doth hence remain.

How can I sing your worth with modesty,
When all my best is really come from you?
What use is praise of mine when made of me,
For when I praise you don't I praise me too?
Because of this we should live lives apart
And our dear love must lose its unity;
So I, through separation, can impart
What's due to you alone, deservedly.
O absence, what a torment you'd impose
If your unwanted leisure did not bring
The time for thoughts of love and love of those
Whose charms beguile the time and turn your sting;
And, too, you help a one become a pair
By here enabling praise for him who's there.

SONNET 40: Here, at last, it seems, is the cause of the disapproval in Sonnets 33-35 and the trigger for subsequent concerns as to Southampton's associations with Shakespeare. The Earl has been bedding his poet's mistress! We know that the third party in this triangular affair is a woman, because the next sonnet makes this clear.

Perhaps Shakespeare had been assured, after the first such occasion, that this was just a one-off slip; hence the moves to rapprochement in Sonnets 37-39. But, here, his grief and indignation are expressed with resurgent force: the Earl has continued to cheat. The concurrent mistress sonnets are 133 and 134.

There are possible double meanings intended in the second quatrain. I suggest that one sense could be rendered as follows. *If it was for love of me that you invited my lovemaking, I couldn't blame you for taking pleasure in my attentions. But, you were wrong, if you deceived me into doing this by saying you can't enjoy a woman's lovemaking, when clearly you can.*

Commentators often emend "*this self*" in line 7 to "thyself", on the grounds that the printer had a tendency to errors of such nature. But, I think, such emendation would change the poet's intentions erroneously. The words make perfect sense as a substitute for "me", and are poetically apt in their resonance with "*thy self*" in the next line.

The word "grace", in line 13, is another reference to Southampton's aristocratic status.

SONNET 40

Take all my loves, my love, yea, take them all:
What hast thou then more than thou hadst before?
No love, my love, that thou mayst true love call;
All mine was thine before thou hadst this more.
Then, if for my love thou my love receivest,
I cannot blame thee for my love thou usest;
But yet be blamed, if thou this self deceivest
By wilful taste of what thy self refusest.
I do forgive thy robb'ry, gentle thief,
Although thou steal thee all my poverty;
And yet, love knows, it is a greater grief
To bear love's wrong than hate's known injury.
Lascivious grace, in whom all ill well shows,
Kill me with spites, yet we must not be foes.

Take all my loves, my love, yes take them all:
What have you then more than you had before?
Not love, my love, that you can true love call:
All mine was yours before you took this more.
As you host her at the behest of me
I cannot carp you let her share your bed,
But shame on you for also making free
With my love, when you said you could not wed.
I do forgive your theft, O gentle thief,
Although you take what little that I own;
And yet, love knows, it is a greater grief
To bear love's wrongs than spite from foe well known.
Your lustful grace, in whom all dark shows bright,
Hurt me to death, yet we must never fight.

SONNET 41: Shakespeare provides more detail, and suggests that it is not Southampton's fault that he has become a lover to the poet's girlfriend. However, in almost the same breath his anguish re-emerges, and he clearly feels deeply hurt by both parties.

Here is a truly unusual love triangle. Surely this must be fiction: an aristocratic young man becoming lover to both his poet and that poet's mistress? Yet, as we saw in Part I, we have corroboration of just such an occurrence, in the sarcastic words addressed to the Earl by Thomas Nashe some months later in June 1593: *"A dear lover and cherisher you are, as well of the lovers of Poets, as of Poets themselves"*. And, these typically direct observations from Nashe are supplemented by more subtle hints from his enemy, Gabriel Harvey, who, in or before July 1593, made veiled allusions to a scandal involving Southampton and Shakespeare (see Appendix B).

SONNET 41

Those pretty wrongs that liberty commits,
When I am sometime absent from thy heart,
Thy beauty and thy years full well befits,
For still temptation follows where thou art.
Gentle thou art, and therefore to be won,
Beauteous thou art, therefore to be assailed.
And when a woman woos, what woman's son
Will sourly leave her till she have prevailed?
Ay me! but yet thou mightst my seat forbear,
And chide thy beauty and thy straying youth,
Who lead thee in their riot even there
Where thou art forced to break a twofold truth:
Hers, by thy beauty tempting her to thee,
Thine, by thy beauty being false to me.

Those little wrongs that freedom lets slip by,
In times when I am from your thoughts afar,
Your good looks and your youth well justify
For sweet temptation follows where you are.
Your gentleness means you're there to be won;
Your beauty means you're there to be assailed;
And when a woman woos, what woman's son
Will leave po-faced before she has prevailed?
But ah! you might forbear to take my place
And curb your youth and charm that so entice
And thrust you, in their urge, at headlong pace
To where their pleasures cause a faith breach twice:
Hers, through your beauty tempting her to you:
Yours with your beauty, now my friend untrue.

SONNET 42: Shakespeare continues his lament, expressing offence at Southampton's actions. He does so tactfully, however: perhaps because he does not want to lose patronage, or because he is less fussed by his male lover's infidelity than by his mistress's, or because he is genuinely a loving forgiver - or, maybe, for some or all of these reasons.

It is interesting that, though the poet claims that the loss of the Earl is the more severe of his pains, he consistently refers to the mistress as his "*love*", while three times describing the youth as "*friend*". And, this is not a matter of poetic necessity: he could easily have used a similar terminology in reverse, without losing rhyme or rhythm.

Given the circumstances of eventual publication (see Part I), it appears that Shakespeare had an arrangement to provide copies of his Dark Mistress sonnets to Southampton. Perhaps this arrangement arose as a by-product of the triangular affair. In any case, with this development he now has an ideal outlet for expressing his hurt, outrage and sonnet creativity, without giving direct offence to his patron. Mistress sonnets 135-144 give vent to his feelings about his situation, blaming her, but leaving his patron in no doubt about his distress.

SONNET 42

That thou hast her it is not all my grief,
And yet it may be said I loved her dearly;
That she hath thee is of my wailing chief,
A loss in love that touches me more nearly.
Loving offenders, thus will I excuse ye:
Thou dost love her, because thou know'st I love her;
And for my sake even so doth she abuse me,
Suffering my friend for my sake to approve her.
If I lose thee, my loss is my love's gain,
And losing her, my friend hath found that loss:
Both find each other, and I lose both twain,
And both for my sake lay on me this cross.
But here's the joy: my friend and I are one;
Sweet flattery! Then she loves but me alone.

That you have her is not my main regret,
And yet it may be said I loved her dearly;
That she has you is what I can't forget:
A loss in love which moves me much more clearly.
O loving sinners, let me clear your name:
You give her love because she's loved by me,
As she, for my sake, gives me grief and shame
To let my good friend prove her charity.
If I lose you my loss is my love's gain;
Though I lose her, my friend recoups that loss;
Each finds the other, I get two-loss pain,
And both for my sake put me on this cross.
But here's the joy: since friend and I are one
She's loved just me since this was all begun.

SONNET 43: This sonnet begins a batch, apparently composed in continued separation. Perhaps Shakespeare's feelings remain too ruffled for close contact, while the Earl's forays with the mistress play out? Or, maybe, they are heeding Burghley's concerns as to his ward's reputation.

There are no reproaches. Shakespeare has made his point to the young lord (and is probably continuing to do so, via the mistress sonnets) and, here, he is focused on repairing or maintaining their relationship. The theme is now more intellectual, perhaps appealing to a common sense of humour or shared interests.

The poem makes play with the words "*shadow*" and "*shade*": a device used in several of the Sonnets. As Ledger remarks, this evokes Plato's philosophy that the world experienced by humans is only a reflection of a greater, but not directly perceived, reality. Plato's analogy was of men being confined to a gloomy cave, in which they perceive the events of a wider, real world, outside the cave, only as images cast on to the cave walls.

Following this concept, the real thing is an original or a "form" (ie something which forms other things) and lesser imitations or perceptions are but shadows or reflections of that reality. The term "shade" continues to evoke this concept in modern English, with its alternative meaning of "ghost" or insubstantiality. So, too, does "shadow", as in "he's but a shadow of his former self".

SONNET 43

When most I wink then do mine eyes best see,
For all the day they view things unrespected;
But when I sleep, in dreams they look on thee,
And, darkly bright, are bright in dark directed.
And thou, whose shadow shadows doth make bright,
How would thy shadow's form form happy show
To the clear day with thy much clearer light,
When to unseeing eyes thy shade shines so!
How would, I say, mine eyes be bless-ed made
By looking on thee in the living day,
When in dead night thy fair imperfect shade
Through heavy sleep on sightless eyes doth stay!
All days are nights to see till I see thee
And nights bright days when dreams do show thee me.

My eyes see best when mostly closed to view,
For in my waking hours they see but dross;
But when I sleep, in dreams they look on you
Dark-brightly through that night they beam across.
And you, whose shadow's cast makes all shades bright,
How splendid would you in your person show
To clear of day with your much clearer light,
When to unsighted eyes your shade shines so!
And oh how blest would be my eyes if laid
Upon your person in the living day,
When in dead night your fair but copy shade,
Engraved on sleeping eyes, won't go away!
All days are nights until it's you I see,
And nights bright days when dreams show you to me.

SONNET 44: In this first part of a sonnet brace, Shakespeare turns his philosophically inclined lamenting to another ancient Greek concept: that all substances, including his person, are made up of four basic elements: fire, air, earth and water.

In this scene it seems that the Earl and poet are indeed separated by physical and, probably, emotional (*"injurious"*) distance. However, Shakespeare continues to work on eliminating the latter, with flattery and clever word play on the properties of the elements.

SONNET 44

If the dull substance of my flesh were thought,
Injurious distance should not stop my way;
For then, despite of space, I would be brought,
From limits far remote where thou dost stay.
No matter then although my foot did stand
Upon the farthest earth removed from thee;
For nimble thought can jump both sea and land,
As soon as think the place where he would be.
But, ah! thought kills me that I am not thought,
To leap large lengths of miles when thou art gone,
But that, so much of earth and water wrought,
I must attend time's leisure with my moan;
Receiving noughts by elements so slow
But heavy tears, badges of either's woe.

If my dense elements of flesh were thought,
No distance in our lives would be too far,
For then, despite the gap, I would be brought
From any place remote to where you are.
No matter then were I at end of land
Across the furthest reaches of the sea,
For nimble thought could leap to where you stand
As soon as think that place it seeks to be.
But, oh, the thought kills me that I'm not thought,
To jump those many miles when you're away,
But, since I'm much of earth and water wrought,
I must endure the absence and delay:
Thus gaining nought from elements so slow
But heavy tears, joint symbols of their woe.

SONNET 45: This, the second part of a brace (with 44) continues the flattery of the Earl, using the theme of the poet's elements.

In line 12, *"their"* is emended in most modern editions to "thy", on the grounds of possible printer's error, and in the belief that the line so emended makes more sense. This seems inappropriate, since such emendation would imply that the poet can be kept informed of the disposition of the youth, merely by thinking of him. I suggest that Shakespeare intended to portray a desiring thought (*fire* and *air*), directed towards the Earl, whose image then reinforces (*"assures of fair health"*) that same thought.

This leads to a straightforward interpretation of the lines. The poet is sad. He thinks, with love and desire, of the youth, whose image, thereby summoned, provides comfort and confirmation of the youth's desirability. This, in turn, reminds of separation. The poet is no longer glad and the cycle begins again.

SONNET 45

The other two, slight air and purging fire,
Are both with thee, wherever I abide:
The first my thought, the other my desire,
These present-absent with quick motion slide.
For when these quicker elements are gone
In tender embassy of love to thee,
My life, being made of four, with two alone
Sinks down to death, oppressed with melancholy.
Until life's composition be recured
By those swift messengers returned from thee,
Who even but now come back again, assured
Of their fair health, recounting it to me:
This told, I joy; but then no longer glad,
I send them back again, and straight grow sad

My other elements of air and fire
Are both with you, wherever I may be:
The first my thought, the other my desire,
Flit here and there and back most rapidly.
And when these fleeter elements have flown
To you, as my love's tender embassy,
My person, needing four, with two alone,
Sinks down in torpor, full of melancholy,
Until full complement is thus restored
When these swift messengers return from you;
Which, even as I write, come back assured
That they thrive still, on seeing you anew:
This done, I joy; but then, no longer glad,
I send them back and straight away grow sad.

SONNET 46: Still in philosophical mode, Shakespeare turns to biological, as opposed to physical, elements of his person, with a debate expressed in military and legal metaphor. Perhaps, again, he is appealing to previously shared interests, witticisms or discussions.

Some of the concepts in this and certain preceding sonnets can be seen in the following lines spoken by Lewis to his father in *King John (II i)*:

> *"I do, my lord; and in her eye I find*
> *A wonder, or a wondrous miracle,*
> *The shadow of myself form'd in her eye;*
> *Which, being but the shadow of your son,*
> *Becomes a sun and makes your sun a shadow:*
> *I do protest I never loved myself*
> *Till now infix-ed I beheld myself*
> *Drawn in the flattering table of her eye."*

SONNET 46

Mine eye and heart are at a mortal war
How to divide the conquest of thy sight:
Mine eye, my heart thy picture's sight would bar,
My heart, mine eye the freedom of that right.
My heart doth plead that thou in him dost lie —
A closet never pierced with crystal eyes —
But the defendant doth that plea deny,
And says in him thy fair appearance lies.
To 'cide this title is impanell-ed
A quest of thoughts, all tenants to the heart,
And by their verdict is determine-ed
The clear eye's moiety and the dear heart's part:
As thus: mine eye's due is thine outward part,
And my heart's right thine inward love of heart.

My eye and heart, in combat, disagree
On how the rights to view you should be split:
The eye would bar the heart so it can't see,
The heart says eye should not have such permit.
My heart claims that its realm is where you dwell,
A haven quite immune from fleshly spy;
But the defendant does this claim dispel,
Says that you see yourself when eye to eye.
To judge the case a jury is convened,
Of tenant thoughts which from the heart do fare,
And from such inquest is this verdict gleaned
Of clear eye's portion and of dear heart's share:
Your outer form is for the eye to sight,
Your inner feelings are the heart's by right.

SONNET 47: This continues the theme of a debate between eye and heart, and concludes this batch of philosophising verses with some more flattery.

SONNET 47

Betwixt mine eye and heart a league is took,
And each doth good turns now unto the other:
When that mine eye is famished for a look,
Or heart in love with sighs himself doth smother,
With my love's picture then my eye doth feast,
And to the painted banquet bids my heart;
Another time mine eye is my heart's guest
And in his thoughts of love doth share a part.
So, either by thy picture or my love,
Thyself away art present still with me;
For thou not farther than my thoughts canst move,
And I am still with them and they with thee.
Or, if they sleep, thy picture in my sight
Awakes my heart to heart's and eye's delight.

And now my eye and heart do re-unite,
To let one look out for the other too:
So when the eye is famished for your sight,
Or when the heart is languishing for you,
My eye feasts on the portrait of your face
And to this painted banquet bids my heart;
Another time my heart hosts eye with grace
And shares its thoughts of love in fullest part.
So either through my love or your portrayal,
Though you are gone from me you're still in view,
For you can't go where thoughts will not prevail,
And these remain with me and close to you.
Or, if they sleep, your portrait in my sight
Awakes my heart, to heart's and eye's delight.

SONNET 48: In the context of an underlying storyline, this sonnet suggests that Shakespeare and Southampton are still apart, emotionally and physically. However, the poet now introduces an overtone of jealousy to his flattery. Is the young lord still pre-occupied with the poet's mistress, or are there other causes for alarm? There is a hint in the final couplet that someone, whom otherwise the poet would trust, may be crowding in on what he sees as his territory.

SONNET 48

How careful was I, when I took my way,
Each trifle under truest bars to thrust,
That to my use it might unus-ed stay
From hands of falsehood, in sure wards of trust.
But thou, to whom my jewels trifles are,
Most worthy comfort, now my greatest grief,
Thou best of dearest and mine only care,
Art left the prey of every vulgar thief.
Thee have I not locked up in any chest,
Save where thou art not, though I feel thou art,
Within the gentle closure of my breast,
From whence at pleasure thou may'st come and part;
And even thence thou wilt be stol'n , I fear,
For truth proves thievish for a prize so dear.

How careful was I, when I went away,
To lock up tight each trinket and be sure
That it would not be taken in foul play,
And so in bonds of trust would be secure.
But you, who make my richest things seem dreary,
Most cherished comfort, now my greatest grief,
My only care and whom I love most dearly,
Are left the prey to every common thief.
I have not locked you up in any chest,
Save one from which you've left, but feels as though
You are there still as my heart's welcome guest,
Whereby at pleasure you may come and go.
But I still fear your theft from even here,
For faith itself turns rogue for prize so dear.

SONNET 49: It seems that Shakespeare has decided that his position is so precarious that all he can do is grovel to Southampton, and hope that the pathos of this poem will win him sympathy. He admits his flaws, and casts himself on the mercy of the young lord.

Shakespeare again demonstrates his knowledge of the commercial world, with metaphoric references to casting of sums and audit, as well as his use of legal terminology. In those days accounts (casting of sums) were delivered orally, as much as in writing. The term, "accounts", derives from the practice of giving an account of business transactions to a skilled objective listener (or Auditor), who would assess the credibility of the accounts. Such a process was known as an "*audit*", as it is today.

Rowse points out that "*leave poor me*" in line 13 can be interpreted as "leave me poor", perhaps designed to remind Southampton, yet again, of the poet's material dependence on him.

SONNET 49

Against that time, if ever that time come,
When I shall see thee frown on my defects,
When as thy love has cast his utmost sum,
Called to that audit by advised respects:
Against that time when thou shalt strangely pass,
And scarcely greet me with that sun, thine eye,
When love, converted from the thing it was,
Shall reasons find of settled gravity:
Against that time do I ensconce me here
Within the knowledge of mine own desert,
And this my hand against myself uprear,
To guard the lawful reasons on thy part:
To leave poor me thou hast the strength of laws,
Since why to love I can allege no cause.

Against that time, if ever this arise
That I will see you frown upon my faults
When your love sums my balance, to despise;
Account now closed; dead audit in the vaults:
Against that time when you will pass me by
Like stranger barely bothering to look,
When love has turned to dust, for it knows why
My sins were judged and trespass brought to book:
Against that time, I put me in my place
Now, knowing of my just deserts in time;
Accuse myself herein of my disgrace,
So you've no need to prosecute my crime.
You've right to leave poor me in equity,
For I can give no cause for love of me.

SONNET 50: The distance between the two continues to increase, as Shakespeare now journeys further from his friend. Maybe he is on a provincial tour with his acting company; or perhaps he is visiting the family home in Stratford.

SONNET 50

How heavy do I journey on the way
When what I seek, my weary travel's end,
Doth teach that ease and that repose to say,
Thus far the miles are measured from thy friend.
The beast that bears me, tired with my woe,
Plods dully on, to bear that weight in me,
As if by some instinct the wretch did know
His rider loved not speed, being made from thee:
The bloody spur cannot provoke him on
That sometimes anger thrusts into his hide,
Which heavily he answers with a groan,
More sharp to me than spurring to his side:
For that same groan doth put this in my mind:
My grief lies onward, and my joy behind.

How heavy seems my journey on the way,
When what I seek, my weary travel's end,
Instead of bringing relief, seems to say
You're now just that much further from your friend.
The horse that bears me, worn down with my woe,
Plods dully on as though grief had weight too
And as if by instinct the beast did know
His rider wants no speed in leaving you.
The bloody spur is not enough alone,
That sometimes anger thrusts into his hide,
Which heavily he answers with a groan
More sharp to me than spurring to his side.
For that same groan serves only to remind:
My sadness lies ahead, my joy behind.

SONNET 51: This continues the theme of its predecessor, and reintroduces the concepts (from Sonnet 45) of thought and desire as elements unbound by fleshly constraints.

The *"posting"*, in line 4, refers to the practice of keeping fresh horses at "posts" or key points on main highways, to enable those on urgent governmental business to exchange mounts for greater speed.

SONNET 51

Thus can my love excuse the slow offence
Of my dull bearer, when from thee I speed:
From where thou art, why should I haste me thence?
Till I return, of posting is no need.
O, what excuse will my poor beast then find,
When swift extremity can seem but slow?
Then should I spur, though mounted on the wind,
In wing-ed speed no motion shall I know:
Then can no horse with my desire keep pace.
Therefore desire, of perfect's love being made,
Shall neigh no dull flesh in his fiery race:
But love, for love, thus shall excuse my jade:
Since from thee going he went wilful-slow,
Towards thee I'll run and give him leave to go.

My love thus tolerates the plodding gait
Of my horse when I'm on my way from you:
When leaving you why should I want quick rate?
No need for haste till time for rendezvous.
But then, oh what excuse for my poor steed,
When fastest journey will seem all too slow?
For even if I flew with windblown speed
On Pegasus the pace would seem too low.
No horse could then keep pace with my desire;
And so desire, which comes from love perfect,
Will gallop me in thoughts of urgent fire,
And love will thus excuse my nag's defect:
Since from you he made pace reluctantly,
To you my thoughts will race and let him be.

SONNET 52: Here, it seems, finally, are reconciliation and renewed contact between Shakespeare and Southampton.

This apparently innocuous sonnet becomes heavy with secondary suggestions when one focuses on the terms, *"blessed"* and *"sweet"*, in lines 1 and 2. Why should a key be blessed and what sort of *"treasure"* is sweet? To the Elizabethans, *"treasure"*, in such a context, was used as a metaphor for a sexual object or adjunct, and, in this light, the *"blessed key"* takes on a distinctly phallic shape, reinforced by the wording of the final line. Christopher Marlowe had used a similar metaphor in his play, *The Massacre at Paris*, where, in Scene 19, Mugeroun is accused of cuckolding the Duke of Guise, by using his *"key"* to access the *"privy chamber"* of the Duchess.

Ledger points out that the use of the expression, *"ward-robe"* (as it was spelt in line 10), in close proximity to *"robe"* seems uncharacteristically clumsy, suggesting that a secondary meaning was intended. I agree. I offer the thought that Southampton was at the time a ward of state. In this light, the line might be construed by someone, privy to an existing in-joke, as: *Or like the robe of a ward, whom the garment hides.*

Interestingly, under either of its parallel themes, the sonnet seems to carry an excuse for the poet not seeking moments of intimacy as often as the Earl thinks appropriate.

SONNET 52

So am I as the rich, whose bless-ed key
Can bring him to his sweet uplock-ed treasure,
The which he will not every hour survey,
For blunting the fine point of seldom pleasure.
Therefore are feasts so solemn and so rare
Since, seldom coming, in the long year set,
Like stones of worth they thinly plac-ed are,
Or captain jewels in the carcanet.
So is the time that keeps you as my chest,
Or as the ward-robe which the robe doth hide,
To make some special instant special blest,
By new unfolding his imprisoned pride.
Blessed are you, whose worthiness gives scope,
Being had, to triumph; being lacked, to hope.

I'm like a fortuned man whose bless-ed key
Will let him come to joy in his hid treasure,
Which he won't wish to do incessantly
And blunt delight that comes from rare-felt pleasure.
For so are feast days made much more profound,
With their sparse scattering throughout the year,
And major jewels, when in a necklace bound,
Shine out the more for spacing wide and clear.
And so our time apart is like a chest,
Or that containment of a robe unspied,
Which makes some special moment specially blest
When it yields up the wonder kept inside.
How blest are you whose person has such worth:
Gloried in the having; longed for on dearth.

SONNET 53: In his interpretation of this sonnet, Rowse suggests that Southampton has made a generous monetary gift to Shakespeare. Certainly, the words are strongly suggestive of the young lord's benevolence, though this may have taken only the form of promised future reward. In any case, here is joyful gratitude. It appears that the reconciliation between the two is complete.

The reference to Adonis seems deliberate, for its resonance with the contemporary *Venus & Adonis*, in which Southampton was identified with the beautiful youth of that poem. We are probably now in the early months of 1593, and much of that poem would have been composed. Perhaps Shakespeare had engineered his renewed contact with Southampton (and the celebrations depicted in Sonnets 52 and 53) with a preview of the substantially complete, and soon-to-be-published, poem.

SONNET 53

What is your substance, whereof are you made,
That millions of strange shadows on you tend?
Since every one hath, every one, one shade,
And you, but one, can every shadow lend.
Describe Adonis, and the counterfeit
Is poorly imitated after you;
On Helen's cheek all art of beauty set,
And you in Grecian tires are painted new:
Speak of the spring and foison of the year,
The one doth shadow of your beauty show,
The other as your bounty doth appear;
And you in every blessed shape we know,
In all external grace you have some part,
But you like none, none you, for constant heart.

What is your essence, from what are you made
Who are reflected in so many ways?
Everyone has but one image or shade,
But yours plays a role wherever we gaze.
Describe Adonis, and the face we see
Is but a poor copy of your profile;
Recreate Helen in all her beauty,
And there is your aspect in Grecian style.
Speak of the spring and the reap of the fall:
In one do echoes of your beauty show,
The other recalls your bounty to all.
And you, in all bless-ed shapes that we know,
In all outer graces, you have some part,
But yours just yours your constancy of heart.

SONNET 54: The mood of gratitude and reconciliation continues. All now, indeed, seems rosy, and the flowery personification (suggested in Sonnet 1 and elsewhere) reappears.

In the absence of definitive, surviving vocabulary, there has been much debate as to what Shakespeare meant by *"canker-blooms"*, in line 5. Most interpreters have concluded that he was referring to wild, or dog, roses. Contrary to line 5, however, the latter are not as deeply dyed as the damask roses, used for perfume.

I prefer Duncan-Jones' identification of canker-blooms as poppies, which are as vivid in colour as the damasks. They don't hang on thorns, but I think that my interpretation of "prickled" is a reasonable reflection of Shakespeare's terminology.

The term *"vade"*, in line 14 meant "depart" (from the Latin vadere, to go away). It is usually emended to "fade" in modern editions. *"By"* in the same line is usually emended to "my", though I do not think this necessary, and have retained the original meaning.

SONNET 54

O, how much more doth beauty beauteous seem
By that sweet ornament which truth doth give!
The Rose looks fair, but fairer we it deem
For that sweet odour which in it doth live.
The Canker-blooms have full as deep a dye
As the perfume-ed tincture of the Roses,
Hang on such thorns, and play as wantonly
When summer's breath their mask-ed buds discloses:
But, for their virtue only is their show,
They live unwooed and unrespected fade,
Die to themselves. Sweet Roses do not so:
Of their sweet deaths are sweetest odours made:
And so of you, beauteous and lovely youth,
When that shall vade, by verse distils your truth.

How much more beautiful does beauty seem
When with the sweet of constance it's imbued!
The Rose looks fair, but gathers more esteem
For that sweet fragrance which it may exude.
Wild poppies are as coloured fair to see
As those more scented petals of the roses,
Are prickled and do play as prettily,
When summer's breeze their budding bloom discloses.
But they are noticed only for their shows;
They live unsought and, disregarded, fade,
To die unmarked, unlike the sweetened rose,
From whose sweet death is sweetest perfume made.
And so from you, O fair and lovely youth,
As beauty fades, through verse distilled: your truth.

SONNET 55: Here, Shakespeare continues his flattery of the Earl, through the recurring theme of immortality by verse (picked up here from the closing lines of the preceding sonnet). Arguably, he undermines this theme by failing to name his subject overtly. He would probably respond, however, that the essence of a person is not his name:

> *"What's in a name? that which we call a rose*
> *By any other word would smell as sweet."*
> *(Romeo and Juliet* – c.1594)

SONNET 55

Not marble, nor the gilded monuments
Of princes, shall outlive this powerful rhyme;
But you shall shine more bright in these contents
Than unswept stone, besmeared with sluttish time.
When wasteful war shall statues overturn,
And broils root out the work of masonry,
Nor Mars his sword nor war's quick fire shall burn
The living record of your memory.
'Gainst death and all-oblivious enmity
Shall you pace forth: your praise shall still find room
Even in the eyes of all posterity
That wear this world out to the ending doom.
So, till the judgement that yourself arise,
You live in this, and dwell in lovers' eyes.

No marble or engilded monuments
To monarchs will outlive this song for you;
And you will shine more bright in these contents
Than in such stone's unkempt and faded hue.
When wasteful wars cause statues tall to spill
And battles leave engravings scarred and bent
No war-stormed fire, nor weapon's blows will kill
These thoughts, which give you living testament.
Death will not stand, nor shroud of mind prevail
Against your march, nor will they stunt your praise,
With worlds to come now able to regale
Your deeds and ways, until the end of days.
So, till you, on the day of judgement, rise
You'll live in this, and dwell in lovers' eyes.

SONNET 56: Disquiet now hits the relationship again. Love is dwindling and unable to match the constancy of *"appetite"*, though Shakespeare is careful to leave ambiguous whose love it is that dwindles. It seems, too, that one of the pair has absented himself from the other.

The reference in the third quatrain to lovers parted by a stretch of ocean suggests the ancient Greek myth of Hero and Leander. In this Leander is separated by the waters of the Hellespont from his love, Hero, a virgin priestess of the goddess, Aphrodite (who was Venus to the Romans). But why would Shakespeare hark on such a theme?

Around 1592/3, at a time when Shakespeare was working on *Venus & Adonis*, Christopher Marlowe was working on his long poem, *Hero & Leander*. Here, Marlowe portrays Leander in sensuous terms, as a fair youth, with smooth white skin and long *"dangling tresses"*: descriptions which fit perfectly what we know of the nineteen-year old Southampton. Marlowe's depictions become positively erotic in his account of Leander's swim across the Hellespont, during which excursion the sea-god, Neptune, takes his opportunity to caress various parts of the youth's body.

Rowse points to a number of parallels in phrasing within the two poems, which suggest that each poet was aware of the other's concurrent work. All these clues, described with other evidence in Part I, suggest that Shakespeare is, here, reproaching Southampton for paying heed to Marlowe's distractions.

The word *"As"*, at the beginning of line 13, is usually emended in modern editions to "Or".

SONNET 56

Sweet love, renew thy force: be it not said
Thy edge should blunter be than appetite,
Which but today by feeding is allayed,
Tomorrow sharpened in his former might.
So, love, be thou: although today thou fill
Thy hungry eyes even till they wink with fullness,
Tomorrow see again, and do not kill
The spirit of love with a perpetual dullness.
Let this sad interim like the ocean be
Which parts the shore, where two contracted new
Come daily to the banks, that when they see
Return of love, more blest may be the view.
As call it winter, which, being full of care,
Makes summer's welcome thrice more wished, more rare.

O jaded love, revive: let not be said
That you are less keen than that coarse desire,
Which on one day is dulled when it is fed,
But on the next rebounds with renewed fire.
So, love, be like this: though today you fill
Your hungry eyes until, replete, they close,
Tomorrow be wide-eyed and do not kill
Love's spirit with an ever-lasting doze.
Let this sad break like ocean inlet be,
Which parts the shores where lovers to be wed
Come daily to the banks, that when they see
Their love's return, more blest be view ahead.
Or call it winter, which being full of drear,
Makes summer's welcome thrice more wished, more dear.

SONNET 57: We glean from this sonnet that it is, indeed, Southampton, who is absenting himself, much to Shakespeare's chagrin.

Line 2 leaves ambiguous the nature of the "*desire*", which brings the young lord back intermittently.

The whole sonnet smacks of Shakespeare's jealousy and irritation, reinforcing the sense of a close relationship between the pair, albeit that their difference in social station is also evoked. Perhaps it is the Earl's choice of "*those*" - his companions, or companion, of line 12 - which has triggered this outburst.

In line 13, the word "*Will*" (which had the secondary meaning in Elizabethan English of sex or sexual desire) is given an initial capital letter in the original, apparently to emphasise the pun on the poet's name. The triple pun reinforces the sense that the jealousy is partly sexual in its nature, and that the sonnet is autobiographical.

SONNET 57

Being your slave, what should I do but tend
Upon the hours and times of your desire?
I have no precious time at all to spend,
Nor services to do, till you require.
Nor dare I chide the world-without-end hour
Whilst I, my sovereign, watch the clock for you,
Nor think the bitterness of absence sour
When you have bid your servant once adieu.
Nor dare I question with my jealous thought
Where you may be, or your affairs suppose,
But like a sad slave stay and think of nought
Save, where you are, how happy you make those.
So true a fool is love that in your Will,
Though you do anything, he thinks no ill.

Being your slave, what should I do but tend
Upon the hours and times of your desire?
I have no precious time at all to spend,
Nor services to do, till you require!
Nor dare I chide the wait of hour on hour
Whilst I, O Master, watch the clock for you,
Nor think the bile of separation sour
Once you have bid your servant, me, adieu.
Nor dare I question with my jealous thought
Where you may be or any thing you do,
But stay here, like a serf, and think of nought
Save what joy your companions have of you.
So true a fool is love that, in your Will,
Though you do anything he thinks no ill.

SONNET 58: Shakespeare continues his railing along the same lines, and sounds, for all the world, like a wronged spouse or lover.

SONNET 58

That God forbid, that made me first your slave,
I should in thought control your times of pleasure,
Or at your hand th' account of hours to crave,
Being your vassal, bound to stay your leisure.
O let me suffer, being at your beck,
Th'imprisoned absence of your liberty,
And patience tame, to sufferance bide each check,
Without accusing you of injury.
Be where you list, your charter is so strong
That you yourself may privilege your time
To what you will, to you it doth belong
Yourself to pardon of self-doing crime.
I am to wait, though waiting so be hell,
Not blame your pleasure, be it ill or well.

May God, who first made me your slave, forbid
That I should think to rule your times of pleasure,
Or seek in-depth accounts of what you did,
Since I'm your servant, waiting on your leisure.
O let me, who am at your beck and call,
Be shackled by your right to liberty,
And patiently then bear curbs great and small,
Without accusing you of wrongs to me.
Go where you will: you have the right alone
To choose both when and what you want to do,
And you retain sole power to condone
Those harms that you yourself bring on to you.
I have to wait, though waiting is a hell,
Not blame your pleasures, bring they ill or well.

SONNET 59: Here, it seems that Shakespeare has decided it politic to take a break from complaining. Or, maybe, the Earl has toned down his abuses of the relationship.

The theme reverts to flattery of a philosophical nature. In this case the concept is the proverbial thought that there is nothing new under the sun. This idea originated in ancient times and, as pointed out by Rowse, is reflected in Ecclesiastes: *"The thing that hath been, it is that which shall be; and that which is done is that which shall be done: and there is no new thing under the sun".*

An extension of this concept is the ancient Greek hypothesis that earthly events moved in cycles, and that, after a period of many years, everything was doomed to repeat. Here Shakespeare speculates on the state of development of poetry in such a cycle, in comparison to the position five hundred years earlier: all while contriving his flattery.

SONNET 59

If there be nothing new, but that which is
Hath been before, how are our brains beguiled,
Which, labouring for invention, bear amiss
The second burden of a former child?
Oh that record could with a backward look,
Even of five hundred courses of the sun,
Show me your image in some antique book,
Since mind at first in character was done.
That I might see what the old world could say
To this compos-ed wonder of your frame,
Whether we are mended, or where better they,
Or whether revolution be the same.
Oh sure I am, the wits of former days
To subjects worse have given admiring praise.

If nothing's new and all that now arises
Occurred before, what duped imaginations
That, labouring in birth of new surprises,
Miscarry what are but re-incarnations!
If only records let me take a look
Back through five hundred years to have a sighting
Of your depiction in some ancient book,
When thoughts were first set down on page in writing.
Then I could see how authors of that day
Described such wondrous looks in word and name,
And whether we've improved or where were they
The better, or if phases were the same.
Of this I'm sure: those olden skills gave birth
To works which praised some things of far less worth.

SONNET 60: Shakespeare, in continuing his philosophising, falls back on his favourite device of immortality through verse, spiced with some classical references.

The first quatrain appears to be inspired by a description in Ovid's *Metamorphoses*, translated into English by Golding and published in 1567:

> *As every wave drives other forth*
> *and that that comes behind*
> *Both thrusteth and is thrust itself,*
> *Even so the times by kind*
> *Do fly and follow both at once.*
> *and evermore renew.*

SONNET 60

Like as the waves make towards the pebbled shore,
So do our minutes hasten to their end,
Each changing place with that which goes before,
In sequent toil all forwards do contend.
Nativity, once in the main of light,
Crawls to maturity; wherewith being crowned
Crooked eclipses 'gainst his glory fight,
And time that gave doth now his gift confound.
Time doth transfix the flourish set on youth
And delves the parallels in beauty's brow,
Feeds on the rarities of nature's truth,
And nothing stands but for his scythe to mow:
And yet to times in hope my verse shall stand,
Praising thy worth, despite his cruel hand.

Just as the waves approach the pebbled shore
So do our moments hasten to their end,
Each one replacing that which went before,
As one on one they toil to self-expend.
Nativity, once in the head of light,
Crawls to maturity, but then its day
Is all too soon eclipsed and turned to night,
As time, which gave its gifts, now takes away.
Time ravishes the face of youthful bloom
And digs deep trenches in a beauty's face,
Feeds on those creatures rare in nature's room,
Scythes down all things which stand, to leave no trace.
And yet in times to come my words will stand,
And praise your worth, in spite of Time's harsh hand.

SONNET 61: It seems, from line 6, that Shakespeare is again living a separate life. He revisits his earlier theme, of nightly visions of the Earl preventing sleep (as in Sonnets 27 and 43), but this time with the added dimension of the jealousy, expressed in Sonnets 57 and 58 (and first hinted at in Sonnet 48).

SONNET 61

Is it thy will thy image should keep open
My heavy eyelids to the weary night?
Dost thou desire my slumbers should be broken,
While shadows like to thee do mock my sight?
Is it thy spirit that thou send'st from thee
So far from home into my deeds to pry,
To find out shames and idle hours in me,
The scope and tenure of thy jealousy?
O no, thy love, though much, is not so great:
It is my love that keeps mine eye awake,
Mine own true love that doth my rest defeat
To play the watchman ever for your sake.
For thee watch I, whilst thou dost wake elsewhere,
From me far off, with others all too near.

Is it your will your image should keep open
My heavy eyelids to the weary night?
Do you desire my slumbers should be broken
By shades of you which fill and taunt my sight?
Is it your spirit that you've sent to me,
So far from home, to pry into my deeds
And spy out idle hours of frailty
As guardian of your rights and jealous needs?
O no, your love, though great, is not so deep:
It is my love that keeps me wide awake,
My own true love that takes away my sleep
And keeps a ceaseless vigil for your sake.
I watch you as you revel far from me,
With others in too close proximity.

SONNET 62: Shakespeare, perhaps conscious he has been too intense, lightens the mood with a clever sonnet, whose humorous and flattering message emerges only in the concluding punchlines. The twist is based on the age-old concept: that two persons in love are, in fact, as one.

Ledger speculates that the poet is responding to accusations by his young man, of excessive self-interest in the previous expressions of jealousy – and this, I suggest, fits well.

The "*antiquity*" of line 10 denotes, in this context, the process or experience of ageing, rather than a state of old age. It is used similarly in Sonnet 108. And, "age", in line 14, represents the duration of life to date, rather than old age. Both expressions seem designed to flatter, with their implied contrast to, and hence emphasis of, Southampton's state of bloom

SONNET 62

Sin of self-love possesseth all mine eye,
And all my soul, and all my every part;
And for this sin there is no remedy,
It is so grounded inward in my heart.
Methinks no face so gracious is as mine,
No shape so true, no truth of such account;
And for my self mine own worth do define
As I all others in all worths surmount.
But when my glass shows me my self indeed,
Beated and chopped with tanned antiquity,
Mine own self-love quite contrary I read:
Self, so self-loving, were iniquity.
'Tis thee, my self, that for my self I praise,
Painting my age with beauty of thy days.

This sin of self-love is in all of me,
My eye, my soul and all my every part;
And for this sin there is no remedy,
It is so grounded deep into my heart.
I think there is no face which charms like mine,
No word so true, no form so fine to gaze;
And I regard my self as more than fine,
Surpassing any other in all ways.
Though when my mirror shows my own true face,
Engraved and chapped with tanned seniority,
I find my love of self is out of place:
To love such self would be iniquity.
It's you, my other self, who gets self praise,
Whose youthful beauty lights my older days.

SONNET 63: The humour and wit continue, though these are not immediately obvious to a modern reader. Shakespeare picks up the concluding thought of the preceding sonnet, and turns it into his favourite fall-back theme of poetic immortality, all while apparently depicting himself as old and decrepit.

Shakespeare had surely lived a stressful life since his marriage at age eighteen. There was a family to support, while he struggled to carve out a career in a precarious profession, away from home in plague-ridden times. No doubt this stress would have left its marks, even on a man only in his late twenties. And, set against the fresh-faced, beardless young earl, these signs of life's experience must have appeared twice as evident. However, none of this quite explains the extremity of the image evoked, and we are left wondering at the latter.

The answer lies in the poet's sense of humour and the language of his time. In Shakespeare's speech, the "*hours*" of line 3 sounded exactly like "whores" (each probably rhyming approximately with "grower" or the "o'er" of line 2)[94]. The word "*blood*", in context, was a synonym of "semen" (see commentary at Sonnet 11). With this background, lines 2 and 3 take on a very different connotation! The joke is revisited in line 8, with its secondary image of a commandeering, or sparseness, of ejaculate.

In the same vein, lines 4 & 5 might be rendered: *When his youthful vigour has toiled away into that dark steeping place of old hags.*

---

[94] See *Shakespeare's Pronunciation* (p 59). This homonymic pun is also used in *As You Like It* (*II, vii, 26-8*) and *The Comedy of Errors* (*IV, ii, 59-60*).

SONNET 63

Against my love shall be, as I am now,
With Time's injurious hand crushed and o'erworn;
When hours have drained his blood and filled his brow
With lines and wrinkles; when his youthful morn
Hath travailed on to age's steepy night,
And all those beauties whereof now he's king
Are vanishing or vanished out of sight,
Stealing away the treasure of his spring:
For such a time do I now fortify
Against confounding age's cruel knife,
That he shall never cut from memory
My sweet love's beauty, though my lover's life:
His beauty shall in these black lines be seen,
And they shall live, and he in them still green.

Against that time my love is as am I,
Whose hours of grind have racked and who's sore-worn,
When tart experience has sucked him dry
And made him wrinkle; when his youthful morn
Has toiled unto the dark depths of the old,
And all those beauties of which now he's king
Are vanishing or not there to behold,
All stealing off the lush spurts of his spring:
Against such time do I now make insurance
And fortify against Time's scathing knife,
So he'll not cut from memory's endurance
My sweet love's beauty, though he takes his life.
His beauty shall in these black lines be seen
And they shall live, and in them he'll stay green.

SONNET 64: Shakespeare now muses on the depredations and cycles of time. It's time to show his patron, again, that he can deliver seriously good poetry. However, his feelings of relationship insecurity also seem to resurface in the subtle ambiguity of the concluding lines.

The second quatrain appears to have its origins in Ovid's *Metamorphoses* (as translated by Golding). Rowse interprets this as a depiction of processes on a geological scale of time: erosion of land by the sea, periodically accompanied by coastline advance through sea level change or new accretions of terrain. The source in Golding's Ovid is ambiguous or silent on the time scale. Rowse's view is, perhaps, supported by the following passage in *II Henry (IV, iii, 1)*:

> *"O God! That one might read the book of fate,*
> *And see the revolution of the times*
> *Make mountains level, and the continent,*
> *Weary of solid firmness, melt itself*
> *Into the sea! And, other times to see*
> *The beachy girdle of the ocean*
> *Too wide for Neptune's hips;"*

However, it may be that the Sonnet lines were, instead, depicting the cycles of the ocean tides.

SONNET 64

When I have seen by Time's fell hand defaced
The rich, proud cost of outworn buried age;
When sometime lofty towers I see down-razed,
And brass eternal slave to mortal rage;
When I have seen the hungry ocean gain
Advantage on the kingdom of the shore,
And the firm soil win of the wat'ry main,
Increasing store with loss and loss with store;
When I have seen such interchange of state,
Or state itself confounded to decay,
Ruin hath taught me thus to ruminate,
That Time will come and take my love away.
This thought is as a death, which cannot choose
But weep to have that which it fears to lose.

When I have seen by Time's defile how worn
Are those proud monuments from bygone age,
And witness lofty towers be down-torn
And metal plaques destroyed by human rage;
When I have seen the hungry ocean gain
Advantage on the kingdom of the shore,
And firm ground overtake the deep blue main,
Thus in then out, and so on evermore;
When I have seen such interchange of state,
Or State itself confounded to decay,
Such change has taught me to now contemplate
That Time will come and take my love away.
This thought feels like a death, since it can't choose
But weep to have that which it fears to lose.

SONNET 65: The theme of the Earl's immortality through verse continues, expressed in a contrast of enchanting and ominous images: a perfect patronage sonnet.

SONNET 65

Since brass, nor stone, nor earth, nor boundless sea,
But sad mortality o'ersways their power,
How with this rage shall beauty hold a plea
Whose action is no stronger than a flower?
O how shall summer's honey breath hold out
Against the wrackful siege of batt'ring days,
When rocks impregnable are not so stout,
Nor gates of steel so strong, but Time decays?
O fearful meditation! where, alack,
Shall Time's best jewel from Time's chest lie hid?
Or what strong hand can hold his swift foot back?
Or who his spoil o'er beauty can forbid?
O, none, unless this miracle have might,
That in black ink my love may still shine bright.

Since brass and stone and earth and boundless sea
Will one day fade away, despite their power,
How long can there be life for frail beauty,
Whose mettle is no stronger than a flower?
O how shall summer's honey breath hold out
Against the spiteful siege of battering days,
When rocks impregnable are not so stout,
Nor gates of steel so strong as Time's decays?
Now here's a dreadful thought, alas, O where
Shall Time's best jewel from Time's harsh hand be hid?
Or what strong arm can force his scythe to spare,
Or who his spoil of beauty can forbid?
No ways, unless men see this wondrous sight:
That in black ink my love may still shine bright.

SONNET 66: Now the tone of dissatisfaction returns in strength. This sonnet is the opener in a series, which complains of malign influences surrounding Southampton. The sense continues of some distance between Shakespeare and the young lord, notwithstanding the customary closing flattery.

Rowse points out an echo in line 12 of Marlowe's *"And all his captains bound in captive chains"* (from *I, Tamburlaine, III, iii, 115*).

SONNET 66

Tired with all these, for restful death I cry,
As, to behold desert a beggar born
And needy nothing trimmed in jollity,
And purest faith unhappily forsworn,
And gilded honour shamefully misplaced,
And maiden virtue rudely strumpeted,
And right perfection wrongfully disgraced,
And strength by limping sway disabl-ed,
And art made tongue-tied by authority,
And folly, doctor-like, controlling skill,
And simple truth miscalled simplicity,
And captive good attending captain ill:
Tired with all these, from these I would be gone,
Save that to die, I leave my love alone.

Tired of such things, for restful death I plea,
As: to see merit, poor of birth, unpaid,
And the unworthy bask in jollity,
And purest faith unhappily betrayed,
And shining honour shamefully debased,
And maiden virtue coarsened and depraved,
And pure perfection wrongfully disgraced,
And strength by dumb paralysis enslaved,
And knowledge censored by authority,
And skill directed by fools and falsehood,
And simple truth miscalled naivety,
And evil lording over subdued good.
Tired with all these, I would from them depart,
But that my death would leave alone my heart.

SONNET 67:   With this first part of a sonnet brace, Shakespeare launches into a diatribe aimed at one or more of the Earl's companions. He also targets practices such as make-up and other artificial beauty aids, which he deplores here and in other parts of the Sonnets.

The references to Southampton in this brace are made in the third person, unlike the normal practice of the Sonnets. I suggest that this was done to soften the implied criticism of the young aristocrat, who, if addressed in the second person (as could easily have been done under the poem's structure), would assume that he was the main target, being castigated for his choice of associate. This can be seen readily by substituting "you/your" for "he/him/his" in the first quatrain.

The roses of line 8 evoke the *Rose* of Sonnet 1.

The meaning of "*proud of many*", in line 12, is elusive. I have interpreted "proud of" as "aloof from", which seems to me to be consistent with the sense of the quatrain.

SONNET 67

Ah, wherefore with infection should he live
And with his presence grace impiety,
That sin by him advantage should achieve
And lace itself with his society?
Why should false painting imitate his cheek,
And steal dead seeing of his living hue?
Why should poor beauty indirectly seek
Roses of shadow, since his Rose is true?
Why should he live, now nature bankrupt is,
Beggared of blood to blush through lively veins?
For she hath no exchequer now but his,
And, proud of many, lives upon his gains.
O, him she stores, to show what wealth she had
In days long since, before these last so bad.

Why must he live with what is putrefied
And, by his presence, grace impiety,
So sin through him becomes more dignified
And gilds itself with his society?
Why should there be make-up to ape his face?
To steal with dyeing from his living hue?
And why should Beauty wish to find disgrace
In paper roses, when in his she's true?
Why should he live, now Nature is so poor,
Unhoused from cheeks once blushed from living veins?
She blooms in him, not others any more,
And stays aloof from most, whom she disdains.
O, he's her keepsake for her rich displays
In times long gone, before these squalid days.

SONNET 68: Shakespeare takes up from Sonnet 67 and continues in the same vein.

Some of the content is later echoed in *The Merchant of Venice* (*III, ii*):

> *"Look on beauty,*
> *And you shall see 'tis purchased by the weight;*
> *Which therein works a miracle in nature,*
> *Making them lightest that wear most of it:*
> *So are those crisp-ed snaky golden locks*
> *Which make such wanton gambols with the wind,*
> *Upon suppos-ed fairness, often known*
> *To be the dowry of a second head,*
> *The skull that bore them in the sepulchre."*

SONNET 68

Thus in his cheek the map of days outworn,
When beauty lived and died as flowers do now,
Before these bastard signs of fair were born,
Or durst inhabit on a living brow:
Before the golden tresses of the dead,
The right of sepulchres, were shorn away
To live a second life on second head,
Ere beauty's dead fleece made another gay:
In him those holy antique hours are seen,
Without all ornament, itself and true,
Making no summer of another's green,
Robbing no old to dress his beauty new;
And him as for a map doth nature store,
To show false art what beauty was of yore.

He thus portrays the ways of long ago,
When beauty lived and died as flowers do now,
Before these bastard aids to beauty's woe
Were born or dared attach to living brow,
Before the golden tresses of the dead,
Belonging to the tomb, were shorn away
To live a second life on second head
And so fair locks on one less fair display.
Those pure old ways in him are plain to sight,
With no adornment, showing only true,
That shine no brightness with another's light,
Nor rob the old to make a beauty new.
So Nature keeps him, template to behold,
That shows false art what beauty was of old.

SONNET 69: Now Shakespeare reverts to his normal form of address. Through the device of warning Southampton of threats to his reputation, he criticises the young lord's behaviour and, by implication, his association with the "*infection*" of Sonnet 67. The concluding couplet, startling in its directness and insult, must have triggered resentment in, and repercussions from his aristocratic patron.

Line 3 originally terminated in the word "end", commonly emended to "due", which can be readily justified on the basis of printer's reading or setting error (typeset had to be read as a mirror image of what was to be printed). The word, "*their*", commencing line 5, is commonly emended to "thy" (though the plural possessive could well relate to the "*parts*" of line 1). Line 14's original "*solye*" is normally presented as "soil".

SONNET 69

Those parts of thee that the world's eye doth view
Want nothing that the thoughts of hearts can mend;
All tongues, the voice of souls, give thee that due,
Utt'ring bare truth, even so as foes commend.
Their outward thus with outward praise is crowned;
But those same tongues that give thee so thine own
In other accents do this praise confound,
By seeing farther than the eye hath shown,
They look into the beauty of thy mind
And that, in guess, they measure by thy deeds;
Then churls, their thoughts (although their eyes were kind)
To thy fair flower add the rank smell of weeds;
But why thy odour matcheth not thy show,
The soil is this: that thou dost common grow.

Those sides of you on show to public view
Need no improvement that one can foresee;
All tongues, with heartfelt voice, give you that due;
It is plain truth, as even foes agree.
And so the outward gets its outward praise;
But those same tongues which compliment you so
Are pitched to hint in praise-detracting ways,
And thus reflect on where the eye can't go.
They look into the beauty of your mind,
And that, in guess, they measure by your deeds,
And then their churlish thoughts, though eyes are kind,
Bring to your rosy hue the smell of weeds.
Your stature does not match what's there to see
For commonness now soils your pedigree.

SONNET 70: Had Shakespeare gone too far with the castigations of Sonnets 67-69? Here he appears to backtrack, with convoluted arguments.

In line 7 the *Rose* conceit is glimpsed again, through the image of the "*sweetest buds*" being loved by "*canker-vice*" – the latter evoking the "*infection*" of Sonnet 67.

SONNET 70

That thou art blamed shall not be thy defect,
For slander's mark was ever yet the fair;
The ornament of beauty is suspect,
A crow that flies in heaven's sweetest air.
So thou be good, slander doth but approve
Thy worth the greater, being wooed of time;
For canker-vice the sweetest buds doth love,
And thou present'st a pure unstain-ed prime.
Thou hast passed by the ambush of young days
Either not assailed, or victor being charged:
Yet this thy praise cannot be so thy praise,
To tie up envy evermore enlarged.
If some suspect of ill masked not thy show,
Then thou alone kingdoms of hearts should'st owe.

That you're maligned need not require contrition,
For slander's target always is the fair,
And beauty gets adorned with black suspicion,
A crow that flies in heaven's clearest air.
But if you're innocent such slurs will show
Your worth the greater, through the test of time;
For bugs prefer the fairest buds that grow,
And you seem in your pure unblemished prime.
You have survived the tests of younger days,
Unassailed or vanquishing your hurt;
But these achievements also pave the ways
To bolster envy, always on alert.
If you had no detraction or shortfall
Then you alone would be beloved of all.

SONNET 71: This begins a batch of four sonnets in which Shakespeare invites contemplation of his death. Is he ill and feeling sorry for himself? Or, are these a reaction to the anger of the Earl, still incensed at insults associated with Sonnet 69? Expanding the latter scenario, perhaps Southampton has ostracised the poet, or even told him, stingingly, that he is dead to him. In such context, the references to death may also be seen as a metaphor for the demise of the friendship.

In the early months of 1593 Shakespeare would have been desperate to retain patronage, given the ebb in earning capacity caused by closure of the London playhouses and the demands of his family, probably exacerbated by his father's financial problems. *Venus & Adonis*, substantially complete, would have been difficult to market without the endorsement of, and support from, its prime subject.

To these ends, and perhaps for the sake of a genuine regard for the Earl, he would have needed to defuse the fallout from the insult of Sonnet 69. We can reasonably surmise that this batch of sonnets seeks to achieve this purpose with their liberal doses of pathos and grovelling. There is also some wry wit - if they are indeed responding to events or remarks associated with the poet's metaphoric death. In addition, they hint strongly at the loss which Southampton would suffer if he became permanently separated from the poet for any reason.

SONNET 71

No longer mourn for me when I am dead
Than you shall hear the surly sullen bell
Give warning to the world that I am fled
From this vile world with vilest worms to dwell:
Nay, if you read this line, remember not
The hand that writ it; for I love you so
That I in your sweet thoughts would be forgot
If thinking on me then should make you woe.
O if, I say, you look upon this verse
When I perhaps compounded am with clay,
Do not so much as my poor name rehearse,
But let your love even with my life decay:
Lest the wise world should look into your moan,
And mock you with me after I am gone.

When I am dead you should not grieve for me
Beyond the time you hear the mournful bell
Proclaim to all that I no longer be
Upon this earth, but underneath do dwell.
No, if you read this verse remember not
The one who wrote it; for I love you so
That I prefer that I should be forgot
If thinking on me then would bring you woe.
And, if you chance to read this, don't be kind
When I have left this world of mortal strife;
Do not so much as bring my name to mind
But rather let love fade, as has my life.
The more such thoughts about me linger on
The more they'll hurt you with me when I'm gone.

SONNET 72: This sonnet is so self-deprecating as to suggest that pathos and some timely grovelling are, indeed, the prime motivations for this batch of poems.

SONNET 72

O, lest the world should task you to recite
What merit lived in me that you should love
After my death, dear love, forget me quite,
For you in me can nothing worthy prove,
Unless you would devise some virtuous lie,
To do more for me than mine own desert,
And hang more praise upon decease-ed I
Than niggard truth would willingly impart.
O, lest your true love may seem false in this,
That you for love speak well of me untrue,
My name be buried where my body is,
And live no more to shame nor me nor you.
For I am shamed by that which I bring forth,
And so should you, to love things nothing worth

In case the world should ask you to explain
What was it that you saw and loved in me,
Dear love, when I am dead you must refrain
From my recall, who lived unworthily,
As you would need to make up some white lies
To give me standing which I don't deserve,
And ply more praise on me, on my demise,
Than honest truth would willingly observe.
So let, in case the truth of your true love
Seems false, because for love you speak untrue,
My name be buried to the world above
And live no more, to shame not me nor you.
For I'm ashamed of works which show my dearth,
And so should you, to love what has no worth.

SONNET 73: The stark beauty of this well-loved poem shows Shakespeare in full possession of his faculties. If he is ill, the ailment has not succeeded in dimming his flair.

In this batch of four sonnets on the theme of his (or the friendship's) death, this is the only one which suggests an association with old age (though the brilliance of the poetry simultaneously denies the latter). Shakespeare would have been in his late twenties when he composed the main sequence of poems addressed to the Earl, and far from being the pitifully decayed figure conjured up by this verse.

However, on closer inspection of the poem, we can also see that nowhere does the poet actually state that he is old or that he has the characteristics of old age. The closing line is strangely phrased, with its implication that Southampton will be doing the leaving. Nor is this phrasing a consequence of poetic constraint: Shakespeare could, for example, readily have used the word "lose" instead of "*leave*".

On this basis, the beautifully depicted core message is of Shakespeare's concerns as to the Earl's (erroneous) perceptions and a consequent, impecunious ending of their relationship, along the following lines:

In me you see things that are past it, like a year in the grips of winter[95], a day at dusk or a guttering fire. But, given you have this perception, the nobility of your love for me will be seen to be enhanced if you give me more care (and, in particular, a golden handshake) before you dump me.

Other messages seem to be "Cherish me while you can" and "Behold the beauty of my poetry – as good, if not better, than anyone else's".

---

[95] In Shakespeare's day the annual calendar began near the end of March, unlike now.

SONNET 73

That time of year thou mayst in me behold
When yellow leaves, or none, or few, do hang
Upon those boughs which shake against the cold,
Bare ruined choirs, where late the sweet birds sang.
In me thou see'st the twilight of such day
As after sunset fadeth in the west,
Which by and by black night doth take away,
Death's second self, that seals up all in rest.
In me thou see'st the glowing of such fire
That on the ashes of his youth doth lie
As the death-bed whereon it must expire,
Consumed with that which it was nourished by.
This thou perceiv'st, which makes thy love more strong
To love that well which thou must leave ere long.

That time of year you may in me behold,
When yellow leaves, or none, or few do hang
Upon those boughs which shake against the cold,
Bare ruined choirs where lately sweet birds sang.
In me you see the twilight of such day
As after sunset's fading in the west,
That by and by black night will take away,
Like Death, who wraps up all in lasting rest.
In me you see the glowing of such fire
Whose ashes of its youth now underlie:
A death-bed, which upon it must expire,
Consumed by that which it was nourished by.
You see this, which now makes your love more strong,
To love that well which you must leave ere long.

SONNET 74: This sonnet concludes the batch on the theme of the poet's death. Shakespeare reminds Southampton of his loyalty, whilst continuing to grovel and jerk the heartstrings with his pathos.

SONNET 74

But be contented when that fell arrest
Without all bail shall carry me away;
My life hath in this line some interest,
Which for memorial still with thee shall stay.
When thou reviewest this, thou dost review
The very part was consecrate to thee:
The earth can have but earth, which is his due,
My spirit is thine, the better part of me:
So then thou hast but lost the dregs of life,
The prey of worms, my body being dead,
The coward conquest of a wretch's knife,
Too base of thee to be remember-ed.
The worth of that is that which it contains,
And that is this, and this with thee remains.

Yet be content when that which is all's due,
With no right of appeal, dispatches me:
My life has in this verse some residue
To stay with you and give you memory.
When you read over this you thereby sight
That part of me devoted to your cause:
The earth can have but earth, which is its right;
The better part of me, my spirit's yours.
So then you've lost what are but dregs of life,
The worm's food from a man disintegrated,
The shallow conquest of Death's hollow knife,
Too base by you to be then celebrated.
The worth of that is that which it contains
And that is this, and this with you remains.

SONNET 75: The grovelling, flattery, pathos and some glorious poetry, within the preceding sonnets, have apparently worked. Southampton is still listening at least, if not fully placated. Here, Shakespeare seems to be justifying his turns of mood and pleading his love for, and delight in, the young lord as the cause of his over-possessiveness and jealousy.

Lines 5 and 6 conjure up the sexual overtones of Sonnet 52.

SONNET 75

So are you to my thoughts as food to life,
Or as sweet-seasoned showers are to the ground;
And for the peace of you I hold such strife
As 'twixt a miser and his wealth is found:
Now proud as an enjoyer, and anon
Doubting the filching age will steal his treasure;
Now counting best to be with you alone,
Then bettered that the world may see my pleasure;
Sometime all full with feasting on your sight,
And by and by clean starv-ed for a look:
Possessing or pursuing no delight,
Save what is had or must from you be took.
Thus do I pine and surfeit day by day,
Or gluttoning on all, or all away.

You're like unto my thoughts as food to life,
Or as the spring rains are to earth's good health;
And for that ease from you I feel such strife
As lies between a miser and his wealth:
Now rampant in possession, then awhile
Afraid the thieving times will steal his treasure;
Now having you alone makes me most smile,
But then I want the world to see my pleasure;
At times I'm full with feasting on your sight,
But shortly after starving for your view,
Enjoying or pursuing no delight
Except what's had or what must come from you.
And so I starve or glut from day to day,
With overfill or famine come my way.

SONNET 76: Shakespeare turns to a new theme – ironic given that the subject is the lack of new themes and techniques. He is clearly concerned either that he is not matching up to some other poet(s) or, more likely, that Southampton has this perception.

Perhaps the Earl has commented on his unchanging style: in which case Shakespeare, here, echoes Southampton's criticism, and then explains and defends himself with flattery and avowals of constancy.

SONNET 76

Why is my verse so barren of new pride,
So far from variation or quick change?
Why with the time do I not glance aside
To new-found methods and to compounds strange?
Why write I still all one, ever the same,
And keep invention in a noted weed,
That every word almost doth tell my name,
Showing their birth and where they did proceed?
O, know, sweet love, I always write of you,
And you and love are still my argument:
So all my best is dressing old words new,
Spending again what is already spent:
For as the sun is daily new and old,
So is my love still telling what is told.

Why is my verse so lacking in bold flair,
So standardised and like not to amaze?
Why don't I follow fashions and thus dare
To try some new techniques and turns of phrase?
Why do my poems always look the same,
All set out in a style that's so well known
That every word might almost bear my name,
It is so clear to all that they're my own?
Because, sweet love, I always write of you,
And you and love remain my theme's content:
So all my best just spins old words anew,
To spend again what is already spent.
For, as the sun is daily new and old,
So is my love: re-telling what's been told.

SONNET 77: Apparently this sonnet is, in effect, the note accompanying the gift of a blank notebook, which Shakespeare offers to Southampton with some sage, if unexciting, advice. No-one reading this can avoid a sense of autobiography.

In line 1 *"were"* is commonly emended to "wear". This emendation carries a similar sense in context, but has the effect of implying that the decay of beauty has commenced. I suggest that this is inappropriate, and that Shakespeare is actually pointing to a time still reasonably distant, when the three articles mentioned will, in different ways, reflect the experience of time elapsed.

SONNET 77

Thy glass will show thee how thy beauties were,
Thy dial how thy precious minutes waste:
The vacant leaves thy mind's imprint will bear,
And of this book this learning mayst thou taste:
The wrinkles which thy glass will truly show
Of mouth-ed graves will give thee memory;
Thou by thy dial's shady stealth mayst know
Time's thievish progress to eternity.
Look what thy memory cannot contain
Commit to these waste blanks, and thou shalt find
Those children nursed, delivered from thy brain,
To take a new acquaintance of thy mind.
These offices, so oft as thou wilt look,
Shall profit thee and much enrich thy book.

Your mirror will in time show beauty's past,
Your watch, your precious minutes' dissipation;
Your thoughts will on these empty leaves be cast
And so this book may bring you education:
Those wrinkles that show clearly in your glass
To yawning graves will turn your memory;
The stealthy crawl of clock will show the pass
Of time in stealing to eternity;
Whatever memory cannot contain
Commit to these blank pages and you'll find
The offspring of such thoughts birthed in your brain
Preserved to stimulate your future mind.
These habits, if performed each time you look
Will profit you and much enrich your book.

SONNET 78: Now, finally, Shakespeare refers openly to the situation which has provoked his jealousy and concern, probably since as far back as Sonnet 56 (and maybe even Sonnet 48). Other poets are competing for Southampton's favours, but, as established in the preceding section and the following sonnets, Shakespeare's focus is on just one rival – the formidable Christopher Marlowe.

In its original printing, "*Alien*", in line 3, is italicised and has a higher case opening letter. My interpretation of its sexual allusions, in conjunction with the phallic "*pen*", evoked by Shakespeare elsewhere in his works, is explained in Part I, preceding this section.

Shakespeare also deprecates his "*ignorance*" and contrasts this with the learnedness of Marlowe and Southampton, who, unlike the Stratfordian, were university men. He uses the contrast in flattery of the young Earl but, in so doing, he suggests a continuing sensitivity to the curtailing of his formal education, despised in Greene's insults of only a few months before.

SONNET 78

So oft have I invoked thee for my Muse,
And found such fair assistance in my verse,
*As every **Alien** pen hath got my use*
And under thee their poesy disperse.
Thine eyes, that taught the dumb on high to sing
And heavy ignorance aloft to fly,
Have added feathers to the learned's wing
And given grace a double majesty.
Yet be most proud of that which I compile,
Whose influence is thine and born of thee:
In other works thou dost but mend the style,
And arts with thy sweet graces grace-ed be.
But thou art all my art, and dost advance
As high as learning my rude ignorance.

So often have I used you to inspire,
And had your fair assistance of my verse,
Now every strange-bent poet seeks your hire
And ply their tools for pleasure of your purse.
Your grace, which taught my dumbness how to sing,
My earthy ignorance to seek the sky,
Has also given learned men something
With which their poetry to dignify.
Yet be more proud of works which I compile,
Whose influence is yours and born of you:
In others' you but modulate their style,
As you with grace do all the arts imbue.
But you are all my art and you raise high
My ignorance to where the tutored fly.

SONNET 79: Shakespeare acknowledges Marlowe's current superiority in their poetic competition for Southampton; although he does his best to undermine his rival's praises of the Earl, while himself contriving flattery.

In Shakespeare's English the word, "*argument*", in line 5 had, in context, a primary meaning of "theme" or "subject matter" (see also line 10 of Sonnet 76).

The energetically wielded "*pen*" of line 6 continues to have the "*use*" of Southampton brought out in the preceding sonnet and is deemed "*worthier*". With these parallel images, it seems that Marlowe is also winning the sexual competition for the young lord.

SONNET 79

Whilst I alone did call upon thy aid
My verse alone had all thy gentle grace;
But now my gracious numbers are decayed
And my sick Muse doth give another place.
I grant, sweet love, thy lovely argument
Deserves the travail of a worthier pen;
Yet what of thee thy poet doth invent
He robs thee of, and pays it thee again.
He lends thee virtue, and he stole that word
From thy behaviour; beauty doth he give,
And found it in thy cheek; he can afford
No praise to thee but what in thee doth live.
Then thank him not for that which he doth say,
Since what he owes thee thou thyself dost pay.

When I alone relied upon your aid
My verse alone had all your gentle grace;
But now my poems fail to make the grade
My ailing skill is down in second place.
I grant, sweet love, your lovely attributes
Deserve the stroke-work of a better pen;
But what of you your poet's verse imputes
He takes from you then gives it back again.
He lends you virtue, but he stole that grace
From your behaviour; beauty does he give
But found this in your face; he cannot place
A praise on you that does not in you live.
So thank him not for what he has to say,
Since what he owes you you yourself do pay.

SONNET 80: In his opening lines, Shakespeare seems to be almost prostrating himself in his admissions of inferiority to Marlowe. However, given what has gone before, we have to now expect the presence of subtle wit or, perhaps, sarcasm.

The word "*spirit*" (line 2) could refer to any or all of his rival poet, the character of that poet or a supernatural entity.

However, this spirit "*uses*" Southampton's name, and, in so doing, "*spends all his might*". These expressions carry hints of rather unspiritual activity - strengthened if one takes Southampton's name to be "rose", the affectionate nickname of the Sonnets and itself a beautiful receptacle[96]. Elsewhere, Shakespeare uses the term "spirit", in context, as a synonym for "semen" (as in Sonnet 129).

In any case, there is strong sexual innuendo in the remainder of the poem, highlighted by the reference to Marlowe's "*ride*" on Southampton's "*soundless deep*" (so providing a sexually loaded maritime metaphor , similar to that of Sonnet 137, where the dark mistress is likened to a "*bay where all men ride*").

The sonnet turns into a clever plea for Southampton's continued support of his former favourite. Shakespeare hints, in reproachful parallel meanings, that his displacement may be due to the inadequacy of his love-making compared to Marlowe's.

---

[96] It is also used by Shakespeare as the symbol for a sexual prize, seen in the following rebuttal by Diana of Bertram's promises, as he urges her to fornicate (*All's Well That Ends Well, IV, ii, 22-25*): "*Ay, so you serve us till we serve you; but when you have our roses you barely leave our thorns to prick ourselves, and mock us with our bareness* ".

SONNET 80

O, how I faint when I of you do write,
Knowing a better spirit doth use your name,
And in the praise thereof spends all his might,
To make me tongue-tied, speaking of your fame.
But since your worth, wide as the ocean is,
The humble as the proudest sail doth bear,
My saucy bark, inferior far to his,
On your broad main doth wilfully appear.
Your shallowest help will hold me up afloat,
Whilst he upon your soundless deep doth ride;
Or, being wracked, I am a worthless boat,
He, of tall building and of goodly pride.
Then if he thrive and I be cast away,
The worst was this: my love was my decay.

O, how I faint when I of you do write,
Aware that stronger issue plugs your name,
And in that rose-esteem is spent his might,
Which makes it hard for me to voice your fame.
But since your worth, as great as ocean's bulk,
Supports the low as well as proudest crafts,
My saucy skiff, so dwarfed by his fine hulk,
Persists in flitting on your boundless draughts.
Your shallowest help will hold me up afloat,
While he upon your soundless deeps can ride;
And, if unmanned, I am a worthless boat,
As he, erect and tall, disports with pride.
But if he thrives and I am cast away,
The worst would be: my love caused my decay.

215

SONNET 81: Here, Shakespeare falls back on his favourite theme of immortality through verse. Is he trying to get back to normal business, albeit in the process continuing to compete with Marlowe, with what is a fine patronage poem?

Rowse suggests that the references to the Earl's epitaph and monument were a reflection of contemporaneous events, and he points to the project for the Southampton family monument, which would have been in progress during 1593. The monument, commissioned in May 1594, was, in its final form, a compromise from the grandiose specifications in the second Earl's will. It survives, splendidly intact at St Peter's Church in Titchfield (near Southampton), and depicts the third Earl as a boy in armour kneeling at the sides of his recumbent father and grandfather.

The ceremonial use of monuments and epitaphs on the death of an aristocratic family member is well described in the following advice from Friar Francis in *Much Ado About Nothing* (*IV, i*):

> *Maintain a mourning ostentation,*
> *And on your family's old monument*
> *Hang mournful epitaphs, and do all rites*
> *That appertain unto a burial.*

SONNET 81

Or I shall live, your epitaph to make,
Or you survive when I in earth am rotten;
From hence your memory death cannot take,
Although in me each part will be forgotten.
Your name from hence immortal life shall have,
Though I, once gone, to all the world must die:
The earth can yield me but a common grave,
When you entomb-ed in men's eyes shall lie.
Your monument shall be my gentle verse,
Which eyes not yet created shall o'er-read;
And tongues to be your being shall rehearse,
When all the breathers of this world are dead.
You still shall live, such virtue hath my pen,
Where breath most breathes, even in the mouths of men.

Whether your epitaph is writ by me
Or you survive to see my bones interred,
From here on Death can't take your memory
Though I be quite forgot, my name unheard.
Your name from here will live eternally
Though I, once gone, be dead to all alive
And there will be but common grave for me,
As you, entombed in human minds, will thrive.
Your monument will be my poetry,
Which eyes not yet created will light on,
And you'll be heard in voices yet to be
When all the breathers of this age are gone.
You'll be alive – such power has my pen –
Where breath most breathes, that stirs in mouths of men.

SONNET 82: It seems that Shakespeare has failed to make headway in his rivalry, either with the double-edged pleadings of Sonnets 78 to 80 or with his more conventional offering of Sonnet 81.

Now the tone becomes more direct and more urgent, as if opening a debate: gone are the innuendos and possible attempts to amuse of earlier sonnets in this rivalry sequence. Shakespeare is now focused on what most concerns him – his professional status with Southampton. We have probably reached April 1593.

At first sight, lines 2 to 4 seem to be couched in the affable phrases of a poet who knows his place. The message that comes across is: *I have no problem with you glancing over the content of any other writer's works and thereby raising their stature with your interest.*

However, a secondary message is discernible, due to the ambiguity of the word, *"o'erlook"*, which could mean either "ignore" or "have a look over". Taken as "ignore", the message becomes a politic reproach, thus: *You can ignore my poetry, dedicated to you alone, in favour of other poets who versify to all and sundry.*

Like many others of the Sonnets, it is hard to construe this poem as anything other than part of an autobiographic sequence.

SONNET 82

I grant thou wert not married to my muse,
And therefore mayst without attaint o'erlook
The dedicated words which writers use
Of their fair subject, blessing every book.
Thou art as fair in knowledge as in hue,
Finding thy worth a limit past my praise;
And therefore art enforced to seek anew
Some fresher stamp of the time-bettering days.
And do so, love; yet when they have devised
What strain-ed touches rhetoric can lend,
Thou, truly fair, were truly sympathised
In true plain words by thy true-telling friend.
And their gross painting might be better used
Where cheeks need blood: in thee it is abused.

I grant you haven't given me sole right
To your theme or your aid to inspiration;
So you can look past mine and give no slight
By blessing others' words of dedication.
You are as learned as your looks are fair,
And know your worth is quite beyond my praise;
And so you are obliged to look elsewhere
For fresher verse from these progressive days.
And do so, love; yet when they have displayed
Those most strained touches rhetoric can lend,
You, truly fair, are better so portrayed
In true plain words by your true-telling friend.
And their gross painting might be better based
Where cheeks need hue: on you this is misplaced.

SONNET 83: The sense of a debate continues: one can almost hear Southampton dismissing Shakespeare's argument in the previous sonnet, whereupon the poet responds with this.

It seems clear that the young lord is being wooed by flattering verse from Marlowe: too thickly applied and unnecessary, according to Shakespeare. Any such poetry from Marlowe remains undiscovered. It would have been expunged from the records of both Southampton and Marlowe, under the scenario of their subsequent enforced separation, described in Part I, preceding.

In line 7 "*modern*", as used by Shakespeare, meant "ordinary", perhaps even "trite".

The final line reinforces the sense, previously conveyed, that Shakespeare has here only one serious rival for Southampton's favours.

SONNET 83

I never saw that you did painting need,
And therefore to your fair no painting set;
I found, or thought I found, you did exceed
The barren tender of a poet's debt.
And therefore have I slept in your report,
That you yourself, being extant, well might show
How far a modern quill doth come too short,
Speaking of worth, what worth in you doth grow.
This silence for my sin you did impute,
Which shall be most my glory, being dumb;
For I impair not beauty being mute,
When others would give life and bring a tomb.
There lives more life in one of your fair eyes
Than both your poets can in praise devise.

I thought for you cosmetics were needless,
And so I used no make-up to disguise
That beauty I thought greatly in excess
Of any words a poet could devise.
And so I did not eulogise your charms,
That you, there in the flesh, would thus impress
On all that shallow rhymers should have qualms:
Be lost for words to paint such worthiness.
My silence for a sin you did impute,
But credit me that I did thus behave:
For I impair not beauty, being mute,
When others wish it life, yet dig its grave.
There lives more life in one of your fair eyes
Than both your poets can in praise devise.

SONNET 84: Shakespeare becomes more forceful in his arguments to undermine Marlowe's successful poetic seduction of Southampton. Though contriving praise, he again insults the young earl, in effect accusing him of narcissism – ironic, given the poet's attempts, starting around a year earlier, to defuse the venom of John Clapham's work.[97].

"*Fond*", in the final line, then meant "foolishly attracted to". The final two lines are astonishing in their bluntness towards one of much higher social standing, whose continuing patronage is presumably not yet foregone. Such freedom of expression suggests anger, desperation, and a sense of injustice. It is also within the reasonable bounds of their intimate relationship, which, to Shakespeare's mind, might excuse such latitude within the private communication of his sonnets.

---

[97] See commentary at Sonnets 5 and 6

SONNET 84

Who is it that says most, which can say more
Than this rich praise, that you alone are you:
In whose confine immure-ed is the store
Which should example where your equal grew?
Lean penury within that pen doth dwell
That to his subject lends not some small glory;
But he that writes of you, if he can tell
That you are you, so dignifies his story.
Let him but copy what in you is writ,
Not making worse what nature made so clear,
And such a counterpart shall fame his wit,
Making his style admire-ed everywhere.
You to your beauteous blessings add a curse,
Being fond on praise, which makes your praises worse.

What teller of the tallest tales can sing
More rich praise than that you alone are you?
For you embody each and every thing
A poem needs to paint your image true.
Poor is that writer's pen which shows not well
His subject, adding colour to the pale;
But he that writes of you, if he can tell
That you are you, makes credible his tale.
Let him but list your attributes by name,
Not overdressing Nature's gifts to you,
And such an offering will bring him fame
And praise of style here and the whole land through.
You, with your wondrous blessings, have an ill:
Too fond of praise, which brings praise overkill.

SONNET 85: Shakespeare gives no clue as to Southampton's reception of the insult in the preceding sonnet. Perhaps that poem and this were submitted to the Earl simultaneously – in which case, they may even have been filed in reversal of their chronology. Here, Shakespeare portrays an image of his watching on while Marlowe's poems in praise of Southampton are read over. Although he depicts himself as humble, complimentary and deferential, some ambiguous phrasing suggests that contrary messages were also intended.

For example, the first quatrain implies of Southampton: *You are being skilfully eulogised in the most wonderful of terms, but these are really rather hackneyed phrases used by a multitude of other poets before – though I'm too polite to say this out loud.*

In lines 10 and 11, the thrust of the thoughts which he adds to his spoken words is unspecified - and can be taken to be derogatory. The gist of the subsequent lines can be rendered as: *Love outranks words. Though you may respect others for their speeches you should respect me for my deeds which are the true representatives of my thoughts.*

By now we have probably reached early May 1593. A brooding Shakespeare is involved with the printing of *Venus & Adonis,* and in devising his bold and insultingly second-edged dedication to Southampton (described in Part I).

Around now, another poem is composed, suggesting Marlowe's involvement with dissident anti-immigrant campaigners, being sought by the Queen's authorities.

SONNET 85

My tongue-tied Muse in manners holds her still,
While comments of your praise, richly compiled,
Reserve their character with golden quill
And precious phrase by all the Muses filed.
I think good thoughts, whilst other write good words,
And like unlettered clerk still cry "Amen"
To every hymn that able spirit affords
In polished form of well-refin-ed pen.
Hearing you praised, I say "Tis so, 'tis true",
And to the most of praise add something more;
But that is in my thought, whose love to you,
Though words come hindmost, holds his rank before.
Then others for the breath of words respect,
Me for my dumb thoughts, speaking in effect.

My stumbling skill stays silently polite,
While praises of your worth are richly wrought
In precious words of golden copyright
And lines of well rehearsed poetic thought.
I think good thoughts while he there writes good things,
And like dull parish clerk I cry amen
To every hymn that able spirit brings
To polished script, with his fine-pointed pen.
I hear your praise and say "It's so, it's true",
And to each peak of praise add something more;
But that is in my thoughts, where love for you
Preceded any words and stands before.
So give the others due for oratory,
And me for my dumb thoughts which act for me.

SONNET 86: Suddenly the subject of the rival poet is couched largely in the past tense and with unreserved respect. He is mentioned in no more sonnets. He is gone. Marlowe has been killed - on 30 May 1593.

The inquest into his death was held two days later and it is from the surviving report, discovered by Leslie Hotson around 1925, that we know of the official findings. Marlowe was deemed killed in self-defence, following an argument in the sole company of three associates of Thomas Walsingham. The quarrel concerned the bill or "reckoning" for the food and drink consumed that day by the quartet.

No doubt, Southampton would have been informed of the official findings by his guardian, Lord Burghley. Whether he believed them is another matter. However, it is this official story which he would have relayed to others, including, most probably, Shakespeare. Some years later, the latter harked back to these circumstances – not then common knowledge – in *As You Like It*.[98]

The references to spirits and their aid have provoked much debate and various theories over the years. Rowse suggests that Marlowe's highly successful play, *Dr Faustus*, was being staged around the time of his death. He proposes that the hero, Faustus, who contracted to sell his soul in exchange for supernatural aid from demons, was regarded as a dramatic projection of Marlowe, himself: hence the current tense, artfully used in line 10, "*nightly gulls him with intelligence*".

Respect notwithstanding, Shakespeare continues to defend his professional ability, blaming any poetic shortcomings in recent times on Southampton's favouring of Marlowe.

---

[98]   See footnote 76

SONNET 86

Was it the proud full sail of his great verse,
Bound for the prize of all too precious you,
That did my ripe thoughts in my brain inhearse,
Making their tomb the womb wherein they grew?
Was it his spirit, by spirits taught to write
Above a mortal pitch, that struck me dead?
No, neither he, nor his compeers by night
Giving him aid, my verse astonish-ed.
He, nor that affable familiar ghost
Which nightly gulls him with intelligence,
As victors of my silence cannot boast;
I was not sick of any fear from thence;
But when your countenance filled up his line,
Then lacked I matter: that enfeebled mine.

Was it the proud full sail of his great verse,
Aimed at that prize he coveted in you,
That boxed my thoughts in brain like corpse in hearse,
To make their tomb the womb in which they grew?
Did his spirit, which spirits taught to write
With an inhuman skill, then freeze mine numb?
No, neither he, nor his aides of the night
Assisting him, did strike my talent dumb.
He, and that affable familiar djinn,
Which nightly gulls him with intelligence,
Are blameless for that writing block within:
I was not stopped by any fear from thence.
But when you smiled upon, and in, his verse
I was deprived, which made mine that much worse.

SONNET 87: Though Marlowe is gone and *Venus & Adonis* has fast proved a popular and admired work, Southampton remains cold to Shakespeare – as is more fully depicted in succeeding sonnets. It seems that the poet is paying the price for his earlier behaviour and insults. And, having had a narrow escape from disgrace in his embroilment with Marlowe, Southampton has probably had his fill of too close an association with poet-playwrights.

In any event, Shakespeare responds with this melancholy sonnet of resignation, perhaps hoping that all will be forgiven.

The references in the sonnet to the poet's possessing, holding and having of the young lord, and the latter's giving of himself, reinforce the signals in earlier sonnets of their, then, intimate and physical relationship.

SONNET 87

Farewell! Thou art too dear for my possessing,
And like enough thou know'st thy estimate:
The charter of thy worth gives thee releasing,
My bonds in thee are all determinate.
For how do I hold thee but by thy granting,
And for that riches where is my deserving?
The cause of this fair gift in me is wanting,
And so my patent back again is swerving.
Thyself thou gav'st, thy own worth then not knowing,
Or me, to whom thou gav'st it, else mistaking;
So thy great gift, upon misprision growing,
Comes home again, on better judgement making.
Thus have I had thee, as a dream doth flatter,
In sleep a king, but waking no such matter.

Farewell! You are too dear for my possessing,
And probably you well know your own worth,
Which, in itself, will defy its repressing:
My claims on you die with my merit's dearth.
For how can I hold you but by your letting,
And for such fortune where is my repaying?
I've spent the reasons for your gifts begetting,
And so my rights are lost through full defraying.
You gave yourself, your own worth not then knowing,
Or else my worthiness in your mistaking,
So your great gift, on realisation growing,
Is taken back on better judgement making.
Thus I had you, and in my dream was king;
But waking up find I am no such thing.

SONNET 88: The rift still yawns wide. Here, Southampton is portrayed as in scorn of Shakespeare's merit.

Conventional biographic interpretations of this sonnet suggest that the poet is, here, displaying acceptance, loyalty and devotion, by offering to take all the blame for the relationship problems. This interpretation - strongly supported by succeeding sonnets - may well be the most appropriate. Nevertheless, I offer below an alternative view, supported primarily by the coherent multiplicity of double-meanings and a justification for the poem's theme which, to my mind, is more persuasive.

The first clue comes immediately. The phrase "*set me light*" in line 1 carries an undertone of *leave me light of pocket*. Could Shakespeare be complaining of Southampton's tightness of purse, as did Nashe before? In line 4, he implies that Southampton has broken faith or a promise. Astonishingly, as the sonnet unfolds, there are then hints of blackmail, all cleverly submerged in the ambiguity facilitated by this form of communication.

Read in this light, Shakespeare seems to hint that he will bring much notoriety to Southampton, by telling the story of what he – the reprobate and vice-ridden poet – has been up to with the Earl. He is prepared to present himself in the worst possible light, knowing that this will benefit his revenge, by gaining the Earl (who, line 10 implies, will be the sole character in his tales of love) even more attention. In his punch line, Shakespeare uses the ambiguous phrase "*for thy right*", which can be rendered as: *in order that you behave properly (and pay up)*.

SONNET 88

When thou shalt be disposed to set me light
And place my merit in the eye of scorn,
Upon thy side against myself I'll fight
And prove thee virtuous, though thou art forsworn.
With mine own weakness being best acquainted,
Upon thy part I can set down a story
Of faults concealed, wherein I am attainted,
That thou in losing me shalt win much glory:
And I by this will be a gainer too:
For bending all my loving thoughts on thee,
The injuries that to myself I do,
Doing thee vantage, double-vantage me.
Such is my love, to thee I so belong,
That for thy right myself will bear all wrong.

When you're not of a mind to see me right,
And scorn my worth and turn your face away,
I'll join your side against me in your spite,
To show you're justified, though you betray.
Because I know my failings all too well,
In your regard I'll tell a tale of shame
Of sins I've hid with vices that repel,
So you, in rid of me, will reap much fame.
And I by this will be a gainer too,
For all my love being yours devotedly,
The injuries that to myself I do
Will serve you right and doubly well serve me.
Such is my love, to you I so belong,
To get what's right of you I'll bear all wrong.

SONNET 89: Conventional biographic interpretations suggest, reasonably, that this sonnet is a straightforward development of that preceding, with the poet continuing to accept all the blame for the sake of his love.

Under the alternative scenario offered for the preceding sonnet, it seems that Shakespeare has had cold feet. Southampton has either not recognized or not responded to his subtle threats, cloaked in the safety of ambiguity and deniability. The poet now decides to retreat and to preclude any such recognition with this follow-up, designed to reinforce the overt sense of loyalty in its predecessor. Nevertheless, a sense of injustice and abandonment remains. "Tell me of anything which I have done to cause you to forsake me and I will give you fair justification" he seems to be saying. "But if your scorn (and parsimony) is because you think my work (*Venus & Adonis*) is mediocre, then I will not argue and I will get out of your life completely, though I love you."

The *"lameness"* of line 3 is most probably a reference to writing ability, rather than the physical lameness suggested by some interpreters. Shakespeare uses similar language in *Two Gentlemen of Verona*, where Speed says of Valentine's lines of verse *"Are they not lamely writ?"* (II, *i*)

The *"look strange"* of line 8 means "behave as a stranger to you".

SONNET 89

Say that thou didst forsake me for some fault,
And I will comment upon that offence;
Speak of my lameness, and I straight will halt,
Against thy reasons, making no defence.
Thou canst not, love, disgrace me half so ill,
To set a form upon desir-ed change,
As I'll myself disgrace; knowing thy will,
I will acquaintance strangle and look strange;
Be absent from thy walks; and in my tongue
Thy sweet beloved name no more shall dwell,
Lest I, too much profane, should do it wrong,
And haply of our old acquaintance tell.
For thee, against myself, I'll vow debate,
For I must ne'er love him whom thou dost hate.

Just say that you forsook me for some fault,
And I will talk to you on this offence;
Tell me that I am lame and I will halt
Excuse of this and make no more defence.
You cannot, love, demean me half so much,
By indicating what you'd wish to change,
As I'd demean myself to give you such:
I'd cut all contact and I would arrange
To keep away from where you're wont to go;
My lips would not breathe forth your sweet, loved name
In case our old relationship should show,
Or lest my common speech should bring it shame.
For you, against myself, I'll agitate:
For I must never love him whom you hate.

SONNET 90: In the absence of specific external reference or some other benchmark, it is impossible to date this and the succeeding dozen or so sonnets with great precision. However, with their themes of dependency or woe, we can reasonably surmise that Sonnets 90-94 were written between June 1593 and late 1594, while Shakespeare was still suffering from the effects of closure of the London stages. These re-opened from April 1594, but probably some time would have elapsed before the financial stability of show business dependants was restored.

The incremental troubles suggested in this sonnet suggest that at least a few weeks, or more, have elapsed since the preceding poem. We are probably in the late summer or autumn of 1593. At this time, Shakespeare may be researching, or in the early throes of, his second dedicated poem, *The Rape of Lucrece*, intended for Southampton. If so, their unresolved problems will be giving rise to much uncertainty as to the value of these efforts. With no immediate prospect of the stages re-opening, the playwright's fortunes are likely at a very low financial ebb.

Probably, too, he continues to be frustrated in his one-sided affair with his dark mistress. It could well have been around this period that Shakespeare composed Sonnets 145-154, which, with one or two lighter interludes, demonstrate anguish aplenty.

SONNET 90

Then hate me when thou wilt, if ever, now
Now while the world is bent my deeds to cross,
Join with the spite of fortune, make me bow,
And do not drop in for an after-loss.
Ah, do not, when my heart hath 'scaped this sorrow,
Come in the rearguard of a conquered woe;
Give not a windy night a rainy morrow,
To linger out a purposed overthrow.
If thou wilt leave me, do not leave me last,
When other petty griefs have done their spite,
But in the onset come, so shall I taste
At first the very worst of fortune's might,
And other strains of woe, which now seem woe,
Compared with loss of thee will not seem so.

If ever you will hate me, hate me now:
Now, while the world is bent on humbling me:
Blow with the flow of winds to break my bough,
And do not give me later misery.
Ah, do not, when my heart has beat this sorrow,
Come in the aftermath of conquered woe;
Give not a windy night a rainy morrow
To prolong an intent to let me go.
If you reject me leave this not till last,
When other petty griefs are brought to close;
But at the outset come and deal me fast
And first the very worst of fortune's blows.
These other forms of pain, which feel like woe,
Compared with loss of you will not seem so.

SONNET 91: Shakespeare reverts to a lighter tone and flattery. Has there been some favourable response from Southampton?

However, the sonnet culminates in what effectively is a plea for reassurance, that he still enjoys the young lord's favour (and, by extension, patronage).

SONNET 91

Some glory in their birth, some in their skill,
Some in their wealth, some in their bodies' force,
Some in their garments, though new-fangled ill,
Some in their hawks and hounds, some in their horse.
And every humour hath his adjunct pleasure,
Wherein it finds a joy above the rest;
But these particulars are not my measure:
All these I better in one general best.
Thy love is better than high birth to me,
Richer than wealth, prouder than garments' cost,
Of more delight than hawks or horses be;
And, having thee, of all men's pride I boast.
Wretched in this alone, that thou mayst take
All this away and me most wretched make.

Some exult in their skill or in their birth,
Some in their hawks and hounds, some in their horse,
Some in their strength or in their high net worth,
Some in high-fashioned clothes, though these look coarse.
To every taste there is a matching pleasure
Which gives more satisfaction than the rest;
For me that thing which I most dearly treasure
Is none of such described: all second best.
Your love is better than high birth to me,
Or any wealth or garb from tailor's stall,
Of more delight than horse or falconry,
And, having you, I boast best prize of all.
My only dread is that you might refute
This claim, and thereby leave me destitute.

SONNET 92: Here, we glean a mix of information arising from Shakespeare's frustrations with Southampton.

The young Earl has been seeking to avoid the poet (as he did before with Nashe – depicted by the latter in his *Pierce Pennilesse* – see Appendix B). Shakespeare responds with the thought that such neglect will cause his death (hinting strongly at the impact of the resultant loss of support). Nor was this necessarily a poetic fancy. His fellow poets, Thomas Watson and Robert Greene, had died in the autumn of 1592, not long before these events. Thomas Kyd, now patronless following the Marlowe affair, died in 1594, followed shortly by George Peele. All were relatively young men.

Nevertheless, as he attempts to win back favour, Shakespeare is using risky tactics, going on to accuse Southampton of being temperamental and potentially false. This is a peculiar way to patch things up. Is he being fatalistic or just wanting to convey a strong message of finally giving up on the young lord?

SONNET 92

But do thy worst to steal thyself away,
For term of life thou art assure-ed mine;
And life no longer than thy love will stay,
For it depends upon that love of thine.
Then need I not to fear the worst of wrongs,
When in the least of them my life hath end;
I see a better state to me belongs
Than that which on thy humour doth depend.
Thou canst not vex me with inconstant mind,
Since that my life on thy revolt doth lie:
O, what a happy title do I find,
Happy to have thy love, happy to die!
But what's so blessed-fair that fears no blot?
Thou mayst be false, and yet I know it not.

Though you may do your best to distance me,
You will be mine as long as I do live;
For my life won't survive your enmity,
As it depends upon that love you give.
So then I need not fear the worst of spite,
For come your smallest blow I'll be lifeless;
I see a state for me of more delight
Than one dependent on your moodiness.
You cannot hurt me with inconstancy,
Though my life hangs on your moods, low or high;
O what a happy state befallen me:
Happy if I'm loved, happy if I die!
But what can be so blessed to fear no blow?
You might be false and this I might not know.

SONNET 93: This sonnet appears to pick up from the closing line of its predecessor. Although Southampton is behaving equably (presumably when unable to avoid his poet, as complained of in the preceding sonnet), Shakespeare is suspicious that this may just be for show.

SONNET 93

So shall I live, supposing thou art true,
Like a deceive-ed husband so love's face
May still seem love to me, though altered new:
Thy looks with me, thy heart in other place.
For there can live no hatred in thine eye,
Therefore in that I cannot know thy change:
In many's looks the false heart's history
Is writ in moods and frowns and wrinkles strange.
But heaven in thy creation did decree
That in thy face sweet love should ever dwell;
Whate'er thy thoughts, or thy heart's workings be,
Thy looks should nothing thence but sweetness tell.
How like Eve's apple doth thy beauty grow,
If thy sweet virtue answer not thy show.

So I'll go on assuming you are true
Like any deceived husband and love will
Appear like love to me, though maybe through,
Your looks the same, but heart not with me still.
For hatred cannot reach into your eye,
And so in there a change I cannot see;
In many one can recognise heart's lie
From what shows in their physiognomy.
But Nature, when she made you, did decide
That in your face sweet love should always dwell;
No matter what your thoughts and heart may hide,
Your looks thus nothing but of kindness tell.
How like Eve's apple would your beauty be,
If outer looks mis-told your charity.

SONNET 94: Ending a period of apparently uneasy truce, Shakespeare again erupts, with thinly disguised contempt for the Earl's lack of responsiveness. The concluding lines are, as twice before[99], astonishing in their bluntness. The lily of line 14 was a symbol of purity and its decay vividly underpins the insults.

The husbanding of "*nature's riches*", in line 6, relates, on the face of it, to under-utilisation of natural talents and abilities. It evokes the theme of Sonnets 1-17, where the young lord was affectionately taken to task for not using his reproductive endowments properly. However, with this sonnet's contextual bitterness, it seems that Shakespeare is here, once again, complaining of the Earl's parsimony.

What can have triggered this outburst?

Lucrece was entered in the Stationer's Register on 9 May 1594 and was publicly dedicated by Shakespeare to Southampton with a fulsome declaration of love and loyalty (see end of Appendix A). He might reasonably have expected some return from the Earl.

However, the young lord's allowance was still being controlled by his guardian, who would by now have been thoroughly disgruntled with his ward. Burghley had been forced, at great pains, to extricate the pair of them from the potential disgrace of the Marlowe affair. And, with the end of the wardship looming and no moves by the Earl to fulfil the marriage contract, it was obvious that Southampton would not be marrying Burghley's granddaughter. In mid-1594, the Earl was unlikely to have had much to spare for a hard-up poet, despite any encouragement the latter might previously have taken.

---

[99]   Sonnets 69 and 84

SONNET 94

They that have power to hurt and will do none,
That do not do the thing they most do show,
Who, moving others, are themselves as stone,
Unmove-ed, cold and to temptation slow:
They rightly do inherit heaven's graces
And husband nature's riches from expense;
They are the lords and owners of their faces.
Others but stewards of their excellence.
The summer's flower is to the summer sweet,
Though to itself it only live and die;
But if that flower with base infection meet,
The basest weed outbraves his dignity.
For sweetest things turn sourest by their deeds,
Lilies that fester smell far worse than weeds.

Those who can hurt but do nought of their own,
Whose deeds match not the attributes they show,
And, moving others, are themselves like stone,
Unbending, cold and to temptation slow:
They rightfully assume good heaven's graces,
And keep their natural riches from dispense;
They are the masters of their fates and places,
While others tend their fruits of providence.
The summer's flower does the summer please,
Though for its purpose only does it thrive;
But if that flower meets with coarse disease
The humblest weed brings much more joy alive.
For sweetest things are turned sour by their deeds;
Lilies that fester smell far worse than weeds.

SONNET 95: With their apparent continuing criticisms of Southampton, one might, at first sight, consider Sonnets 95 and 96 to be part of the immediately preceding sequence of plaintive, suspicious and castigatory poems.

However, on closer inspection, the flaws highlighted are significantly different. In Sonnet 94, the complaint was of parsimony and self-containment. Here, the young lord's faults are licentiousness and over-indulgence. Nor do Sonnets 95 and 96 carry that sense of personal suspicion and bitterness, which pervades those immediately preceding. Shakespeare is more dispassionate, less condemning and even affectionate in his observations and avuncular advice. The references to a "*rose*" and the youth's "*budding name*", in lines 2 and 3, again strongly evoke the deeper meaning, suggested by the *Rose* of Sonnet 1.

All this suggests that some time has elapsed since the events of the previous sonnet, and that the poet and his aristocratic patron are now on better terms, as a result of undisclosed interim events.

Southampton's wardship ended on his 21st birthday, 6 October 1594. With this approaching, he had begun to spread his wings. A letter from Sir George Carey to his wife in April 1594 records that "*Bes[s] Bridges [a Queen's maid of attendance] hast forsaken the Earl of Bedford and takes the Earl of Southfil [Southampton]*"[100]. In July, another Maid of Attendance, Lady Bridget Manners, went on record with the view that the Earl was too young and "fantastical" for marriage.   [Continued at Sonnet 96 following]

---

[100] As recorded in Ian Wilson's *Shakespeare: the Evidence*

SONNET 95

How sweet and lovely dost thou make the shame
Which, like a canker in the fragrant rose,
Doth spot the beauty of thy budding name:
O, in what sweets dost thou thy sins enclose!
That tongue that tells the story of thy days,
Making lascivious comments on thy sport,
Cannot dispraise but in a kind of praise:
Naming thy name blesses an ill report.
O, what a mansion have those vices got,
Which for their habitation chose out thee,
Where beauty's veil doth cover every blot
And all things turns to fair that eyes can see!
Take heed, dear heart, of this large privilege:
The hardest knife ill-used doth lose his edge.

How cute and lovely do you make that shame,
Which, like a maggot in the fragrant rose,
Despoils the brightness of your budding name:
So sweet the joys which hold such sinful woes!
Those tongues that tell the stories of your ways,
With lewd and probing comments on your sport,
Can only give their slights as kinds of praise:
Your name brings good to any bad report.
O, what a mansion have those vices got,
Which chose you out for their life tenancy,
Where beauty's veil can hide each blight and spot,
And all things show up fair that eyes can see!
Beware the scope, dear, of the libertine;
The hardest blade, ill-used, becomes less keen.

SONNET 96: [Continued from Sonnet 95] In October, the Earl was instrumental in helping two lifelong friends, the brothers, Sir Charles and Sir Henry Danvers, flee the country to avoid the consequences of a family feud, which had ended in a high profile murder. Then, on reaching his majority, he took charge of the family estate. Though this involved paying a hefty tax to the Crown, funds were generated through leasing out his London residence, Southampton House, and by vesting title to all his extensive properties in a trust, designed to maximise tithes, rental and other incomes.

All these events suggest that, by late 1594, Southampton was attracting notice for a more expansive lifestyle, and was better placed to reward his friends. However, the crippling fine of £5000, imposed by Burghley in revenge for the Earl's breach of marriage contract (and, no doubt, other annoyances), was levied following Elizabeth Vere's marriage to William Stanley in 1595. We can reasonably guess that, either towards the end of 1594 or after 1595, Southampton was able to mollify Shakespeare with some long overdue reward, and that part of the poet's response included Sonnets 95 and 96.

In this sonnet, Shakespeare continues with his affectionate advice to Southampton, who seems to be living a full and independent sexual life (without now triggering any resentment from the poet).

The concluding couplet is identical to that of Sonnet 36. There have been many speculations as to why: unconscious duplication, some sort of linkage of the two sonnets, deliberate substitution by Thorpe, in order to remove too lewd a remark or too strong a clue as to Southampton's identity – and so on. The reason remains unknown.

SONNET 96

Some say thy fault is youth, some wantonness,
Some say thy grace is youth and gentle sport;
Both grace and faults are loved of more or less:
Thou mak'st faults graces that to thee resort.
As on the finger of a thron-ed queen
The basest jewel will be well esteemed:
So are those errors that in thee are seen
To truths translated and for true things deemed.
How many lambs might the stern wolf betray,
If like a lamb he could his looks translate!
How many gazers mightst thou lead away,
If thou wouldst use the strength of all thy state!
But do not so: I love thee in such sort
As, thou being mine, mine is thy good report.

Some say you're immature, some dissolute:
Some say you gently sport with youthful charm;
All love your flaws and charms, there's no dispute:
You turn each fault to grace so none sees harm.
Just as the finger of an enthroned queen
Gives status to the poorest jewel displayed,
So are those failings that in you are seen
Transformed to lustre, and as such portrayed.
How many lambs might the fierce wolf take in
If he could make himself look like they do!
How many of your fans would turn to sin
If you used all that power bestowed on you!
But don't do this; my love is such to tell
That you being mine, your good name's mine as well.

SONNET 97: More time has passed: several months, at least, have elapsed since Shakespeare and Southampton last saw each other. The tone of the sonnet is affectionate. These factors again suggest that the relationship has moved on from one of close, perhaps cloying, intensity to one of more relaxed friendship.

Their separation is portrayed as occurring in *"summer's time"* (line 5), which, the poet flatteringly suggests, has had the bleakness of winter, given his friend's absence. This may indicate a separation over the course of one summer. However, the expression may also have been used in allegory, here representing a period of growth and abundance lasting considerably longer than one season. In this context, the *"rich increase"* of line 6 would suggest an increase of riches or wealth, the seeds for which were sown by an absent patron or father – Southampton.

From 1594, Shakespeare's star rose rapidly. His stage company, the Lord Chamberlain's Men (reconstituted that April from a predecessor company), quickly became one of the two show business leaders. Shakespeare had become a profit-sharing partner in the new company before December 1594, at latest. By 1596, he was pursuing the grant of a family coat of arms – a symbol of social status and achievement.

As for the Earl, he had turned his attentions increasingly towards military matters, albeit with some initial frustration. In April 1596, he was forbidden by the Queen from engaging in an assault on Spanish troops besieging Calais. Then, although apparently involved in its planning, he was absent from a successful sacking of Cadiz that June, probably for the same reason. It was 1597 before he saw action.

SONNET 97

How like a winter hath my absence been
From thee, the pleasure of the fleeting year!
What freezings have I felt, what dark days seen,
What old December's bareness everywhere!
And yet this time removed was summer's time,
The teeming autumn, big with rich increase,
Bearing the wanton burden of the prime,
Like widowed wombs after their lord's decease:
Yet this abundant issue seemed to me
But hope of orphans and unfathered fruit;
For summer and his pleasures wait on thee
And thou, away, the very birds are mute;
Or, if they sing, 'tis with so dull a cheer
That leaves look pale, dreading the winter's near.

How like a winter has my absence been
From you, the pleasure of the fleeting year;
What freezings have I felt, what dark days seen,
What bare December gloomings everywhere!
And yet our time apart was summer's time,
With riches grown to fullness in their thrive
From springtime's wanton birth to Autumn's prime,
Like mother's offspring with no sire alive.
Yet this abundant issue seemed to me
But dreams of orphans and unfathered fruit;
For summer needs you for entirety
And you not there the very birds are mute;
Or if they sing it's with so chill a cheer
That leaves look pale, in fear of winter's drear.

SONNET 98: Shakespeare overtly continues and develops the seasonal theme of the preceding sonnet. However, there are clues to a parallel, sexual message in the *"spring"* and *"spirit"* of lines 1 and 3 (cf Sonnet 129) and the echo of Lord Capulet in *Romeo & Juliet*:

> *Such comfort as do lusty young men feel*
> *When well-apparelled April on the heel*
> *Of limping winter treads, even such delight*
> *Among fresh female buds shall you this night*
> *Inherit at my house.* (I , ii, 26-30)

The flowers of different odour and hew (line 6) are suggestive of lovers, who are pale shadows of Southampton, his original flower - his *"Rose"*. These flowers of different *"hew"* (Appendix E) are probably women: *"lap"* (line 8) was, in context, a term for the female genital area, linked here with *"where they grew"* or "where they produced children"[101].

The final couplet can be construed as Shakespeare's excuse: *I was depressed with you away, so I fooled around with these lesser substitutes for you.*

From this, we can surmise that Earl and poet have become close again, after their extended separation. On hearing Shakespeare's claims of missing him, Southampton has commented on the women in the poet's life, whereupon he responds thus.

"Saturn" (line 4) was probably invoked in astrological terms, rather than as a reference to the god. In astrology, Saturn was, and is, symbolic of discipline, privation, dourness, age and steadiness.

---

101 For example, in *Romeo & Juliet*, Romeo says, of his first love, she will not *"ope her lap to saint-seducing gold"* (I, i, 211)*;* Nurse says in ribaldry *"No less? Nay, bigger! Women grow by men"* (I, iii, 96). See also commentary at Sonnets 109 and 133.

SONNET 98

From you have I been absent in the spring,
When proud pied April, dressed in all his trim
Hath put a spirit of youth in every thing,
That heavy Saturn laughed and leaped with him.
Yet nor the lays of birds, nor the sweet smell
Of different flowers in odour and in hew,
Could make me any summer's story tell,
Or from their proud lap pluck them where they grew.
Nor did I wonder at the lily's white,
Nor praise the deep vermilion in the rose;
They were but sweet, but figures of delight
Drawn after you, you pattern of all those.
Yet seemed it winter still and you away,
As with your shadow I with these did play.

From you I was apart in lusty spring,
When April, boasting dappled finery,
Pumped youthful essence into everything
And sombre Saturns gambolled merrily.
Yet neither lays of birds, nor the sweet smell
Of other flowers of different scent and type,
Could move me to enjoy a summer's spell,
Or take them in their beds, where seed grew ripe.
Nor did I marvel at the lily's white,
Or praise the rich red tones within the rose,
For these were but reflections of delight,
Pale tastes of you, from whom all joys arose.
Yet it seemed winter still with you away,
As with these shades of you I'd sport and play.

SONNET 99:   Since this poem seems to pick up the overt flower theme from the preceding sonnet, it was probably composed shortly thereafter.

The thoughts expressed are remarkably similar to those of a sonnet by Henry Constable, published in his *Diana* sonnet cycle editions of both 1592 and 1594:

> *My lady's presence makes the roses red,*
> *Because to see her lips they blush with shame.*
> *The lily's leaves for envy pale became,*
> *And her white hands in them this envy bred.*
> *The marigold the leaves abroad doth spread,*
> *Because the sun's and her power is the same.*
> *The violet of purple colour came,*
> *Dyed in the blood she made my heart to shed.*
> *In brief, all flowers from her their virtue take;*
> *From her sweet breath their sweet smells do proceed;*
> *The living heat, which her eye-beams doth make,*
> *Warmeth the ground and quickeneth the seed.*
> *The rain, wherewith she watereth the flowers,*
> *Falls from mine eyes, which she dissolves in showers.*

The similarities are an unlikely coincidence. Shakespeare's thoughts were probably drawn to the above sonnet, triggered by the flower associations he, himself, had conjured in Sonnet 98. However, he brings his own stamp to the theme, including the removal of Constable's female subject, in order to adapt it to Southampton's patronage.

Sonnet 99 is unusual in that it contains fifteen lines, one more than the conventional fourteen. It is also one of the few to have an obvious predecessor model.

SONNET 99

The forward violet thus did I chide:
Sweet thief, whence didst thou steal thy sweet that smells
If not from my love's breath? The purple pride
Which on thy soft cheek for complexion dwells
In my love's veins thou hast too grossly dyed.
The lily I condemn-ed for thy hand,
And buds of marjoram had stol'n thy hair;
The roses fearfully on thorns did stand,
One blushing shame, another white despair;
A third, nor red nor white, had stol'n of both,
And to his robbery had annexed thy breath;
But for his theft, in pride of all his growth
A vengeful canker ate him up to death.
More flowers I noted, yet I none could see
But sweet or colour it had stol'n from thee.

I chided thus the pert young violet:
"Where did you steal your fragrance from, sweet thief,
If not from my love's breath? And you did get
From my love's veins the purple on your leaf,
Too grossly dyed, which thus compounds your debt."
I charged the lily: white robbed from your hand,
And buds of marjoram stole from your hair;
The guilty roses in thorned dock did stand,
Displaying blushing shame or white despair;
And one, not red nor white, but partly both,
Had added to his loot your honeyed breath;
But for this crime, when in full bloom of growth,
A vengeful maggot ate it all to death.
More flowers did I see, but none in view
Which hadn't stolen scent or hue from you.

SONNET 100: After a brief flurry of sonnets (97-99), a long period has elapsed. Here Shakespeare lectures and cajoles the personified source of his creativity (see also Sonnet 38), presumably for the attempted amusement of Southampton.

The inspection of the Earl's face for wrinkles (in lines 9 and 10), though presented in a humorous context, points to a passage of several years since the early sonnets were composed. All this reinforces the sense that their relationship is now on a very different, if still amicable, footing. We have probably reached the late 1590s.

The *"worthless song"* of line 3 presumably refers to Shakespeare's play-writing, much of which was expressed in blank verse. This, together with Southampton's continuing *"esteem"* of the playwright's work (line 7) suggests that the pair have met again at one or more of Shakespeare's stage productions.

"Satire" (line 11), in its original printing, was italicised with its opening letter in upper case. Duncan-Jones suggests a pun on "satyr" as the reason for this distinction (discussed more generally in Appendix E).

By late 1598, Southampton had been involved in two military campaigns under the command of his friend, Robert Devereux, Earl of Essex. He was also unexpectedly married. In February of that year, he had departed England, still single, intent on an extended tour of France and Italy, and leaving behind a desolate and tearful lady. She was Elizabeth Vernon, a cousin of Essex and a Queen's maid of attendance. Several months later, on learning that she was pregnant, Southampton slipped back to England to marry her in secret. She gave birth to their first daughter in November.

SONNET 100

Where art thou, Muse, that thou forget'st so long
To speak of that which gives thee all thy might?
Spend'st thou thy fury on some worthless song,
Dark'ning thy power to lend base subjects light?
Return, forgetful Muse, and straight redeem
In gentle numbers time so idly spent;
Sing to the ear that doth thy lays esteem
And gives thy pen both skill and argument.
Rise, resty Muse, my love's sweet face survey,
If Time have any wrinkle graven there;
If any, be a satire to decay,
And make Time's spoils despis-ed everywhere.
Give my love fame faster than Time wastes life,
So thou prevent'st his scythe, and crooked knife.

Where are you, Inspiration, that so long
You have not mused upon your driving force?
Do you spend your zeal on worthless song,
Or waste on works too trite too much resource?
Return, forgetful Muse, and now redeem
Yourself with verse to pay for frittery;
Sing to the ear that does your work esteem
And gives your pen both theme and artistry.
Rise, lazy Muse, and check my love's dear face
And, if you see Time's passage wrinkled there,
Pump out fresh lines with unrelenting pace
And take-off of his spoils, no matter where.
Give my love fame more fast than Time drains life,
And you will beat his scythe and sickle-knife.

SONNET 101: Shakespeare continues to berate and blame his Muse for the lack of sonnets to his friend. He concludes by demonstrating to his inactive guide how it should be done!

Southampton's unauthorised marriage in 1598 may have been as much out of respect for Essex as for regard for the young woman he had impregnated. The couple's flouting of the Queen's prerogative was punished by a brief spell in confinement, where they were visited by Essex, now bound even closer to Southampton.

In the spring of 1599, Essex led his ill-fated expedition to subdue rebellion in the Queen's provinces in Ireland. He appointed Southampton as General in charge of his cavalry, contrary to the Queen's wishes that Southampton should have no command. Several weeks into the campaign, and after Southampton had distinguished himself, she learned of the appointment, and countermanded it.

In September 1599, having failed to carry out his remit, Essex unilaterally relinquished his own command. With Southampton and others in tow, he hastened to confront Elizabeth in a strange, emotional encounter, which he forced on her, unprepared, at Nonsuch Palace. This heralded the end of his special standing with the Queen.

SONNET 101

O truant Muse, what shall be thy amends
For thy neglect of truth in beauty dyed?
Both truth and beauty on my love depends;
So dost thou too, and therein dignified.
Make answer, Muse: wilt thou not haply say
"Truth needs no colour, with his colour fixed;
Beauty no pencil, beauty's truth to lay;
But best is best if never inter-mixed"?
Because he needs no praise, wilt thou be dumb?
Excuse not silence so, for't lies in thee
To make him much outlive a gilded tomb
And to be praised of ages yet to be.
Then do thy office, Muse: I teach thee how
To make him seem long hence as he shows now.

O lazy Muse, how will you now atone
For your neglect of Faith with Beauty's face?
Both faith and beauty stem from him, my own,
And so do you, ennobled by his grace.
So answer, Muse: will you perhaps now say
"Faith needs no touching up: he's done it proud,
And beauty needs no brush for true display:
What's best would be debased were paint allowed"?
Will you stay dumb because he needs no praise?
Do not, for you have that ability
To give him life beyond a gold tomb's days,
And praise to come from ages yet to be.
So do your duty, Muse, for here is how
To show him far down time as he seems now.

SONNET 102: It seems that Southampton was unimpressed by the resumption of the sonnets or, perhaps, by the attempts to amuse, after such a long break. Here, one can sense Shakespeare back-pedalling into seriousness, with an attempt to justify his apparent neglect.

After his failed bid to explain and excuse his conduct to the Queen, Essex was put into close confinement for several months. Southampton tried, with Sir Charles Danvers, to arrange his friend's escape and flight to France – rather as had been secured for Danvers, himself, back in 1594[102]. However, Essex was uninterested, and Southampton ended up kicking his heels in London.

A contemporary, Rowland Whyte, commented in his correspondence of the time that Southampton and his friend, Rutland "pass away the time in London merely in going to plays every day". No doubt, here the Earl encountered his poet and lover of old – and perhaps it was the renewed contact at this time which triggered the composition of Sonnets 100-103.

---

[102] Following the provision of loyal intelligence services and the payment of fines, the Danvers brothers were pardoned in 1598, whereupon they returned to England from Paris, where they had based themselves.

SONNET 102

My love is strengthened though more weak in seeming,
I love not less, though less the show appear;
That love is merchandised whose rich esteeming
The owner's tongue doth publish everywhere.
Our love was new, and then but in the spring,
When I was wont to greet it with my lays;
As Philomel in summer's front doth sing,
And stops her pipe in growth of riper days:
Not that the summer is less pleasant now
Than when her mournful hymns did hush the night,
But that wild music burdens every bough,
And sweets grown common lose their dear delight.
Therefore, like her, I sometimes hold my tongue,
Because I would not dull you with my song.

My love is stronger though it seems more weak;
I love no less, though it may less appear;
The sort of love extolled in salesman-speak
And shouted out to all, seems much less dear.
Our love was new and then but in its spring
When I was wont to greet it with my lines,
As nightingales in early summer sing
But hold their peace as sun the hotter shines:
Not since the summer is less pleasant now
Than when their mournful tunes did hush the night,
But since wild music trills from every bough
And thrills too common lose their sweet delight.
And so like them I sometimes stop my song,
In case I dull allure, go on too long.

SONNET 103: Shakespeare seems to be giving up on Southampton: admitting that he has run out of inspiration. Apparently, the Earl has continued to be less than enthusiastic in his responses to the poet's overtures. The diplomatically expressed message here is: don't expect more sonnets from me in a hurry.

By the spring of 1600, Southampton's mind was on other things. Continually aware of Essex's plight, he also needed to rebuild his bridges with the Queen. In May he returned to Ireland to serve under the new commander there, Lord Mountjoy, and immediately earned plaudits from the latter for brave and timely action in battle. In July, Mountjoy recommended that Southampton be awarded the vacant governorship of Connaught, but this recommendation was rejected by the Queen.

A frustrated Southampton travelled briefly to the Low Countries, in August, ostensibly to join Dutch forces allied with England. However, in September Essex was freed from house arrest, and Southampton returned to England to rejoin his friend.

That October, after Elizabeth had failed to renew Essex's main source of income – a licence to levy duties on sweet wine imports – the die was cast. Essex decided on the Queen's overthrow, in favour of James of Scotland. He, Southampton and others spent the winter plotting and, on 8 February 1601, made an abortive coup attempt.

` On 25 February, Essex was beheaded. Sir Charles Danvers and others followed him to the executioner. Southampton, on the intervention of Sir Robert Cecil, had his death sentence commuted to life detention in the Tower, where he languished until the Queen's death in March 1603.

SONNET 103

Alack, what poverty my Muse brings forth,
That having such a scope to show her pride
The argument, all bare, is of more worth
Than when it hath my added praise beside.
O, blame me not, if I no more can write!
Look in your glass and there appears a face
That over-goes my blunt invention quite,
Dulling my lines and doing me disgrace.
Were it not sinful then, striving to mend,
To mar the subject that before was well?
For to no other pass my verses tend
Than of your graces and your gifts to tell.
And more, much more, than in my verse can sit,
Your own glass shows you when you look in it.

Alas, how unproductively I write,
When, with this chance to let my talent shine,
My subject on his own looks much more bright
Than when he's praised within a verse of mine.
But, failure though I be, do not blame me,
Since in your mirror you will see a face
Which quite out-blazes all my poetry,
And dulls my lines, thus bringing me disgrace.
Would striving to improve not be a crime,
If this then marred a subject of repute?
For there's no other purpose to my rhyme
Than singing of your each sweet attribute:
And you'll see so much more within your glass
Than in my verse whose lines are all too sparse.

SONNET 104: As justified in Part I, this beautiful sonnet, so fresh and different in tone to its immediate predecessors, celebrates Southampton's liberation, in 1603, from his two year incarceration in the Tower. Shakespeare gives reassurance of his unending love for the Earl, and of the latter's beauty – supposedly as fresh as if only three years had elapsed since their first acquaintance, some twelve years before. The key to the form of this flattery is line 6, which may be construed as: *insofar as I can perceive any impact on you of the processes of time.*

In reality, the Earl, in his thirtieth year, had changed much from the narcissistic and fresh-faced youth of the early 1590s. With the experience of responsibility, marriage, military campaigns, political crosses and imprisonment, he had matured both physically and emotionally. In a surviving portrait of his sojourn in the Tower, a middle-aged man and his cat stare lugubriously at the viewer[103]. Each sports thin whiskers, in contrast to the beardless young lord, who received the first sonnets. Only the unfashionably long tresses, still dangling to the Earl's shoulders, hint at the eternal summer, sung in Sonnet 18.

As we shall see, Shakespeare has misjudged the Earl's continuing susceptibility to this sort of flattery. After a bright start, this final tranche of some twenty or so poems becomes increasingly defensive, in reaction to Southampton's cynicism.

---

[103]   A depiction may be seen at the following website:
http://www.boughtonhouse.org.uk/htm/gallery2/paintings/earlofsoton.htm

SONNET 104

To me, fair friend, you never can be old,
For as you were when first your eye I eyed,
Such seems your beauty still: three winters cold
Have from the forests shook three summers' pride,
Three beauteous springs to yellow autumn turned
In process of the seasons have I seen,
Three April perfumes in three hot Junes burned,
Since first I saw you fresh, which yet are green.
Ah, yet doth beauty like a dial-hand
Steal from his figure, and no pace perceived;
So your sweet hew, which methinks still doth stand,
Hath motion, and mine eye may be deceived:
For fear of which, hear this, thou age unbred:
Ere you were born was beauty's summer dead.

To me, fair friend, you never can be old;
For as you were when first your eye I eyed,
So shines your beauty still: three winters cold
Have from the forests shook three summers' pride,
Three beauteous springs to yellow autumns turned,
So seems the seasoning of years between:
Three April perfumes in three hot Junes burned,
Since first I saw you fresh, who still are green.
Ah, but then beauty, like an hour hand
Crawls from the figure with no pace perceived;
So your sweet looks, which to me seem to stand
Still move on forth, perhaps my eye deceived:
In case of which, hear this, you worlds ahead!
Ere you were born was beauty's summer dead.

SONNET 105: Shakespeare reiterates his love and admiration for the Earl. He praises the constancy and kindness of his friend, perhaps tacitly pressing the latter to show such virtues in his reception of the poet's renewed attentions.

In lines 3 and 4, he reminds Southampton that all his poetry and praises have been directed towards one person only – the Earl himself. Sonnets 127-154 might appear to contradict this statement, but as these were also supplied to the Earl, Shakespeare can justify his claim to singular dedication. With these thoughts he reminds the Earl of his hundred-plus sonnets to date, *Venus* and *Lucrece* (and probably *A Lover's Complaint*), and he rebuts any notion that he is a Johnny-come-lately, trying to jump on Southampton's bandwagon.

After his release in April 1603, Southampton's star rose rapidly, as the new King James rewarded him for his role in the coup attempt led by Essex. In May, he was granted restitution of property and estates confiscated by Elizabeth's government. In July, his earldom was formally restored and he was installed as a Knight of the Garter. In August, he was granted the lucrative licence to excise sweet wine imports (which had been taken from Essex by Elizabeth). In September, he was appointed Keeper of the Isle of Wight, following the death of George Carey, Lord Hunsdon. Though he never became part of the inner circle of the King's advisers, he was a frequent attendee at Court and companion to both King and the new Queen: in short, a man of high influence and wealth.

SONNET 105

Let not my love be called idolatry,
Nor my belov-ed as an idol show,
Since all alike my songs and praises be
To one, of one, still such, and ever so.
Kind is my love today, tomorrow kind,
Still constant in a wondrous excellence;
Therefore my verse to constancy confined,
One thing expressing, leaves out difference.
"Fair, kind and true" is all my argument,
"Fair, kind and true", varying to other words;
And in this change is my invention spent,
Three themes in one, which wondrous scope affords.
"Fair, kind and true" have often lived alone,
Which three till now never kept seat in one.

Let no one call my love idolatry,
Or my beloved an idol put on show,
Because my verse, in all, is seen to be
To one, in praise of one, and ever so.
Today my love is kind, tomorrow too,
Ever constant with true dedication;
And so my poems deal with what stays true,
A single subject, with no variation.
"Fair", "kind" and "true" combine as all my theme,
Though these may be expressed in other ways
Which tax my inspiration to extreme:
Three themes in one; enough scope to amaze.
"Fair", "kind" and "true" alone are oft in some;
Till now there's never been the three in one.

SONNET 106: Shakespeare spares no efforts in his renewed flattery, with reassurances that Southampton's beauty remains beyond the description even of past masters. There are echoes in the first quatrain of a sonnet by Henry Constable:

> *Miracle of the world! I never will deny*
> *That former poets praise the beauty of their days:*
> *But all those beauties were but figures of thy praise,*
> *And all those poets did of thee but prophesy.*[104]

The fortunes of Shakespeare and his stage company were mixed during these early months of James' reign. On 19 May 1603, the company was appointed as the King's own group of players, and was thereafter known as the King's Men. This was a spectacular promotion, especially since it is unlikely that James had seen even one of their performances. Many have guessed it could only have arisen as a result of a recommendation to the King by someone in a position of influence – perhaps Southampton?

On the other hand, the London playhouses were again closed due to an outbreak of plague. By mid-July, there were more than one thousand deaths per week in London, leading to a large exodus. The King's Court stayed away from the capital, and the procession celebrating his coronation was postponed until March 1604. The pockets of the King's Men and their shareholders must have been hard hit.

---

[104] It is unclear when this poem would have been circulated. It is included in an undated manuscript edition of Constable's Diana cycle (but excluded from the smaller 1592 and 1594 printings, whose sonnets all appear in the manuscript).

SONNET 106

When in the chronicle of wasted time
I see descriptions of the fairest wights,
And beauty making beautiful old rhyme
In praise of ladies dead and lovely knights,
Then in the blazon of sweet beauty's best,
Of hand, of foot, of lip, of eye, of brow,
I see their antique pen would have expressed
Even such a beauty as you master now.
So all their praises are but prophecies
Of this our time, all you prefiguring:
And, for they looked but with divining eyes,
They had not still enough your worth to sing:
For we, which now behold these present days,
Have eyes to wonder, but lack tongues to praise.

When in the chronicles of olden times
I see described the fairest human sights,
Whose beauty does enrich those golden rhymes
In praise of ladies dead and handsome knights,
Then in their icons of past beauty's best,
Of hand, of foot, of lip, of eye, of brow,
I see those ancient pens have well expressed
That kind of beauty you exhibit now.
So all their praises are but prophecy
Of this, our time, all you prefiguring;
But, since they had but farsight to foresee,
They still fell short in your worth's rendering,
As we, who now exist in these, your days,
Have eyes to wonder, but lack words to praise.

SONNET 107: As established in Part I, this poem commemorates the death of the "*mortal moon*" and "*tyrant*" - Elizabeth - and the release of Southampton from his "*confined doom*" in the Tower.

With Sonnets 104, 105 and 106, it forms the opening salvo in Shakespeare's renewed sonneteering of the Earl. The four poems are generally celebratory and affectionate – albeit with an undertone of self-justification in Sonnet 105 – and there is no substantive indication within them of the Earl's response. They could well have been supplied simultaneously (and perhaps, as a consequence, filed out of the internal sequence of their original presentation).

From now on, however, the sonnets become increasingly defensive, suggesting a cynical reception from the Earl.

With his newly restored and improved status, the Earl was feted by many during 1603-4. Sir Francis Bacon, who had helped the prosecutions of his benefactor, Essex, and Southampton, now wrote to the latter to express his unswerving support. A multitude of other literary men offered their praises in dedications or poems, including Samuel Daniel, John Davies, Francis Davison, Thomas Powell, Robert Pricket and Thomas Wright. Such idolatry, notably absent in the preceding years, and perhaps alluded to in Sonnet 105, must have triggered cynicism in even the most generous of hearts.

SONNET 107

Not mine own fears, nor the prophetic soul
Of the wide world dreaming on things to come,
Can yet the lease of my true love control,
Supposed as forfeit to a confined doom.
The mortal moon hath her eclipse endured,
And the sad augurs mock their own presage;
Incertainties now crown themselves assured,
And peace proclaims olives of endless age,
Now with the drops of this most balmy time
My love looks fresh, and Death to me subscribes,
Since, spite of him, I'll live in this poor rhyme,
While he insults o'er dull and speechless tribes.
And thou in this shalt find thy monument,
When tyrants' crests and tombs of brass are spent.

Not all my fears, nor that prophetic soul
Of our wide world in dreams of things in wait,
Can designate my true love's life or role,
Thought lost to the imprisonment of fate.
The mortal moon has met with her eclipse;
The doomsayers belie their own forecast;
Ifs, ors and buts no longer trip men's lips,
As peace is crowned and said now here to last.
Now, with the dawn of this most balmy time,
My love looks fresh and Death defers to me,
Since, though I die, I'll live in this poor rhyme,
While he gloats on those with no literacy.
And you in this will have your monument
When tyrants' crests and tombs of brass are spent.

SONNET 108: Southampton's reaction to Sonnets 104-107 has apparently been along the following lines: "Why are you serenading me with this same old stuff? We all know I'm not your beautiful young lad of years ago, and this poetry on keeping me young forever looks increasingly stupid!"

In an injured tone Shakespeare here responds and justifies himself. "What else can I write to show my true feelings? To me you are still my sweet boy and I need to tell you this and to make you understand that my love for you looks past your signs of ageing!"

Tellingly, however, the poet subsequently ignores his own justification. In none of the regular sonnets which follow does he again imply that Southampton is young; nor does he revisit his once favourite fall-back theme of immortality through verse.

SONNET 108

What's in the brain that ink may character
Which hath not figured to thee my true spirit?
What's new to speak, what now to register
That may express my love, or thy dear merit?
Nothing, sweet boy: but yet, like prayers divine,
I must each day say o'er the very same,
Counting no old thing old, thou mine, I thine,
Even as when first I hallowed thy fair name.
So that eternal love in love's fresh case
Weighs not the dust and injury of age,
Nor gives to necessary wrinkles place,
But makes antiquity for aye his page;
Finding the first conceit of love there bred,
Where time and outward form would show it dead.

What thought is there that can be put in ink
Which hasn't conveyed to you my true spirit?
What's new to say, what now to make you think,
That might portray my love or your dear merit?
There's nought, sweet boy; and yet, like holy prayer,
I have to daily say what's just the same:
You're mine, I'm yours, no old words deemed past care,
Just like when I first came to praise your name:
So that eternal love, rejuvenated,
Can from Time's tribulations disengage,
Look past those wrinkles to which all are fated,
And make a servant of unfolding age;
To see there that first flush of love live on,
Where time and outer form would show it gone.

SONNET 109: Shakespeare continues to react to Southampton's dismissals. One can almost hear the Earl saying "Where have you and your sonnets been all this time? And what about all those others you have been carrying on with?" To such challenges the poet responds with these eloquent, if possibly unconvincing, protestations.

Shakespeare's defence is that though he has "*ranged*" and is afflicted by "a*ll frailties that besiege all kinds of blood*" he remains true to his over-riding love, Southampton. In these words there is a strong hint (not for the first time) that amongst his frailties is a weakness for women. There is a further such hint with the word "*nothing*" in line 12. In context, this word was an allusion to the vaginal circle or cavity (as "thing" was slang for penis). Such usage is well illustrated in the following interplay in Act III, Scene ii of *Hamlet*, which also brings out the bawdy meanings in "*lap*" (Sonnet 98) and "*country*" (cf "*count*" in Sonnet 2) :

Hamlet: *Lady, shall I lie in your lap?*
Ophelia: *No, my lord.*
Hamlet: *I mean, my head upon your lap?*
Ophelia: *Ay, my lord.*
Hamlet: *Do you think I mean country matters?*
Ophelia: *I think nothing, my lord.*
Hamlet: *That's a fair thought to lie between maids' legs.*
Ophelia: *What is, my lord?*
Hamlet: *Nothing.*
Ophelia: *You are merry, my lord.*

In his concluding line, with his direct address of Southampton by nickname, Shakespeare appeals to his "*Rose*" to remember their long, intimate relationship.

SONNET 109

O, never say that I was false of heart,
Though absence seemed my flame to qualify:
As easy might I from myself depart
As from my soul, which in thy breast doth lie.
That is my home of love: if I have ranged,
Like him that travels I return again;
Just to the time, not with the time exchanged,
So that myself bring water for my stain.
Never believe, though in my nature reigned
All frailties that besiege all kinds of blood,
That it could so preposterously be stained
To leave for nothing all thy sum of good:
For nothing this wide universe I call,
Save thou, my Rose; in it thou art my all.

O, never say that I was false of heart,
Though absence seemed to say I loved you less;
As easy might I split myself apart
As leave my soul, which your heart does possess.
You are my spirit's home: if my forays
Have led me here and there, I have come back
Unchanged by passing time, with no delays,
To make my reparations for my slack.
Do not believe, though in my nature's core
Are all men's frailties of every kind,
That it could carry such a monstrous flaw
To leave for nothing all your good behind.
For without you my world is less than small;
Dear Rose, my universe, you are my all.

SONNET 110: Shakespeare goes on defending his conduct, albeit that he is confessing to carnal delights taken elsewhere (which, however, are asserted to have paled in comparison to those previously available from Southampton).

"*Blench*" (line 7) meant a side glance or deviation.

The double superlative in line 14 may be poetic exaggeration but, as others have pointed out, it can also be read as carrying a cynical overtone alluding to his friend's own abundance of lovers. Such cynicism then suffuses the "*to whom I am confined*" of line 12, and we see a subtle parallel message of "you expect me to confine myself to you, while you stray all over the place".

SONNET 110

Alas, 'tis true I have gone here and there,
And made myself a motley to the view,
Gored mine own thoughts, sold cheap what is most dear,
Made old offences of affections new.
Most true it is that I have looked on truth
Askance and strangely; but, by all above,
These blenches gave my heart another youth,
And worse essays proved thee my best of love.
Now all is done, have what shall have no end:
Mine appetite I never more will grind
On newer proof, to try an older friend,
A god in love, to whom I am confined.
Then give me welcome, next my heaven the best,
Even to thy pure and most most loving breast.

Alas, it's true I have gone here and there,
And made myself a fool to public view,
Lost self-respect, sold cheap what needs most care,
Committed old affronts with passions new.
Most true it is that I have looked on truth
Askance and skewly; but, by all above,
These sideshows gave my heart another youth,
And testing worse proved you my foremost love.
Now this is done; my faith will have no end:
I never more will whet my appetite
On newer tastes to try an older friend,
A god in love, to whom I am bound tight.
So welcome me, you, who's my best apart
From heaven, to your pure all-loving heart.

SONNET 111: It seems that Southampton has attributed Shakespeare's behaviour to his common background or surroundings – perhaps too trenchantly and condescendingly, given the hint (in the third quatrain) of sarcasm as to the Earl's over-zealous correction of the poet's faults.

Most commentators take the word "*public*", used twice in line 4, to be a reference to stage work and the world of the playhouse. It is possible that all Shakespeare meant was that he had to work for a living, dealing with the public, and that this bred a style of social intercourse which was common (rather than refined). However, judging by the surrounding lines, as well as preceding sonnets, the flaws to which he was alluding went beyond such normality.

"*Eisel*" (line 10) was a wine infused with ingredients from the bitter tasting plant, wormwood, often taken as a treatment or prophylactic for various illnesses.

SONNET 111

O, for my sake do you wish Fortune chide,
The guilty goddess of my harmful deeds,
That did not better for my life provide
Than public means, which public manners breeds.
Thence comes it that my name receives a brand,
And almost thence my nature is subdued
To what it works in, like the dyer's hand:
Pity me then and wish I were renewed.
Whilst, like a willing patient, I will drink
Potions of eisel 'gainst my strong infection:
No bitterness that I will bitter think,
Nor double penance to correct correction.
Pity me then, dear friend, and I assure ye
Even that your pity is enough to cure me.

For my sake you blame Fortune's stinted giving
Which fostered all my damaging displays,
By leaving me no better means of living
Than showbiz work, which leads to showbiz ways.
For this gives me a showman's reputation,
And lifestyle that I almost make my norm,
As dyer's hand takes on false pigmentation:
Give pity then and wish for my reform.
While, like a willing patient, I will sup
Harsh medicine to deal with my infection,
I will with any bitterness put up,
In double dose if this puts right correction.
Just pity me, dear friend, and you will see
Your pitying is cure enough for me.

SONNET 112: With some convoluted grammar and opaque phrases the full meanings of this sonnet are far from easy to decipher. Ostensibly, Shakespeare praises Southampton for his care and pity. The poet acknowledges his scandalous behaviour and throws himself on the Earl's superior judgement and support with fawning subservience. Perhaps this is completely sincere. However, given his track record and the probably deliberate opacity, one must suspect underlying sarcasm aimed by Shakespeare at his aristocratic friend: "You, the centre of the universe, who pity me, clearly know me much better than I know myself and I must give up all independent thought and ignore all other opinions of me, you prying busybody".

"*O'ergreen*", in line 4 (or rather "ore-greene" as it was originally printed), is apparently a word coined by Shakespeare. He uses it also in *Anthony & Cleopatra* (*IV, xiv*) in a reference to ships covering the ocean. Some have suggested that its use here is intended to carry a parallel meaning, alluding to Robert Greene, who attacked Shakespeare in print in 1592 (see Sonnet 29).

The "*abysm*" of line 9 was printed with an opening capital and italics (like certain other words with an extension of sense – see Appendix E). I have interpreted it as "Hell".

The adder (line 10), lacking external ears like all snakes, was metaphorically regarded as deaf: "*What! art thou like the adder, waxen deaf?*" (*II Henry VI, III, ii*).

SONNET 112

Your love and pity doth th' impression fill
Which vulgar scandal stamped upon my brow;
For what care I who calls me well or ill,
So you o'er-green my bad, my good allow?
You are my All-the-world and I must strive
To know my shames and praises from your tongue:
None else to me, nor I to none alive,
That my steeled sense or changes right or wrong.
In so profound abysm I throw all care
Of others' voices, that my adder's sense
To critic and to flatterer stopp-ed are:
Mark how with my neglect I do dispense.
You are so strongly in my purpose bred
That all the world besides me thinks y'are dead.

Your care and pity fill those furrowed lines
Which uncouth slander in my brows made berth;
For what care I who lauds me or maligns,
When you de-green my flaws and know my worth?
You are my everything, and I must strive
To judge my feats and failings through your eyes,
Ignoring all, so none but you alive
May change my mind thus steeled on truth or lies.
To such far depths of hell I cast all care
Of others' views, that with my adder's ear
I hear nought of me, be this ill or fair:
Note my indifference to all I hear.
You're so concerned to see my wrongs put right
You're dead to all but me, my guiding light.

SONNET 113: This sonnet is part one of a brace, which suggests that the pair have had an amicable meeting. With this brace, and the following sonnet, we see a temporary respite from Shakespeare's defensive attitude, as he reverts to flattery.

Some commentators interpret the phrase "*quick object*" (line 7) to mean a living thing. The word "quick" was used as a synonym for "alive", but here it seems more appropriate in its other sense of changing position rapidly (as in the use of "*quicker*" in Sonnet 45).

SONNET 113

Since I left you mine eye is in my mind,
And that which governs me to go about
Doth part his function and is partly blind,
Seems seeing, but effectually is out:
For it no form delivers to the heart
Of bird, of flower, or shape which it doth latch:
Of his quick objects hath the mind no part,
Nor his own vision holds what it doth catch:
For if it see the rud'st or gentlest sight,
The most sweet-favour'd or deformed'st creature,
The mountain or the sea, the day or night,
The crow or dove, it shapes them to your feature.
Incapable of more, replete with you,
My most true mind thus maketh mine untrue.

Since I left you daydreams beguile my mind
And vision, which I need to get about,
Is partly functional but partly blind:
It seems to work but in effect is out.
For it does not perceive forms which exist
Of bird, of flower, or any shape in sight,
And things which move about are wholly missed,
Nor does my mind retain what comes to light.
For if it sees best or worst scenery,
The fairest charm or ugliest of creatures,
The day or night, the mountain or the sea,
The crow or dove, it shapes them to your features.
With room for nothing more, so full of you,
My inner thoughts thus make my mind untrue.

SONNET 114:   This is the second part of the brace, and continues the theme of the preceding poem.

I have interpreted the *"first"* in line 14 as being poetic shorthand for the associations of the *"first"* of line 9, ie the plying of flattery. Differing interpretations of *"first begin"* have been offered by other commentators, but these seem unnecessarily complicated.

These two sonnets carry the flavour of earlier poems of a philosophic bent, such as Sonnets 44-47. Perhaps Shakespeare, seeking non-contentious flattery, has retrieved unsent drafts from that period and updated these for use in current circumstances. Later on, it seems, he is accused of recycling poems (Sonnet 125).

SONNET 114

Or whether doth my mind, being crowned with you,
Drink up the monarch's plague, this flattery?
Or whether shall I say mine eye saith true,
And that your love taught it this alchemy,
To make of monsters and things indigest
Such cherubins as your sweet self resemble,
Creating every bad a perfect best,
As fast as objects to his beams assemble?
O, 'tis the first; 'tis flattery in my seeing,
And my great mind most kingly drinks it up:
Mine eye well knows what with his gust is 'greeing,
And to his palate doth prepare the cup.
If it be poisoned, 'tis the lesser sin
That mine eye loves it and does first begin.

Is it that my mind, ennobled by you,
Drinks up that vice of monarchs: flattery?
Or rather that my eyes see things more true,
And that your love taught them ability
To see in monsters and brutes imperfect
Fair cherubim that all resemble you,
Creating beauty from each foul defect
As fast as such things come into their view?
No, it's the first: my eyes ply flattery,
And my mind, like a king, will drink it up:
My eyes know just what my mind wants to see,
And to mind's taste will mix the perfect cup.
And if it's poisoned it's the lesser sin
That eyes love it and stir the sugar in.

SONNET 115: Shakespeare finds a new, witty way to continue his protestations that his love for Southampton is greater than ever. Presumably, the lines to which he alludes (of previously asserted pinnacles of love) were those in such as Sonnet 31 or in his dedication of *Lucrece*.

The grammar of the third quatrain makes some of the detail difficult to follow. Commentators differ in their interpretations of lines 11 and 12.

My interpretation construes the second and third quatrains essentially as an argument by Shakespeare on the form of words he should have used in prior writings, having regard to the uncertainties of the future.

SONNET 115

Those lines that I before have writ do lie,
Even those that said I could not love you dearer;
Yet then my judgement knew no reason why
My most full flame should afterwards grow clearer.
But reckoning Time, whose millioned accidents
Creep in 'twixt vows and change decrees of kings,
Tan sacred beauty, blunt the sharp'st intents,
Divert strong minds to the course of altering things:
Alas, why, fearing of Time's tyranny,
Might I not then say "Now I love you best",
When I was certain o'er incertainty,
Crowning the present, doubting of the rest?
Love is a babe; then might I not say so,
To give full growth to that which still doth grow?

Those lines I wrote before are now a lie,
Those ones which said I could not love you more,
Although I had no reason to think why
Most fierce flames would burn brighter than before.
But, knowing that Time's countless incidents
Can loosen vows and change decrees of kings,
Make beauty worn, blunt keenest of intents,
Divert strong wills to flow with changing things,
Then why, alas, wise to Time's tyranny,
Did I not then say "Now I love you best",
Which well I knew was true of history,
And would downplay what future might suggest?
But, Cupid is a babe: so why not say
Love's at a peak, though growing day by day?

SONNET 116: In this famous sonnet, Shakespeare declares that true love should overcome and outlast any obstacle. The opening two lines evoke words from the Christian church marriage service.

Some commentators suggest that the poet is here referring to his own love for his friend, which, he asserts, will not be dented or deflected by the deeds of the latter. However, given what has gone before, I suggest that the sonnet is more an appeal to Southampton to forgive the lapses of the poet. "Don't", Shakespeare appears to be saying, "let the impediments of my behaviour sour our relationship".

With this interpretation, it seems that Shakespeare is again on the defensive after the pleasantries of Sonnets 113-115.

SONNET 116

Let me not to the marriage of true minds
Admit impediments: love is not love
Which alters when it alteration finds,
Or bends with the remover to remove.
O no, it is an ever fix-ed mark
That looks on tempests and is never shaken;
It is the star to every wand'ring bark,
Whose worth's unknown, although his height be taken.
Love's not Time's fool, though rosy lips and cheeks
Within his bending sickle's compass come:
Love alters not with his brief hours and weeks,
But bears it out even to the edge of doom:
If this be error and upon me proved,
I never writ, nor no man ever loved.

Let me not to the marriage of true minds
Admit impediments: love is not true
Which alters when it alteration finds
Or goes off when one's other does so too.
O no! it is an ever-present mark
That looks on storms and never bows to force;
It is the star to every wandering barque
Which takes its fix but knows aught of its source.
Love has no clock, though rosy lips and cheeks
Fall in Time's thrall, where all that's flesh decays.
Love does not veer with those brief hours and weeks,
But bears on straight until the end of days.
If I am wrong in these thoughts owned above,
I wrote this not, and no man knows of love.

SONNET 117: With this sonnet, it becomes clear that the relationship is in a bad way. Shakespeare has been accused of waywardness and ingratitude, which he admits but attempts to mitigate.

What is the nature of the *"dear-purchased right"* of line 6? It might be purely emotional. However, the phrase reeks strongly of significant past monetary support of the poet, and earlier in the sequence we saw indications of a reward after *Lucrece*, albeit delayed.

It also brings to mind the anecdote recorded by Shakespeare's first biographer, Nicholas Rowe in 1709. According to Rowe *"There is one instance so singular in the magnificence of this patron of Shakespeare's that if I had not been assured that the story was handed down by Sir William D'Avenant, who was probably very well acquainted with his affairs, I should not have ventured to have inserted: that my Lord Southampton, at one time, gave him a thousand pounds to enable him to go through with a purchase which he heard he had a mind to. A bounty very great and very rare at any time..."*.

Such an amount (£1,000 - of huge value in those days) would have been far too high a reward purely for the dedications of *Venus & Adonis* and *Lucrece*. But, as we have seen, Shakespeare was much more to Southampton than merely the dedicator of two long poems. Even if the tale is distorted, it seems probable that there was a sizeable grain of truth at its core.

SONNET 117

Accuse me thus: that I have scanted all
Wherein I should your great deserts repay,
Forgot upon your dearest love to call,
Whereto all bonds do tie me day by day;
That I have frequent been with unknown minds,
And given to time your own dear-purchased right;
That I have hoisted sail to all the winds
Which should transport me farthest from your sight.
Book both my wilfulness and errors down,
And on just proof surmise accumulate;
Bring me within the level of your frown,
But shoot not at me in your wakened hate:
Since my appeal says I did strive to prove
The constancy and virtue of your love.

Accuse me thus: that I have skimped in all
Those duties, which command priority,
Forgot upon your dearest self to call,
To whom all bonds do tie me constantly;
That I have been too oft with folk unknown
On time to which you have the dear-bought right;
That I have hoisted sail to all winds blown
Away from you and furthest from your sight.
Note both my wilfulness and errors down
Plus sins you guessed and can substantiate:
Then I deserve your strictures and your frown,
But do not fire me in your wakened hate;
For my appeal is that I did but test
Endurance of your love with which I'm blessed.

SONNET 118: Shakespeare, here ostensibly still on the defensive, continues to contrive explanations for his conduct. His excuse, however, is flimsy: he needed to have the unpleasant experience of other lovers in order better to appreciate Southampton's sweetness.

Is he trying to amuse Southampton whilst flattering him that he is, nevertheless, the best of company? It seems difficult otherwise to justify such a patently contrived excuse.

However, there are hints of irritation in lines 5, 12 and 14. The *"ne'er cloying sweetness"* of line 5 was originally spelt "nere cloying" which sounds like a pun of near-cloying[105]. In any event the line gives a faintly unfavourable impression merely by its use of the word cloying. *"Rank"*, in line 12, carries the implication of being made detrimental through excess. And, though the overt meaning of the final clause (line 14) is "who became so lovesick for you", this could be interpreted as "who became so sick of your company".

So, it seems, Shakespeare is being sarcastic under the guise of his flattery.

---

[105] As pointed out by Duncan-Jones

SONNET 118

Like as to make our appetites more keen
With eager compounds we our palate urge;
As to prevent our maladies unseen
We sicken to shun sickness when we purge:
Even so, being full of your ne'er cloying sweetness,
To bitter sauces did I frame my feeding,
And sick of well-fare found a kind of meetness
To be diseased, ere that there was true needing.
Thus policy in love, t'anticipate
The ills that were not, grew to faults assured,
And brought to medicine a healthful state
Which, rank of goodness, would by ill be cured.
But thence I learn, and find the lesson true,
Drugs poison him that so fell sick of you.

Just as we seek our appetites to please
With piquant foodstuffs and tart additives,
And aim to stop the threat of a disease
By making ourselves ill with purgatives,
So, replete with your overwhelming sweetness,
I took to bitter sauces in my feed,
And, having things too good, then found some meetness
In toxic deeds before there was true need.
So tactics hatched for love produced a mess,
To make imagined ills become assured
And forced a bitter pill on healthiness,
Which, far too good, ill needed to be cured.
But I have learned from this a lesson true:
Drugs poison him who fell so sick of you.

SONNET 119: Shakespeare develops the closing image of the previous sonnet to provide yet another excuse for his gallivanting - he was bewitched! Here he suggests that he has been behaving as if under the influence of hallucinatory drugs or "*siren tears*". He conveys penitence and a desperation to rebuild "*ruined love*".

Sirens, in ancient Greek mythology, were females with supernatural powers of attraction and bemusement, which enabled them to lure men to their doom. Poets, such as Robert Greene in his *Groatsworth of Wit*, used the term to describe predatory, attractive women who besotted men for selfish reasons. Here, the word, "Siren", was italicised in its original printing, perhaps indicating its classical source.

"*Limbecks*" were distillation containers used in alchemy or chemical processing. They were gourd-shaped vessels and the imagery, in close association with "sirens", is of female receptacles.

Rowse suggests that this poem is referring to Shakespeare's dark mistress, and it is true that several of the Mistress sonnets describe her ability to misdirect the poet's faculties in similar terms.

However, the plurality of the word "limbecks" implies that Shakespeare has been distracted by more than one woman. Perhaps these were the "*blenches*" of Sonnet 110.

SONNET 119

What potions have I drunk of Siren tears
Distilled from limbecks foul as hell within,
Applying fears to hopes and hopes to fears,
Still losing when I saw myself to win?
What wretched errors hath my heart committed,
Whilst it hath thought itself so blessed never?
How have mine eyes out of their spheres been fitted
In the distraction of this madding fever?
O benefit of ill: now I find true
That better is by evil still made better.
And ruined love, when it is built anew,
Grows fairer than at first, more strong, far greater.
So I return rebuked to my content,
And gain by ills thrice more than I have spent.

What potions have I drunk of Siren tears,
Distilled from vessels foul as hell within,
Applying fears to hopes and hopes to fears,
Still losing when I thought that I would win?
What wretched errors did my heart pursue,
While thinking that it never was so blessed?
How far from truth have my eyes been askew
Distracted by this feverish unrest?
Yet benefits from ill do then accrue,
Since goodness is by evil made more strong,
And ruined love, when it is built anew,
Grows fairer than before, more great, more long.
So, chastised I return to my content,
To gain from ills much more than I have spent.

SONNET 120: Shakespeare, struggling to rebuild the *"ruined love"* of Sonnet 119, and apparently continuing to receive rebuffs, resorts to reminding Southampton of a time when the latter was the offender in their relationship. He suggests that they are now even.

Earlier in the sequence we saw two possible such occasions of offence: the Earl's seduction by the Dark Mistress, and his seduction (professional and personal) by Marlowe. However, the suggestion of Southampton's immediate repentance (line 11) points more strongly to the first of these occurrences. And, if Shakespeare is trying to excuse his own dalliances with women, this would be the more apt reminder to make.

What is the *"night of woe"* (line 9)? The term, *"remembered"*, means here "caused me to remember" or "reminded me". Given the above context, the reference is presumably to the occasion on which Shakespeare first discovered (or confronted Southampton with) the Earl's romps with the poet's dark-eyed girlfriend.

SONNET 120

That you were once unkind befriends me now,
And for that sorrow which I then did feel
Needs must I under my transgression bow,
Unless my nerves were brass or hammered steel.
For if you were by my unkindness shaken
As I by yours, you've passed a hell of time;
And I, a tyrant, have no leisure taken.
To weigh how once I suffered in your crime.
O, that our night of woe might have remembered
My deepest sense, how hard true sorrow hits,
And soon to you, as you to me then, tendered
The humble salve which wounded bosoms fits!
But that your trespass now becomes a fee;
Mine ransoms yours, and yours must ransom me.

That you were once unkind assists me now,
And thought of that pain which I then did feel
Must, for my sin, into my heart allow
Remorse, unless my feelings were of steel.
For if you were by my unkindness shaken
As I by yours, you've passed a hell of time;
And I, self-centred, have no moments taken
To weigh that sorrow I felt from your crime.
O, that our night of woe might me have proffered
Remembrance of how hard true sorrow hits,
And I to you, as you to me then, offered
Contrition swift, as wounded heart befits.
But your trespass now likens to a fine:
Mine pays for yours, and yours must pay for mine.

SONNET 121: It seems that all of Shakespeare's overtures and arguments have proved fruitless, and he is now reduced to challenging the reliability of Southampton's *"spies"* who are, as the poet portrays it, small-minded and misrepresenting of his activities.

The proudly independent statement *"I am that I am"* in line 9 was exactly the assertion of God to Moses in the Biblical book, Exodus.

SONNET 121

'Tis better to be vile than vile esteemed,
When not to be receives reproach of being;
And the just pleasure lost, which is so deemed
Not by our feeling, but by others' seeing.
For why should others' false adulterate eyes
Give salutation to my sportive blood?
Or on my frailties why are frailer spies,
Which in their wills count bad what I think good?
No, I am that I am, and they that level
At my abuses reckon up their own:
I may be straight, though they themselves be bevel,
By their rank thoughts my deeds must not be shown:
Unless this general evil they maintain –
All men are bad, and in their badness reign.

It's better to be vile than so assessed,
When guilt is charged despite one's innocence,
And pleasure that hurts none is thus suppressed
Not by one's conscience - but intolerance.
For why should others' lusting, faithless eyes
Declaim the dissoluteness of my ways?
Or on my sins why are worse sinners spies,
Who disdain things that I prefer to praise?
No, I am what I am, and they that rail
At my faults are revealing of their own;
I may be straight, unlike their bent portrayal;
My deeds should not be seen through minds so prone:
Unless this general theory one holds true:
All men are bad and all the things they do.

SONNET 122: The arguments between the pair have descended into the banal, as Shakespeare responds to the accusation: "What did you do with that notebook which I gave you? You can't think much of me if you don't have it to hand." The portrayal of such pettiness and trivia yet again reinforces the sense of autobiography.

There is no consensus amongst commentators as to whether the "*tables*" of original line 1 (being a collection of note papers, ie a note book in modern parlance) constituted blank pages for the poet to inscribe or a notebook in which were already recorded the thoughts of his friend.

I favour the first of these interpretations (following Ledger), mainly because of the reference to "*idle rank*" in line 3 (which reference is either to the pages of the notebook or what is written therein). Most commentators (including Ledger) appear to interpret "idle" here as meaning "trivial", though I think that Shakespeare meant "unused". However, if it did mean "trivial" it is unlikely that Shakespeare would be so openly derogatory in referring to notes made by Southampton – either way, the implication is that the pages were unused or blank.

On this basis, the thrust of the sonnet is that, though the poet has failed to make notes on or for his friend, or even to keep the book so gifted, he has done so mentally and in his heart, which has enabled the "notes" (unnecessary anyway because Southampton is so close to mind) to be much more comprehensive and long-lasting.

SONNET 122

Thy gift, thy tables, are within my brain
Full charactered with lasting memory,
Which shall above that idle rank remain
Beyond all date even to eternity.
Or, at the least, so long as brain and heart
Have faculty by nature to subsist,
Till each to razed oblivion yield his part
Of thee, thy record never can be missed.
That poor retention could not so much hold,
Nor need I tallies thy dear love to score,
Therefore to give them from me was I bold,
To trust those tables that receive thee more:
To keep an adjunct to remember thee
Were to import forgetfulness in me.

My mind holds that blank book you gave to me
Completed with a script within my brain;
And there it will persist eternally,
Much longer than those pages will remain.
Or, at the least, so long as brain and heart
Are given leave by Nature to survive,
My images of you will stay a part
Of these, until I am no more alive.
Those pages had much less capacity,
Nor need I dear love-gifts to keep love's score,
So I presumed to pass your book from me
And trust those stores of love which hold much more.
To need an aid to keep your memory
Would show how little you impinged on me.

SONNET 123: And now Shakespeare, fed up with the rebuffs, gives up his attempts to placate. He retreats into assertions brimming with wounded dignity, in both this and the succeeding sonnet. Though other things change with time (including by implication Southampton's affections), he and his loyalties will stay firm.

There has been much speculation by commentators on what the poet had in mind when referring to *"pyramids"* in line 2. In Shakespeare's time the word denoted high towers, steeples and obelisks as well as the monuments and shape for which we now reserve the term exclusively. Consequently, he was probably using the term primarily as a metaphor for impressive achievements of the past echoed in the present.

However, maybe there was a secondary connotation of contemporary relevance. Various commentators have pointed to the support towers which were described by Ben Jonson as "pyramids" and which were parts of the pageantry for the delayed celebration in March 1604 of the accession of James I[106]. Such an interpretation fits the sonnet sequence well (and aligns with another hint of that pageantry in Sonnet 125), but any steeple or spire on any of the impressive buildings of the times could have been so described.

To my mind the sonnet strongly echoes the theme on the cycles of time commented on at Sonnet 59. Consequently, I have interpreted the *"registers"* and *"records"* (lines 9 and 11) as being imprints, copies or recalls of an original or precursor.

---

[106]   As, for example, discussed by Duncan-Jones on page 26 of her *Shakespeare's Sonnets*

SONNET 123

No, Time, thou shalt not boast that I do change;
Thy pyramids built up with newer might
To me are nothing novel, nothing strange:
They are but dressings of a former sight.
Our dates are brief, and therefore we admire
What thou dost foist upon us that is old,
And rather make them born to our desire
Than think that we before have heard them told.
Thy registers and thee I both defy,
Not wond'ring at the present nor the past,
For thy records and what we see doth lie,
Made more or less by thy continual haste.
This I do vow and this shall ever be,
I will be true despite thy scythe and thee.

No, Time, you cannot change my points of view,
Though you unfold afresh your works of might:
To me they're nothing strange, they're nothing new;
They're but reflections of a bygone sight.
Our lives are brief, and so we are impressed
By what you foist on us from long ago:
We'd rather credit our creative zest
Than see re-birth in your recycling flow.
But I defy both you and your impressions;
I'm awed by neither present nor the past:
Our views and your replays are but digressions
From truth, deformed as you pass ever fast.
I hereby pledge my faithful constancy,
And this, despite your power, will always be.

SONNET 124: Shakespeare continues with his avowals of constancy. The term, "*child of state*" (line 1), is primarily a metaphor for "political product" or "political expediency".

As for secondary connotations, it seems that the poet was making an artful reference to his faithless friend's history. Southampton, who on the death of his father became a ward of state when aged only eight, was arguably "*unfathered*" twice. His wardship ended in acrimony as we have seen earlier.

"*The fools of time*", who "*die for goodness*" (lines 13 and 14), are considered by many commentators to be a reference to martyrs, such as the Earl of Essex, executed in 1601, or the Gunpowder Plot gang of Guy Fawkes, executed in 1606.

However, it is unlikely that Shakespeare would call upon martyrs to witness his constant love if he regarded them as "fools of time" (and hence apparently unreliable or stupid). I suggest that the concluding couplet was, in fact, aimed at the poet's detractors (Sonnet 121), including, by implication, Southampton, whose inconstancy the poet was challenging. They are the "fools of time", similar in their vulnerability to Time's deceits and depredations as is the "*Time's fool*" of Sonnet 116, which this sonnet echoes.

SONNET 124

If my dear love were but the child of state,
It might for fortune's bastard be unfathered
As subject to time's love or to time's hate,
Weeds among weeds, or flowers with flowers gathered.
No, it was builded far from accident;
It suffers not in smiling pomp, nor falls
Under the blow of thrall-ed discontent
Whereto th' inviting time our fashion calls:
It fears not policy, that heretic,
Which works on leases of short-numbered hours,
But all alone stands hugely politic,
That it nor grows with heat nor drowns with showers.
To this I witness call the fools of time,
Which die for goodness who have lived for crime.

If my dear love were but the child of State,
It might, as Fortune's spawn, be cast away,
An object of Time's whims, a babe of fate:
A weed in weeds or bloom in brief bouquet.
But it is not a thing of accident;
It withstands smiling pomp and is not blown
Aside by strictures or disparagement,
To which these fickle times are all too prone.
Nor is it swayed by fads or policy,
Which change as minutes turn into their hours;
But, statesmanlike, stands independently,
Immune to fiery heat or weeping showers.
Take heed, all those who bend as time goes by,
That live in sin, repent when death is nigh.

SONNET 125:   This, the last sonnet in the Southampton sequence, is a piece of powerfully expressed independence: difficult, in part, to decipher.

Rowse suggests that the *"canopy"* of line 1 is a metaphor for the poet's burden of office and his status as herald and associate of his aristocratic friend. A canopy, in this context, was a ceremonial awning held over persons of high rank (normally monarchs) by a number of bearers. However, various commentators have pointed to an actual ceremony, the procession of James I in 1604. Preceding this, Shakespeare, as a senior member of the King's Men, is known to have been granted four yards of rich red cloth, perhaps to outfit him for a role therein. Both visions may well be relevant here.

The sonnet as a whole seems to be a vigorous riposte to accusations that the poet was a sycophantic, glory-seeking social climber, who had taken advantage of the generosity of his friend to achieve status, while fobbing him off with second-hand or repetitive poems.

Who is the *"suborned Informer"*, forcefully dismissed in the concluding couplet? Southampton is the addressee of the preceding lines. Has he been castigating Shakespeare publicly as well as privately? It could be one of the *"frailer spies"* from Sonnet 121 (who might also be the *"pitiful thrivers"* of this poem). Or it could be a personalisation of the poet's own thought process (the word "Informer" is italicised in the original). I like Duncan-Jones' suggestion that the offender is Time (who was the addressee of Sonnet 123). However, I think this would have been the poet's fall-back interpretation had he subsequently needed to defuse or massage what looks more like a terse message to his former friend to get lost.

SONNET 125

Were't aught to me I bore the canopy
With my extern the outward honouring,
Or laid great bases for eternity,
Which prove more short than waste or ruining?
Have I not seen dwellers on form and favour
Lose all and more by paying too much rent
For compound sweet: foregoing simple savour,
Pitiful thrivers in their gazing spent?
No, let me be obsequious in thy heart,
And take thou my oblation, poor but free,
Which is not mixed with seconds, knows no art
But mutual render, only me for thee.
Hence, thou suborned **Informer***! A true soul*
When most impeached stands least in thy control.

What's it to me I bore the canopy,
Had public honour in my public role,
Or paved the way to reach posterity,
Though, thus far, falling far short of that goal?
Have I not seen men fawn on form and favour,
Who lose their all in complex over-plays,
Ignoring simple truths, each status craver:
Poor jobsworths who no longer raise their gaze?
No, let me pander only to your heart;
Accept my offerings, too poor but free,
No re-used works and with no aims apart
From mutual regard, by you by me.
Begone, you Judas! he who's firm of soul
When most impugned is least in your control.

SONNET 126: This valedictory piece is technically not a sonnet. It is a poem of six rhyming couplets. As well as differing from a sonnet in rhyme structure, it contains only twelve lines.

Its original printing showed two sets of empty parentheses occupying the space which might otherwise have been taken up by the concluding couplet of a sonnet. A number of imaginative suggestions have been put forward as to the underlying intentions: a symbol of the emptiness of the grave or incompleteness of the relationship, a deliberate suppression of identifying information, and so on. I prefer more mundane explanations: that a prior reader of the manuscript (or even the printer), expecting to see two more lines, inserted the parentheses to indicate what he thought was an omission; or that this was an indication by the publisher, Thorpe, of the end of the first sequence.

Following most commentators, I have interpreted the *"glass"* of line 2 as Time's symbolic hour-glass, whose flow of sand grains measured the span of a person's life.

The piece comes over well as a post-script to the sequence. The different structure of the poem reinforces the sense that the time of the sonnets is over. There is a sense, too, of farewell advice, made perhaps several weeks after the last of the sonnets.

And there is residual affection for a friend who, though apparently estranged in some acrimony, was a significant part of the poet's life. Southampton, though now *"waning"* and middle-aged, will, it seems, remain young in Shakespeare's heart and will always be his *"Lovely Boy"*.

SONNET 126

O thou, my lovely boy, who in thy power
Dost hold Time's fickle glass, his sickle hour:
Who hast by waning grown, and therein show'st
Thy lovers withering as thy sweet self grow'st:
If Nature, sovereign mistress over wrack,
As thou goest onwards still will pluck thee back,
She keeps thee to this purpose that her skill
May time disgrace and wretched minute kill.
Yet fear her, O thou minion of her pleasure:
She may detain, but not still keep, her treasure!
Her audit, though delayed, answered must be,
And her quietus is to render thee.

(   )
(   )

O you, my lovely boy, who in your power
Holds back Time's fickle glass, his sickle-hour,
Who has through ageing grown, and thereby shows
Your loved ones withering as your flame grows:
If Nature, queen of ruin and decay,
Lets you persist and does your doom delay,
She does this so that she may show her skill,
To mock Time as she holds his sand grains still.
But fear her, O you plaything of her pleasure!
She holds a while, but cannot keep, her treasure:
Accounts must be discharged, though overdue,
And she'll pay hers when she discharges you.

Postscript: There is nothing to suggest that Southampton and Shakespeare were ever reconciled. Some seven years after their friend's death in 1616, Heminges and Condell dedicated the First Folio of Shakespeare's plays, not to his former patron, but to the Earls of Pembroke and Montgomery.

In or around 1604 (suggest many experts) Shakespeare wrote *All's Well That Ends Well.* The hero of this play, Bertram, Count of Rousillon, shares an unlikely number of characteristics with Southampton[107]. He is a royal ward; he resists a marriage which has been arranged for him; he travels abroad, leaving behind a loving and distressed young lady; he yearns to serve in military campaigns, but is commanded by his monarch to remain at Court; and, when he succeeds in joining a foreign campaign, he is appointed General of the Horse and wins honour in battle. Shakespeare even refers to him as an earl on two occasions (*III, v, 12 and 19*). However, Bertram's character is far from admirable. He is depicted as lascivious, vainglorious, rash and unworthy: a snob and a liar, who does not keep his promises or pay his debts. Southampton would not have been amused.

In 1605, the Earl finally fathered a son, as had been urged in the procreation sonnets of some thirteen years earlier. A second son, who died without male issue, eventually became the last Earl of Southampton.

Southampton's mother died in late 1607. With her passing came the final links in the extraordinary chain of events (described in Part I), which culminated in the publication of the Sonnets in 1609. It seems unlikely that this event – highly unwelcome to the Earl - would have occasioned any contact with Shakespeare: Southampton would have realised exactly how the Sonnets came to be published, after he had read Thorpe's dedication. However, the absence in the Earl's lifetime of any reprint of so significant a work does suggest that its main subject applied himself to its suppression as best he could.

The Sonnets and Essex rebellion apart, perhaps Southampton's most striking contribution to history came from his support of overseas ventures. He became an active and

---

[107] As pointed out by Akrigg

enthusiastic member of the Virginia, East India and North West Passage Companies. His stamp on posterity is marked to this day in the city of Hampton in Virginia (on what used to be named the Southampton River) and Southampton Island (at the entrance to Hudson Bay), both of which are named after him.

In 1624, he was reluctantly persuaded to take command of English troops, despatched to support the Dutch in a new campaign against Spain. He was accompanied by his elder son and heir, James, then aged nineteen. Unhappily, the young man perished from a fever (probably plague), which struck the troops in their winter quarters. The stricken Earl set off for home with his son's body, but en route himself succumbed to the combined effects of grief, sickness and the rigours of war in later age. His span had been 52 years – the same as his old poet.

On 28 December 1624, Shakespeare's Rose was buried - with his "bud" - in the Southampton family vault at Titchfield. In such melancholy and unexpected fashion were the predictions of Sonnet 1 fulfilled.

SONNET 127: Here starts the Dark Mistress sequence of sonnets.

As justified in Part I, much, if not all, of this sequence dates to the period 1592-4 and thus falls chronologically within the time-scale of the Southampton sequence. The poems were copied to Southampton who, probably because he was not their main subject or addressee, caused them to be filed outside the primary sequence dealing with him.

In this opening piece we read the words of a poet smitten with a woman who has dark eyes and hair (the latter being the mourning "suit" of line 10). To Shakespeare she is beautiful, even though prevailing fashions favour fairness of complexion and hair, leading to the fad for dyes and cosmetics decried by the poet.

These sentiments are echoed by Berowne in *Love's Labours Lost* (thought by many commentators to be a play of private satire based on the Southampton social circle). Berowne has fallen in love with the dark-haired Lady Rosaline, whom he extols to the detriment of cosmetic fair looks, as in this excerpt (*IV, iii, 258*):

> *O, if in black my lady's brows be decked,*
> *It mourns that painting and usurping hair*
> *Should ravish doters with a false aspect;*
> *And therefore is she born to make black fair."*

As with many of Shakespeare's plays the precise dating of *Love's Labours Lost* is a matter of educated guesswork. Scholars place the core of the play around 1593, although some peripheral characters and material were added after 1594. Its first known publishing was in 1598, when its title page proclaimed it to be "newly corrected and augmented by W. Shakespeare".

SONNET 127

In the old age black was not counted fair,
Or if it were it bore not beauty's name;
But now is black beauty's successive heir,
And beauty slandered with a bastard shame:
For since each hand hath put on nature's power,
Fairing the foul with art's false borrowed face,
Sweet beauty hath no name, no holy bower,
But is profaned, if not lives in disgrace.
Therefore my mistress' eyes are raven black,
Her eyes so suited, and they mourners seem
As such who, not born fair, no beauty lack,
Slandering creation with a false esteem:
Yet so they mourn, becoming of their woe,
That every tongue says beauty should look so.

In olden days dark looks were not admired
As beautiful, though fairness might be claimed,
But now they're with true beauty more attired
And Beauty's smeared with made up lines and shamed:
For, since mankind has stolen Nature's part
By painting ugliness more fair to eye,
Or turning dark to fair by means of art,
Beauty lives disgraced, undermined to dye.
So shine they black, my mistress' eyes and hair,
And, thus outfit, her eyes do seem to mourn
The falseness of those ones who weren't born fair,
Who win esteem with Nature now forsworn.
Yet so becoming is she in their woe
That everyone thinks beauty should look so.

SONNET 128: In assessing this parallel sequence of sonnets, we can reasonably take account of the following factors:

i) The young Southampton, to whom the poems were copied, was, on the evidence, egoistic and therefore unlikely to be interested in subjects with which he was not in some way connected;

ii) Some of the poems mirror the biography of the main sequence;

iii) There is a coherent overlapping of depicted characteristics, which suggests that the female subject of most of the poems in this sequence is the same woman – Shakespeare's dark mistress, who seduces Southampton.

On the basis of the above arguments, the subject of this sonnet is probably the same dark lady. She is thereby revealed to be a competent player of a musical instrument.

The instrument she plays is generally thought to be a harpsichord or its smaller variant, the virginals. These were keyboard instruments in which the depression of a key would cause a quill or plectrum mounted on a jack to pluck a string. The physical layout was broadly similar to a small piano.

Most commentators consider that in referring to "*jacks*", Shakespeare was in fact envisaging the keys, since it would be these which made most, if not all, contact with the player's hand. However, Madeau Stewart speculated that she was playing a primitive version of another keyboard instrument, the clavichord, in which a technique of hand damping was used to modulate timbre, giving rise to an image of wood "*leaping*" to the fingers.

SONNET 128

How oft when thou, my music, music play'st
Upon that bless-ed wood whose motion sounds
With thy sweet fingers, when thou gently sway'st
The wiry concord that mine ear confounds,
Do I envy those jacks that nimble leap
To kiss the tender inward of thy hand,
Whilst my poor lips, which should that harvest reap,
At the wood's boldness by thee blushing stand?
To be so tickled they would change their state
And situation with those dancing chips,
O'er whom thy fingers walk with gentle gait,
Making dead wood more blest than living lips.
Since saucy jacks so happy are in this,
Give them thy fingers, me thy lips to kiss.

How oft when you, my music, music play
Upon that lucky wood, whose movement sings
With your sweet fingers, as you gently sway,
Entrancing through the harmony of strings,
Do I envy those jacks that lithely shoot
To kiss the tender inside of your hand,
While I, whose lips should harvest that rich fruit,
Display their blush, aroused by woods' upstand?
To have them tickled so I'd change their place
And situation with those dancing chips,
On which your fingers walk with soothing pace,
To make dead wood more blest than living lips.
But since pert jacks so happy are in this
Give them your fingers, me your lips to kiss.

SONNET 129: Shakespeare bemoans the passions which drive men (and, by implication, him in particular) to expend themselves in a sate of lust, at the cost of immoral behaviour and subsequent sadness and disgust.

In Elizabethan English the word *"hell"* (line 14) carried a secondary bawdy allusion to female anatomy, perhaps based on a punning of "hole".

Was the poet here castigating himself and, if so, for his pursuit of whom? Though he could have been referring to women generally, the theme of madness or feverish lust is one which will be echoed in later sonnets only in respect of his dark mistress.

SONNET 129

Th' expense of spirit in a waste of shame
Is lust in action; and till action, lust
Is perjured, murd'rous, bloody, full of blame,
Savage, extreme, rude, cruel, not to trust;
Enjoyed no sooner but despis-ed straight,
Past reason hunted, and no sooner had
Past reason hated, as a swallowed bait
On purpose laid to make the taker mad,
Mad in pursuit and in possession so,
Had, having, and in quest to have, extreme:
A bliss in proof, and proved, a very woe.
Before, a joy proposed, behind, a dream.
All this the world well knows, yet none knows well
To shun the heaven that leads men to this hell.

The spend of spirit in a waste of shame
Is lust in action; and, till action, lust
Is perjured, murd'rous, wounding, full of blame,
Savage, extreme, crude, cruel, not to trust;
As soon despised as spent in joy to sate,
Hunted past reason, and no sooner had,
Hated past reason, like a swallowed bait,
On purpose laid to make the taker mad:
Mad in pursuit and in possession so
Wanting, wanted, wanton in the extreme:
A bliss to have, once had a very woe:
Before, a joy in store; behind, a dream.
All this men know is true but none learns well
To shun the heaven that tempts to clefts of hell.

SONNET 130: Shakespeare returns to the appreciation of his girlfriend's unfashionably dark-haired beauty and, in so doing, mocks poetic exaggerations: eyes bright as the sun; breath as sweet as honey; hair like threads of gold, and so on. Such conceits were made popular by the 14th century poet, Petrarch, who declaimed of his Laura:

> *The way she walked was not the way of mortals*
> *But of angelic forms, and when she spoke*
> *More than an earthly voice it was that sang.*

The word *"dun"* (line 3) evokes a range of colour tones from dull off-white to brown. However, it is being used here conditionally to mock the popular skin-as-white-as-snow conceit. In reality, no human skin, however freakish, can reflect such whiteness, as Shakespeare brings out with his comparison. His girlfriend's colouring could be anything from albino to swarthy and line 3 would still be apt – on which basis, and given the ironic tone, she was probably very pale-skinned.

The word *"reeks"* (line 8) carries far more unpleasant connotations in current English than when used by Shakespeare. We now almost invariably associate the word with the emission of a foul smell. To him it was less offensive and not necessarily associated with the sense of smell, as shown in the following excerpt from *Love's Labour's Lost* (*IV, iii*) where Navarre teases two besotted admirers:

> *I have been closely shrouded in this bush*
> *And marked you both and for you both did blush:*
> *I heard your guilty rhymes, observed your fashion,*
> *Saw sighs reek from you, noted well your passion:*
> *Ay me! Says one; O Jove! the other cries*
> *One her hairs were gold, crystal the other's eyes.*

SONNET 130

My mistress' eyes are nothing like the sun,
Coral is far more red than her lips' red;
If snow is white, why then her breasts are dun,
If hairs be wires, black wires grow on her head.
I have seen roses damasked, red and white,
But no such roses see I in her cheeks;
And in some perfumes is there more delight
Than in the breath that from my mistress reeks.
I love to hear her speak, yet well I know
That music hath a far more pleasing sound;
I grant I never saw a goddess go:
My mistress, when she walks, treads on the ground.
And yet, by heaven, I think my love as rare
As any she belied by false compare.

My mistress' eyes are nothing like the sun,
Her lips are far more pale than coral red;
If snow is white, well then her breasts are dun,
If hairs are threads, black threads grow on her head.
I have seen roses: damask, red and white,
But no such roses in her cheeks see I;
And in some perfumes is there more delight
Than in my mistress' breath as it stirs by.
I love to hear her speak and yet I'll prove
That music has a far more pleasing sound;
I grant I never saw a goddess move:
My mistress, when she walks, treads on the ground.
And yet, by all, I think my love as rare
As any woman hyped in false compare.

SONNET 131: Shakespeare suggests that the relationship with his dark girlfriend is somewhat one-sided, and that she takes advantage of his besottedness. Apparently, too, she is immoral in some way, has a poor reputation, and her beauty is not generally acclaimed.

Nevertheless, he remains transfixed.

SONNET 131

Thou art as tyrannous, so as thou art,
As those whose beauties proudly make them cruel;
For well thou know'st to my dear doting heart
Thou art the fairest and most precious jewel.
Yet, in good faith, some say that thee behold
Thy face hath not the power to make love groan:
To say they err I dare not be so bold,
Although I swear it to myself alone.
And to be sure that is not false I swear,
A thousand groans but thinking on thy face,
One on another's neck, do witness bear
Thy black is fairest in my judgement's place.
In nothing art thou black save in thy deeds,
And thence this slander, as I think, proceeds.

Tyrannical you are, as much as they
Whose beauty gives them pride and makes them cruel;
For well you know you have my heart in sway,
Which sees you as most fair and precious jewel.
And yet, in truth, some say, who've seen your face,
That this is not so fair as makes men sigh:
To tell them they are wrong is not my place,
Though when alone I swear it is a lie.
And, to give proof that what I swear is so,
On picturing your face, a thousand sighs,
One after one, depart my lips and show
Your beauty dark is fairest in my eyes.
In nothing are you black except your deeds,
From which the slander on your looks proceeds.

SONNET 132:   Here, Shakespeare confirms that his mistress feels none of the passion which she so stirs in him, as he longs painfully for a change in her heart.

In line 3, he again evokes the image, first portrayed in Sonnet 127, of her eyes appearing as mourners, with their surrounding garb of black eyebrows and/or head-hair.

In line 5, I have, unlike others, interpreted the "*morning sun*" not as the sun, itself, but as the morning star (being Venus – which also appears as the evening star at different times of the year). I have done this for two main reasons:

    ı)   because there are no "*gray cheeks*" in the eastern skies once the sun has appeared – whereas the morning star glows like a jewel in the gray morning twilight; and

    ıı)   for symmetry - given the image of "*those two mourning eyes*" (line 9), and the possibility that Shakespeare wanted to avoid the duplication of the word, "*star*".

If I am wrong, the underlying sentiments of the poem are unaffected.

SONNET 132

Thine eyes I love, and they, as pitying me,
Knowing thy heart torment me with disdain,
Have put on black and loving mourners be,
Looking with pretty ruth upon my pain.
And truly, not the morning sun of heaven
Better becomes the gray cheeks of the east,
Nor that full star that ushers in the even
Doth half that glory to the sober west
As those two mourning eyes become thy face.
O, let it then as well beseem thy heart
To mourn for me, since mourning doth thee grace,
And suit thy pity like in every part.
Then will I swear beauty herself is black,
And all they foul that thy complexion lack.

I love your eyes which, as if hurt for me,
Because your heart torments me with disdain,
Have put on black, and loving mourners be,
Which look with cute compassion on my pain.
And that bright morning star which hails the sun
Does not better become the fading night,
Nor does its evening self, as dusk's begun,
Bring half the glory to that wan twilight
As those two mourning eyes become your face.
O, let it then as well bestir your heart
To mourn for me, since mourning does you grace;
And usher pity to your every part.
Then I will swear that beauty must be black
And ugly those who your complexion lack.

SONNET 133: Shakespeare's female love has seduced his male one, much to the poet's chagrin! Now she is *Rosaline* – the Rose Besmircher (see Part I) – and his depictions of her change radically. The situation, described here and in Sonnets 134 and 144, mirrors the triangular relationship portrayed in the Southampton sequence[108].

Though apparently upset, Shakespeare cannot resist his fondness for wordplay, and the sonnet is scattered with sexual innuendo.

The word "*wound*" (line 2) is used thus in *The Passionate Pilgrime* (Poem 9, lines 12-14):

> "*See in my thigh*", quoth she, "*here was the sore.*"
> *She showed hers: he saw more wounds than one,*
> *And blushing fled, and left her all alone.*

Similarly, the "*eye*" of line 5 had a secondary meaning of an orifice (as in the eye of a needle). Shakespeare incorporates this secondary suggestion in a number of bawdy double-edged remarks within his works[109].

"*Engross*", in line 6, carries a sense of "absorbing" or "consuming", which can be understood in a physical as well as an emotional sense, as can "*pent*" in line 13.

---

[108] See commentary at Sonnets 40 and 41

[109] Perhaps the best example is in *Measure for Measure*, where Mistress Overdone, a prostitute, is bewailing her future after the city authorities clamp down on brothels. Her pimp, Pompey, reassures her, saying there will still be work for her in the city: "*Courage! There will be pity taken on you; you that have worn your eyes almost out in the service, you will be considered*" (*I, ii, 99*). Similarly, in *Much Ado About Nothing*, the bawdy meanings of "*die*" (Sonnets 3 & 7), "*lap*" (Sonnet 98) and "*eyes*" are all brought out as Benedick says in jest to Beatrice "*I will live in thy heart, die in thy lap and be buried in thy eyes*" (*V, ii, 94-95*).

SONNET 133

Beshrew that heart that makes my heart to groan
For that deep wound it gives my friend and me!
Is't not enough to torture me alone
But slave to slavery my sweet'st friend must be?
Me from myself thy cruel eye has taken,
And my next self thou harder hast engrossed:
Of him, myself and thee I am forsaken,
A torment thrice, threefold thus to be crossed.
Prison my heart in thy steel bosom's ward,
But then my friend's heart let my poor heart bail;
Whoe'er keeps me, let my heart be his guard,
Thou canst not then use rigour in my gaol.
And yet thou wilt, for I, being pent in thee,
Perforce am thine and all that is in me.

Be damned to hell that heart which makes mine groan
For that deep cleft it gives both friend and me!
Is torture not enough of me alone,
Must you bind my best friend in slavery?
Your ruthless eye has me dance to your whim,
My other self held harder and secured;
I am bereft of you, myself and him:
A threefold torment thus to be endured.
Lock up within your steely breast my heart,
But let it bail my friend's, so where mine be
My heart will keep his safe and in good part,
And my heart's jailer can't discomfort me.
But yet you will, for I, held tight in you,
Am therefore yours, and all that's in me too.

SONNET 134: This sonnet implies that Shakespeare had originally called upon Southampton to advance his cause with Rosaline by, in effect, certifying the poet's worthiness.

On this basis, I have interpreted the "*he learned*" of line 7 – puzzling in isolation – to mean the eventual or reluctant acceptance by the Earl of a persuasive argument (that he should write to Rosaline on behalf of the poet). It seems then that the resultant letter triggered closer contact between the correspondents, with the results bewailed by Shakespeare.

The sonnet makes much play with the legal terminology associated with the management of debt, an established conceit in poetry of the time[110].

It is intriguing to consider how Shakespeare may have inadvertently helped to widen Southampton's sexual tastes, and to fulfil his own original remit with the young lord. The procreation sonnets (1-17) and the *Narcissus* message[111] suggest that the Earl, then, had no sexual interest in women. There is a further hint of this attitude in line 8 of Sonnet 40. However, after his seduction by Rosaline, the Earl became receptive to both sexes, and eventually impregnated Elizabeth Vernon, necessitating their marriage. Later, he fathered more daughters and two sons by her.

It seems that the blandishments of Sonnets 1-17 achieved the procreation goal only indirectly - by enabling Shakespeare to befriend Southampton. The real catalyst for inauguration of the Earl's reproductive faculty – to the dismay of the poet - was probably his introduction of the young lord to the predatory Rosaline!

---

110 See commentary at Sonnet 30

111 See commentary at Sonnet 5

SONNET 134

So, now I have confessed that he is thine
And I myself am mortgaged to thy will,
Myself I'll forfeit, so that other mine
Thou wilt restore to be my comfort still.
But thou wilt not, nor he will not be free,
For thou art covetous and he is kind;
He learned but surety-like to write for me,
Under that bond that him as fast doth bind.
The statute of thy beauty thou wilt take,
Thou usurer that put'st forth all to use.
And sue a friend came debtor for my sake:
So him I lose through my unkind abuse.
Him have I lost; thou hast both him and me;
He pays the whole, and yet am I not free.

So, now I have confessed that you have him
While I myself am subject to you still,
I'll submit to your least desire or whim
If you'll release my friend to his own Will.
But you will not, and he'll be free no more,
For you are covetous and he is kind;
He wrote for me, as if my guarantor
And by that bond is now as fast entwined.
Your beauty you will use, as lenders make
The most of wealth to maximise return,
And use a friend now debtor for my sake,
Lost to me through abuse of his concern.
Him I have lost; you have both him and me;
He's paid it all, and yet I am not free.

SONNET 135: It is impossible to modernise this sonnet faithfully because of its primary theme and its play on the word, "will". In addition to its current meaning of strong wish, desire or intent, this word had, for the Elizabethans, secondary connotations of sexual desire and, by extension, sexual anatomy (hence, perhaps, the modern slang "willy"). Also, of course, it was the diminutive of Shakespeare's first name.

"*Will*", in the original printing of this sonnet, is italicised on the occasions it bears an initial letter in upper case - apparently indicating a stretching of meaning by way of pun (as discussed in Appendix E).

In an attempt to convey a semblance of the original, my modernised version plays instead on the word, "fill" – to be taken, besides its normal meaning, as denoting fulfilment or something which fills or is filled. It also plays on the word, "*fulfil*", as Shakespeare does in the accompanying Sonnet 136, which carries much the same theme as this one.

It seems very unlikely that this, and sonnets with a similar derogatory theme, would have been sent to Rosaline, though she is the most likely addressee. Such sonnets were probably shown in some form to friends (in line with Meres' remarks[112]) and were copied to Southampton, under the circumstances of their relationship.

---

[112]   See note 1

SONNET 135

Whoever hath her wish, thou hast thy **Will**,
And **Will** *to boot, and* **Will** *in overplus:*
More than enough am I that vex thee still,
To thy sweet will making addition thus.
Wilt thou, whose will is large and spacious,
Not once vouchsafe to hide my will in thine?
Shall will in others seem right gracious
And in my will no fair acceptance shine?
The sea, all water, yet receives rain still
And in abundance addeth to his store:
So thou, being rich in **Will**, *add to thy* **Will**
One will of mine, to make thy large **Will** *more.*
Let no unkind, no fair beseechers kill:
Think all but one, and me in that one **Will**.

Whoever has her wish, you have your fill
Fulfilled at need and me to fill the more:
More than enough am I, who plies you still,
To let me give you sweet fulfil encore.
Will you, whose fill is wide in its delight,
Not once let me shape my fill to share yours?
Is fill of others deemed so very right
While mine is subject to your curt deplores?
The sea, all water, still receives the rain
And such abundance adds more to its store:
So you, though rich in fill, make full again
With my full fill to make your fulfil more.
Do not fair rising hopes of seekers kill:
Think them but one and mine with them fulfil.

SONNET 136: As is the case for Sonnet 135, it is impossible to render this bawdy and derogatory sonnet faithfully in modern terms, due to the extra meanings of "will" now lost to the language. In addition, there are double-meanings associated with the words, "thing" and "*nothing*" (to indicate male and female sexual organs), and "count" (or the similar word "*account*") - see commentary at Sonnet 109. In line 1 the word, "*come*", probably had a similar secondary sexual meaning to that of today.

I have given a pale, modernised semblance of the original by punning on the word "goodwill" (good Will) and retaining the poet's multi-use of "*fulfil*".

The derogatory nature of many of the mistress sonnets suggests that Southampton was not long in the sexual clutches of Rosaline, given their separate implication that Shakespeare remained hooked by her. He would not have wanted to take the risk of an earl, still "engrossed", showing her sonnets which insulted her. This sign of the brevity of the sexual phase of the young lord's relationship with Rosaline is reinforced by the incidence of his affair with Marlowe, which, as we have seen, must have commenced soon after he was seduced by Shakespeare's girlfriend.

SONNET 136

If thy soul check thee that I come so near,
*Swear to thy blind soul that I was thy **Will**,*
And will, thy soul knows, is admitted there:
Thus far for love, my love-suit, sweet, fulfil.
***Will** will fulfil the treasure of thy love,*
Ay, fill it full with wills, and my will one,
In things of great receipt with ease we prove
Among a number one is reckoned none.
Then in the number let me pass untold,
Though in thy store's account I one must be;
For nothing hold me, so it please thee hold
That nothing me, a something sweet to thee.
Make but my name thy love, and love that still,
*And then thou lovest me, for my name is **Will**.*

If your conscience carps I come so near,
Tell it you play host to your good Will;
And it knows good will must be held as dear,
So hold me tight and thus good will fulfil.
Goodwill full fills that love by which you're moved:
Fulfil what's yours with many and me, one;
In great capacity, with ease it's proved,
Amongst the many one's as good as none.
So in the multitudes I'll pass untold,
As in your count this will be small ado:
Hold me as nought as long as you do hold
That nothing me, a something sweet for you.
Just put my name to good for love's fulfil,
And you'll love me, because my name is Will.

SONNET 137: Shakespeare remains besotted with Rosaline, despite his accusations, here, that she – the *"bay where all men ride"* and the *"wide world's common place"* - has many other lovers. But perhaps this is an exaggeration, fuelled by his bitterness, or designed to deter Southampton from taking her back into his bed.

The identity of this dark-eyed, black-haired, ambitious and promiscuous woman remains unproven. As discussed in Part I and Appendix C, however, the only realistic candidate to date is Emilia Bassano, who became Emilia Lanier upon her forced marriage in October 1592.

SONNET 137

Thou blind fool, love, what dost thou to mine eyes
That they behold and see not what they see?
They know what beauty is, see where it lies,
Yet what the best is take the worst to be.
If eyes, corrupt by over-partial looks,
Be anchored in the bay where all men ride,
Why of eyes' falsehood hast thou forg-ed hooks
Whereto the judgement of my heart is tied?
Why should my heart think that a several plot,
Which my heart knows the wide world's common place,
Or mine eyes seeing this, say this is not,
To put fair truth upon so foul a face?
In things right true my heart and eyes have erred,
And to this false plague are they now transferred.

You blind fool, Love, how do you make my eyes
  Gaze on a sight and see what isn't there?
They know what beauty is, see where it lies,
  Yet take the darkest thing to be most fair.
    If eyes, corrupt with partiality,
Are anchored on the bay where all men ride,
  Why do you give my heart their falsity,
And bind its judgement to the place they're tied?
Why should my heart think private that estate,
  Which well it knows is there for public use,
    Or my eyes seeing this, then fabricate
      A beauty true on ugliness so loose?
My heart and eyes have strayed from what is true,
And sicken from a plague of false-held view.

SONNET 138: A version of this sonnet, with some minor differences, was published in *The Passionate Pilgrime*, in or shortly before, 1599. As explained in more detail in Appendix A, *Pilgrime*, attributed in full to Shakespeare, is known to contain poems by other authors, and its publication is generally considered to be an act of literary piracy, unauthorised by any of the writers. The collection also contains a closer version of Sonnet 144 and sonnets from *Love's Labours Lost*.

There is no evidence of how Jaggard, the publisher of *Pilgrime*, obtained his material, or of the provenance of his somewhat different versions of Sonnets 138 and 144. From the comments of Francis Meres[113], Shakespeare is known to have shared certain "sugared" sonnets with his "private friends". Was such a friend responsible for this leak, perhaps relying on a faulty memory to reconstruct the lines? Or did Shakespeare titivate the wording of these poems at some stage?

We can conclude that both sonnets must have been composed before 1599, but, as Sonnet 144 clearly describes the triangular relationship of pre-June 1593, this information is not particularly helpful in relation to that poem.

Given its theme and the reasonable probability that Sonnet 138 refers to Rosaline – by virtue of its inclusion in the secondary sequence supplied to Southampton – we can also conclude that she was probably younger than Shakespeare.

---

[113]   Footnote 1

SONNET 138

When my love swears that she is made of truth
I do believe her, though I know she lies,
That she might think me some untutored youth,
Unlearned in the world's false subtleties.
Thus vainly thinking that she thinks me young,
Although she knows my days are past the best,
Simply I credit her false-speaking tongue:
On both sides thus is simple truth suppressed.
But wherefore says she not she is unjust?
And wherefore say not I that I am old?
O, love's best habit is in seeming trust,
And age in love loves not to have years told.
Therefore I lie with her and she with me,
And in our faults by lies we flattered be.

When my love swears that she is true to me
I take her word, although I know she lies,
So she might think I show naivety,
As befits youth deceived by worldly guise.
Thus, vainly hoping that she thinks me young,
Although she knows that I am past my best,
I show no doubt of her false-speaking tongue:
On both sides thus is simple truth suppressed.
But why does she not say she is untrue?
And why do I not say that I am old?
Love looks its best when it stands with faith too,
And ageing lovers like their years untold.
And so I lie with her and she with me
And in our faults let lies bring flattery.

SONNET 139:   Here, Shakespeare continues to bewail his girlfriend's preference for another man.

Is the other man Southampton? It seems improbable, if Shakespeare is indeed trying to dissuade his friend from the delights of a girlfriend shared with the poet. More likely, he is a fourth party, and this extension of her attentions would align with the references in surrounding sonnets to Rosaline's promiscuity.

There are echoes of sonnet number 48 of Sydney's *Astrophel & Stella*, where the speaker also bewails the injuries received from his love's eye darts and pleas with her to kill him off quickly.

SONNET 139

O call not me to justify the wrong
That thy unkindness lays upon my heart:
Wound me not with thine eye, but with thy tongue;
Use power with power, and slay me not by art.
Tell me thou lov'st elsewhere, but in my sight,
Dear heart, forbear to glance thine eye aside;
What need'st thou wound with cunning, when thy might
Is more than my o'er-pressed defence can bide?
Let me excuse thee: ah, my love well knows
Her pretty looks have been my enemies.
And therefore from my face she turns my foes,
That they elsewhere might dart their injuries:
Yet do not so, but since I am near slain
Kill me outright with looks and rid my pain.

I should not have to try to justify
Your reasons for the heartache you cause me.
Hurt me with your tongue and not your eye;
Use direct force and not this subtlety.
So tell me you love him, but while I'm here
Spare me those sidelong glances sent his way.
Why hurt slyly when your strength, my dear,
Is far more than my heart can keep at bay?
Let me excuse you: ah, my love is wise
And knows her pretty looks have undone me,
And therefore from my face she turns her eyes,
So they might elsewhere dart their injury.
Yet don't do this, but since I am near slain
Kill me outright with looks and spare my pain.

SONNET 140: Continuing the theme of the preceding sonnet, Shakespeare threatens to publicise Rosaline's flaws – presumably her promiscuity - if she will not, at least, treat him with respect when they are together. This brings to mind the similar threat against Southampton, suggested in the commentary to Sonnet 88.

SONNET 140

Be wise as thou art cruel, do not press
My tongue-tied patience with too much disdain,
Lest sorrow lend me words and words express
The manner of my pity-wanting pain.
If I might teach thee wit, better it were
Though not to love, yet, love, to tell me so;
As testy sick men, when their deaths be near,
No news but health from their physicians know.
For if I should despair I should grow mad,
And in my madness might speak ill of thee;
Now this ill-wresting world is grown so bad
Mad slanderers by mad ears believ-ed be.
That I may not be so, nor thou belied,
Bear thine eyes straight though thy proud heart go wide.

Be wise as much as cruel and don't press
My tongue-tied patience with too much disdain,
Lest anguish make me speak and so express
Your lack of pity and what's caused me pain.
May I suggest it would be better, dear,
If you told me you loved me and did lie:
As tetchy patients, when their ends are near,
Are told only they'll get well by and by.
For if I should despair I would go mad,
And in my frenzy might speak ill of you:
The world is all too quick to find things bad
And would assume mad slander to be true.
For fear of which, and so you're not maligned,
Don't glance aside, though your heart's left behind.

SONNET 141: The diatribe continues, once again hardly likely to be conveyed to the ostensible addressee, his mistress, if Shakespeare remains hopeful of her favours.

The "*five wits*" of line 9 were an Elizabethan fancy that the five physical senses were mirrored by five forms of intellectual perception, such as imagination or logic.

SONNET 141

In faith, I do not love thee with mine eyes
For they in thee a thousand errors note,
But 'tis my heart that loves what they despise
Who, in despite of view, is pleased to dote.
Nor are mine ears with thy tongue's tune delighted,
Nor tender feeling to base touches prone,
Nor taste, nor smell desire to be invited
To any sensual feast with thee alone.
But my five wits, nor my five senses can
Dissuade one foolish heart from serving thee,
Who leaves unswayed the likeness of a man,
Thy proud heart's slave and vassal wretch to be:
Only my plague thus far I count my gain
That she that makes me sin awards me pain.

In truth I do not love you with my eyes,
For they in you a thousand defects note;
It is my heart which loves what they despise,
And which, in spite of view, goes on to dote.
Nor do my ears find music in your voice,
Nor is my feel to clumsy groping prone,
Nor taste, nor smell would share of their own choice
In any sensual feast with you alone.
But neither sense nor my five senses can
Dissuade one foolish heart from serving you,
That leaves the driveless shadow of a man
To be your proud heart's slave and vassal true.
But my plague brings to me this saving gain:
That she who makes me sin deals me my pain.

SONNET 142: This sonnet develops the closing thought of that preceding, and suggests that both Shakespeare and Rosaline have been guilty of numerous sexual forays, unsanctified by marriage.

Other candidates for the poet's mistress, suggested over the years, include a prostitute known as Lucy Negro, Jane Davenant, hostess of an Oxford inn, said to have been used by Shakespeare in his travels and Lady Penelope Rich, sister of the Earl of Essex. None of these candidates fit the template suggested by the Sonnets, without considerable straining of interpretation. Rich, for example, was older than Shakespeare, had golden hair and a conflicting and complicated love life.

SONNET 142

Love is my sin, and thy dear virtue hate,
Hate of my sin, grounded on sinful loving.
O, but with mine compare thou thine own state
And thou shalt find it merits not reproving;
Or, if it do, not from those lips of thine
That have profaned their scarlet ornaments
And sealed false bonds of love as oft as mine,
Robbed others' beds' revenues of their rents.
Be it lawful I love thee, as thou lov'st those
Whom thine eyes woo as mine importune thee:
Root pity in thy heart that, when it grows,
Thy pity may deserve to pitied be.
If thou dost seek to have what thou dost hide,
By self-example mayst thou be denied.

Love is my sin and righteous is your hate
To scorn my love, which violates God's law.
But heed yourself before you castigate,
And you will find me not so great in flaw.
Or if I am then reproof should not fly
From your red lips, which tease and titillate
And helped you stray, as often as have I,
Led you to beds most inappropriate.
Accept my right to love, as you love those
Whom your eyes woo as mine importune you;
Give pity, so your heart reaps what it sows
And you'll receive back pity when it's due.
If you withhold what you of others yearn
May you get what you give, in full return.

SONNET 143: Here, Shakespeare takes a break from his brooding intensity with this comical sketch, which nevertheless paints a vivid picture of the situation.

Who is the intended prey, fleeing from Rosaline? Presumably it is the recipient of her sidelong glances in Sonnets 139 and 140.

In line 13 there is further play on the word, "will", which is italicised with opening capital letter and carries all the meanings described in the commentary to Sonnet 135, including Shakespeare's name.

SONNET 143

Lo, as a careful housewife runs to catch
One of her feathered creatures broke away,
Sets down her babe and makes all swift dispatch
In pursuit of the thing she would have stay;
Whilst her neglected child holds her in chase,
Cries to catch her whose busy care is bent
To follow that which flies before her face,
Not prizing her poor infant's discontent:
So runn'st thou after that which flies from thee,
Whilst I thy babe chase thee afar behind;
But if thou catch thy hope, turn back to me
And play the mother's part, kiss me, be kind.
So will I pray that thou mayst have thy **Will**,
If thou turn back and my loud crying still.

Behold the scene, as watchful housewife sights
Her chicken make a break for liberty;
Puts down her babe and, clutching skirt to tights,
Pursues the bird before it can get free;
While her neglected child begins to chase
His mother, crying, as she is intent
To follow that which flies before her face,
Ignoring her poor infant's discontent:
And so do you chase that which tries to flee,
While I, your babe, chase you from far behind;
But if you catch your prey turn back to me
And play the mother's part, kiss me, be kind.
I'll pray your wants and Will be satisfied,
If you turn back and soothe my needs much cried.

SONNET 144: A closely similar version of this sonnet was published, apparently without Shakespeare's approval, in 1599 (see commentary on Sonnet 138).

It seems to portray a time when the poet suspected Rosaline and Southampton of cheating on him, but had no proof. If so, it may mirror the situation of Sonnets 33 and 34, and would appear to fit chronologically before Sonnets 133 and 134 in the secondary sequence.

The *"hell"* of line 12 probably carries the same double meaning as that of Sonnet 129. Following on from this, some commentators see, in line 14, an allusion to venereal disease. If so, had Shakespeare himself been infected or was he just trying to scare off the Earl?

Some point to a tantalisingly similar situation (with or without disease) hinted at in *Willobie his Avisa*, a publication of 1594, which includes the following comments (spelling modernised):

"H. W. [Henrico Willobego]being suddenly infected with the contagion of a fantastical fit, at the first sight of A [Avisa], ... bewrayeth the secrecy of his disease unto his familiar frend W. S., who not long before had tried the courtesy of the like passion, and was now newly recovered ... he determined to see whether it would sort to a happier end for this new actor, than it did for the old player."

The possibility that the player, "WS", was a reference to Shakespeare is strengthened by a reference to the latter in an introductory poem included with the *Avisa*.

However, to date, the circumstances of the poems and their ostensible author are too uncertain to allow any satire of real characters to be deciphered with confidence.

SONNET 144

Two loves I have, of comfort and despair,
Which like two spirits do suggest me still:
The better angel is a man right fair,
The worser spirit a woman coloured ill.
To win me soon to hell, my female evil
Tempteth my better angel from my side,
And would corrupt my saint to be a devil,
Wooing his purity with her foul pride.
And whether that my angel be turned fiend
Suspect I may, yet not directly tell;
But being both from me, both to each friend,
I guess one angel in another's hell.
Yet this shall I ne'er know, but live in doubt,
Till my bad angel fire my good one out.

Two loves of mine bring comfort and despair
And, like two spirits, guide and tempt me too:
The better angel is a man who's fair,
The succubus a woman dark in hue.
To make my life a hell, my female djinn
Is tempting my good angel from my side,
And would seduce my saint from good to sin,
Corrupting him to slake her greed and pride.
And if my angel's now the fallen kind
Suspect I may, but not directly tell;
But each, avoiding me, to each inclined,
I guess one's in the other's hole from hell.
Yet this I'll never know, but live in doubt,
Till my bad angel burns my good one out.

SONNET 145: Some commentators regard this sonnet as an immature piece, composed by Shakespeare before his marriage to Anne Hathaway in 1582.

This belief is founded on their perception of a pun on Anne's maiden name in the words "*hate away*" in line 13. A second pun, on her Christian name, is also perceived by some in the immediately following word "*And*". The proponents then point to the unusual format of the sonnet (with eight syllables per line instead of the standard ten) and a perceived poor quality of poetry to support their theory.

If this theory is correct, perhaps Shakespeare supplied a copy of the sonnet to Southampton, following a related discussion on the Stratfordian's early poetry and/or loves.

However, given that the sonnet tradition only became established in England with the publication of Sidney's sonnet sequence *Astrophel and Stella* in 1591, it seems unlikely that Shakespeare would have been using his three-quatrains-and-a-concluding-couplet format back in 1581/2. Moreover, as I expand upon in Appendix F, the words in question seem more likely to have arisen from linguistic constraints than the wish to apply an apparently poor pun.

On this basis, the poem's inclusion in the sequence suggests that its subject is the poet's dark girlfriend, albeit in one of her kinder moods. It evokes an image of Rosaline holding forth with complaints but, on seeing his stricken expression, hastily defusing any personal connotation.

SONNET 145

Those lips that Love's own hand did make
Breathed forth the sound that said "I hate"
To me that languished for her sake.
But when she saw my woeful state,
Straight in her heart did mercy come,
Chiding that tongue that, ever sweet,
Was used in giving gentle doom.
And taught it thus anew to greet:
"I hate" she altered with an end,
That followed it as gentle day
Doth follow night who, like a fiend,
From heaven to hell is flown away.
"I hate" from hate away she threw,
And saved my life, saying "not you".

Those lips that Love's own hand did make
Breathed forth the sound that said "I hate"
To me who languished for her sake.
But, when she saw my woeful state,
So quick came mercy to her heart
To check that tongue, which, ever sweet,
Would with kind words my fate impart,
And caused it thus anew to greet:
"I hate" she altered with a jewel,
That followed on like gentle day
Will follow night, which, like a ghoul,
From heaven to hell is blown away.
"I hate" from hatred she withdrew,
To save me with the end, "not you".

SONNET 146: Here is a piece of philosophic introspection from Shakespeare – a patronage poem, which, probably because it does not deal with Southampton, was filed in the secondary sequence.

Has this breast-beating been triggered by a bout of self-disgust akin to that evoked by Sonnet 129? Or, is it essentially a display of his talents on matters more spiritual - which was not an uncommon occurrence among sonneteers of the time? No one scenario stands out, among many possibilities.

The original printing contained an erroneous repetition of words from line 1, at the beginning of the second line. As a result one or two words which should have been in that place were omitted. Rowse suggests that a word along the lines of "confound" would fit the sense. My interpretation, independently reached, is in line with that of Duncan-Jones and Ledger.

With its suggestions that the life of a body should be foreshortened through deliberate deprivation, the theme of my modernisation diverges from orthodox Christianity. There is nothing in Shakespeare's history, or elsewhere in the Sonnets, to suggest that the poet believed in such a philosophy. Some will prefer to interpret the original only as an injunction against excess: I took my lead from the overall sense and the message in the concluding couplet.

SONNET 146

Poor soul, the centre of my sinful earth,
[???] these rebel powers that thee array,
Why dost thou pine within and suffer dearth,
Painting thy outward walls so costly gay?
Why so large cost, having so short a lease,
Dost thou upon thy fading mansion spend?
Shall worms, inheritors of this excess,
Eat up thy charge? Is this thy body's end?
Then, soul, live thou upon thy servant's loss,
And let that pine to aggravate thy store;
Buy terms divine in selling hours of dross,
Within be fed, without be rich no more:
So shalt thou feed on death, that feeds on men,
And death once dead, there's no more dying then.

Poor Soul, O centre to my flesh of sin,
Who feeds those wayward urges clothing you,
Why do you pine and starve yourself within
To give your outer garb such costly hue?
Why spend so much on so short tenancy
And glut your fading mansion with such surplus?
Should worms, who will inherit this bounty,
Eat what you pay: is this your body's purpose?
So, Soul, to body's detriment live on,
And let this starve to feed you, who are core;
Buy heaven's ages with earth's hours foregone,
Inside be fed, outside be rich no more:
So you will feed on death, which feeds on men,
And death once dead, there's no more dying then.

SONNET 147: Shakespeare, distanced - at least emotionally - from his Rosaline, is racked with the suffering of an addict in deprival.

Why are they apart? Have some of his thoughts, vividly expressed in the more derogatory of his sonnets, been conveyed to her? Has she succeeded in securing her preferred prey of Sonnet 143? Perhaps she is just tired of being pestered by a man, whose passion she has never really reciprocated.

Conversely, perhaps the poet is in the throes of trying to reduce his contact with her, hoping to wean himself of his dependency.

SONNET 147

My love is as a fever, longing still
For that which longer nurseth the disease;
Feeding on that which doth preserve the ill,
Th' uncertain sickly appetite to please.
My reason, the physician to my love,
Angry that his prescriptions are not kept,
Hath left me, and I desperate now approve
Desire is death, which physic did except.
Past cure I am, now reason is past care,
And frantic-mad with ever more unrest;
My thoughts and my discourse as madmen's are,
At random from the truth vainly expressed,
For I have sworn thee fair, and thought thee bright,
Who art as black as hell, as dark as night.

My love is like a fever, longing still
For that which tends and succours the disease
And, feeding upon that which keeps me ill,
A dark unhealthy appetite to please.
My reason, like a doctor to my care,
Now angry his advice a waste of breath,
Has left me and I know now in despair
Desire that is not treated feels like death.
Past cure am I, now reason is past care,
And frantic-mad with nag like aching tooth,
My thoughts and my discourse, like madmen's, bear
Delusions, unlike vainly spoken truth.
For I have sworn you fair and thought you bright,
Who are as black as hell, as dark as night.

SONNET 148: Shakespeare continues the theme of the preceding sonnet.

In line 6, he affirms his previous suggestions (eg in Sonnet 131) that Rosaline is not commonly thought to be attractive.

SONNET 148

O me! what eyes hath love put in my head,
Which have no correspondence with true sight;
Or, if they have, where is my judgement fled
That censures falsely what they see aright?
If that be fair whereon my false eyes dote,
What means the world to say it is not so?
If it be not, then love doth well denote
Love's eye is not so true as all men's: no,
How can it? O, how can love's eye be true,
That is so vexed with watching and with tears?
No marvel then, though I mistake my view;
The sun itself sees not till heaven clears.
O cunning love, with tears thou keep'st me blind,
Lest eyes well-seeing thy foul faults should find!

What kind of eyes has love put in my head
Which give no correspondence with true sight?
Or, if they do, where is my judgement fled,
To misinterpret what eyes see quite right?
If what I see with doting eyes is fair,
What means the world to say that it's not so?
And if it's not, the truth is staring there
That love's eye cannot see what all men know.
And how can it? How can love's eye be true,
When it's so strained with watching and with tears?
No wonder, then, that I mistake my view;
The sun, itself, is blind till heaven clears.
O cunning love, you put tears in my eyes
To keep your foul faults hid through this disguise!

SONNET 149: Here, Shakespeare defends himself. Perhaps this was a sonnet, which was actually given by Shakespeare to his dark girlfriend.

The passion evoked in this batch of sonnets is striking for the contrast with that evinced for Southampton. Its intensity reinforces the suggestion that, when it comes to physical attraction, Shakespeare is far more moved by his Rosaline.

SONNET 149

Canst thou, O cruel, say I love thee not,
When I against myself with thee partake?
Do I not think on thee when I forgot
Am of myself, all tyrant for thy sake?
Who hateth thee that I do call my friend;
On whom frown'st thou that I do fawn upon?
Nay, if thou lour'st on me, do I not spend
Revenge upon myself with present moan?
What merit do I in myself respect
That is so proud thy service to despise,
When all my best doth worship thy defect,
Commanded by the motion of thine eyes?
But, love, hate on, for now I know thy mind;
Those that can see thou lov'st, and I am blind.

How can, O Cruel, you say I love you not,
When I, to disadvantage, take your side?
Do I not put you first, when all's forgot
By me of mine, for over-bearing pride?
Who that dislikes you is now called my friend;
On whom d'you frown whom I defend or praise?
No, if you scowl at me do I not rend
Myself with instant punishment always?
What virtue in me gets such self-applause
I think it too good for your enterprise,
When all my best's in thrall to your worst flaws,
Commanded by the flashing of your eyes?
But, love, hate on, for now I know your mind:
You love who see you true, and I am blind.

SONNET 150: Again, there is a suggestion that Rosaline is held in disdain by others.

Rowse identifies the *"unworthiness"* of line 13 with the pregnancy of Emilia Bassano outside of marriage. However, in his paper *Aemilia Lanyer and Queen Elizabeth at Cookham*, Roger Prior makes a persuasive argument, based on analysis of Lanier's poems, that she in fact received great support in this adversity from various ladies of the aristocracy, including Elizabeth Tudor (Appendix C). The two interpretations are not necessarily inconsistent: the first view might have been held by an unsympathetic public, the second by women who knew her and her background.

Having regard to the subject matter of the next sonnet there may, however, be a bawdy double meaning in line 13.

SONNET 150

O, from what power hast thou this powerful might
With insufficiency my heart to sway?
To make me give the lie to my true sight,
And swear that brightness doth not grace the day?
Whence hast thou this becoming of things ill,
That in the very refuse of thy deeds
There is such strength and warrantise of skill
That, in my mind, thy worst all best exceeds?
Who taught thee how to make me love thee more,
The more I hear and see just cause of hate?
O, though I love what others do abhor,
With others thou shouldst not abhor my state.
If thy unworthiness raised love in me,
More worthy I to be beloved of thee.

What mighty source fires your ability
To move my heart with all your many flaws?
And make me disbelieve what I can see,
To swear that day is night for no good cause?
How can you make things foul seem oh so fair,
That in the meanest act I might detest
There is such strength and artistry in there
That to my mind your worst beats others' best?
Who taught you how to make me love you more,
The more I hear and see good cause for hate?
O, though I love what other folk deplore,
You should not join in to deplore my state.
If my love rose at your unworthiness,
More worthy I to have your tenderness.

357

SONNET 151: Here, at last, we have a lighter note again, reaffirming that Shakespeare did, on occasion, experience pleasurable times with his mistress. It seems, too, that the poet's soul has failed to take the advice of Sonnet 146.

Cupid, the god of love, also known as Love, was depicted as a baby: hence the reference to youth in line 1.

Ledger points out that the sexual references in this sonnet go well beyond the norm for poems of that time. He speculates, based on similar puns in Shakespeare's plays, that "*conscience*" (in lines 1 and 2) was pronounced "cunscience", a mock word suggesting knowledge of female genitalia.

The word, "*urge*", in line 3, then had meanings of "charge with", "press a claim for" or "accuse". From its context here, however, I suspect that it also carried its modern primary sense.

The general bawdiness of the poem is yet another indication that the Sonnets were intended only for a private readership.

SONNET 151

Love is too young to know what conscience is,
Yet who knows not conscience is born of love?
Then, gentle cheater, urge not my amiss,
Lest guilty of my faults thy sweet self prove.
For, thou betraying me, I do betray
My nobler part to my gross body's treason:
My soul doth tell my body that he may
Triumph in love: flesh stays no further reason,
But rising at thy name doth point out thee
As his triumphant prize. Proud of this pride,
He is contented thy poor drudge to be,
To stand in thy affairs, fall by thy side.
No want of conscience hold it that I call
Her "love", for whose dear love I rise and fall.

Cupid's too young to know morality,
But all know love provokes our inner sense.
So, sweet cheat, don't promote what's wrong in me
In case you share the guilt of my offence.
For, you betraying me, I then betray
My higher self to my coarse body's treason:
My soul will tell my body that it may
Win through with love: flesh needs no further reason,
But rising at your name will point to you
As its triumphant prize. Puffed out with pride,
It is content to toil until you're through,
To stand for you and then fall by your side.
Don't say I lack uprightness when I call
Her "love", for whose dear love I rise and fall.

SONNET 152: In this, the last of the mistress sonnets to address her directly, Shakespeare's bitterness resurges in full, seeming to herald the end of the affair.

The poet admits that, in loving Rosaline, he has broken a vow. This admission continues the sense of autobiography, as does the unglamorous ending portrayed here. Shakespeare married at the age of eighteen.

The compression of syntax in lines 2 to 4 makes it difficult for readers like us, who are not privy to the situation, to understand the nature of the two vows broken by his mistress.

Most commentators think, as do I, that the bed-vow of original line 3 is a reference to her marriage vows. However, the expression is not used elsewhere by Shakespeare and so its meaning is heavily dependent on its context here. Rowse sees it as a promise made in bed to the poet (the breach of which promise was followed by a reconciliation and a new breach). Either way it seems that "*in act*" (a colloquialism for sexual activity) she broke a vow.

What was the vow of "*hate*"? Perhaps, in response to Shakespeare's complaints, and having pointed out his own infidelity, she told him that she would do what, or whom, she liked.

SONNET 152

In loving thee thou know'st I am forsworn,
But thou art twice forsworn to me love swearing:
In act thy bed-vow broke and new faith torn,
In vowing new hate after new love bearing.
But why of two oaths' breach do I accuse thee,
When I break twenty? I am perjured most,
For all my vows are oaths but to misuse thee,
And all my honest faith in thee is lost.
For I have sworn deep oaths of thy deep kindness,
Oaths of thy love, thy truth, thy constancy,
And, to enlighten thee, gave eyes to blindness,
Or made them swear against the thing they see.
For I have sworn thee fair: more perjured eye,
To swear against the truth so foul a lie.

In loving you, you know I am forsworn,
But twice so you, bed-stray, who swore to me
Your love in hollow words: a vow still-born
When new love brought new vow of cruelty.
But why of two oaths' breach make I ado,
When I break twenty? My words are more crossed,
Since all my vows are oaths that mis-sell you,
And all my honest faith in you is lost.
For I have sworn deep oaths of your deep kindness,
Oaths of your love, your truth, your constancy,
And, to enhance you, cloaked my eyes in blindness,
Or made them misreport that which they see.
For I have sworn you fair: more perjured I,
To swear against the truth so foul a lie.

SONNET 153: Sonnets 153 and 154 appear to provide a postscript to Shakespeare's affair with his mistress, through the witty use of a myth found in a classical collection of poetry known as the Greek Anthology.

The Anthology depiction shows the love god, Cupid, in sleep, having given the Love-Nymphs care of his flaming torch (this brand being a more ancient accessory than the bow and arrows used by him to ignite love in later myths). The Nymphs decide, instead, to extinguish the brand in water, aiming to quench desire in the hearts of men. However, they merely succeed in creating a permanent hot spa.

The re-lighting of Cupid's *"brand"*, in line 9, plays on the romantic conception, common in sonnets of the time, that fiery beams would dart from the female subject's eyes, either to wither a disdained object of her attention or to stoke up passion.

Many commentators see in this sonnet a reference to venereal disease, as well as a sickness of the heart. If the poet took to seeking hot waters as a cure (whether at Bath, a venue of Shakespeare's stage company when on tour, or elsewhere) it would seem likely that some form of physical ailment was involved.

Some commentators perceive sexual allusions in the process of steeping of Cupid's "brand", as described in the first two quatrains.

To my mind, such allusions are clearly intended in the final quatrain and concluding couplet. The poet makes repeated reference to his mistress's *"eye"* in the singular (even at the cost of mis-rhyme in the original printing of line 14) – see commentary on this term at Sonnet 133.

SONNET 153

Cupid laid by his brand and fell asleep:
A maid of Dian's this advantage found,
And his love-kindling fire did quickly steep
In a cold valley-fountain of that ground:
Which borrowed from this holy fire of love
A dateless lively heat, still to endure,
And grew a seething bath, which men yet prove
Against strange maladies a sovereign cure.
But at my mistress' eye love's brand new fired,
The boy for trial needs would touch my breast:
I, sick withal, the help of bath desired
And thither hied, a sad distempered guest.
But found no cure: the bath for my help lies
Where Cupid got new fire, my mistress' eye.

Diana's maid found Cupid fast asleep,
And took her chance to take hold of his brand,
And its love-kindling fire, which she did steep
In a cold cleft-spring flowing near to hand:
Which took from this divine, love-giving fire
An everpresent heat which still endures,
And in whose seething bath men yet aspire
To find for strange diseases sure-fire cures.
But Cupid from my mistress' eye re-lit
His brand, which he then tested on my breast,
And sickened me, who went to Bath unfit,
In search of aid, a sad distempered guest:
But found no cure; the bath for me must lie
Where Cupid got new fire, my mistress' eye.

SONNET 154: In this, the last in the sequence of the mistress sonnets, Shakespeare replays the preceding poem in different words.

The *"general of hot desire"* (line 7) can be interpreted, Rowse points out, either as a title (given to Cupid in *Love's Labour's Lost*, (*III, i, 175*) or as the Generator of hot desire. Other commentators point out the sexual allusion arising, if his *"hot desire"* is taken as the object of the disarming in line 8.

It seems that Shakespeare, infected physically or otherwise, remains sorely in need of his lost mistress.

SONNET 154

The little Love-god lying once asleep
Laid by his side his heart-inflaming brand,
Whilst many nymphs that vowed chaste life to keep
Came tripping by; but in her maiden hand
The fairest votary took up that fire
Which many legions of true hearts had warmed;
And so the general of hot desire
Was sleeping by a virgin hand disarmed,
This branch she quench-ed in a cool well by,
Which from love's fire took heat perpetual,
Growing a bath and helpful remedy
For men diseased; but I, my mistress' thrall,
Came there for cure, and this by that I prove,
Love's fire heats water, water cools not love.

Once, as Cupid slept recumbently,
Aside him lain his heart-inflaming brand,
Some nymphs, who'd vowed a life of chastity,
Came tripping by: but in her maiden hand
The fairest of these sylphs took up that fire,
Which had infused the hordes of Love's great band.
And so the General of hot desire
Was, when asleep, disarmed by virgin hand.
His brand she steeped within a close cool well,
Which took eternal heat from lovefire's stave
To form a bath for illnesses' dispel
From men diseased: but I, my mistress' slave,
Came there for cure and from it I prove this:
Water fired by love cannot cool love's kiss.

PUBLISHED BY WHOSE WILL?

Introduction

On a casual reading of the title, *Shakespeare's Sonnets*, one might suppose that the work so entitled had been published by its author. However, the detached air of the caption, its terseness (out of line with the then standard practice of expansiveness by author-publishers), the unattractiveness to public airing of much of the contents, the absence of copyright law, the precedent for unauthorised publications in Shakespeare's name, and the lack of the usual author dedication or endorsement, together suggest strongly that Shakespeare was uninvolved in the process of publication.

In 1841 a scholar, Charles Knight, put forward the notion that the Sonnets were published without Shakespeare's consent. He was championed in this view by Sidney Lee, who, in 1905, produced a detailed analysis to support his view that the Sonnets had, in effect, been pirated by Thorpe or his procurer. These views swayed the opinions of experts for the next seventy or so years, albeit with dissenting exceptions, such as Sir Edmund Chambers.

However, the academic wheel has continued to turn and there is now a strong groundswell of support among many current Shakespearean scholars for the theory that the author was proactive in the process of publication. Many (though far from all) of Lee's observations have been discounted.

This process has been given energy by the dependence of a number of Sonnet interpretation theories on the assumption that the author instigated publication. Let us consider the more promising of a number of arguments made to this end.

The theory of numerical correlation

The support for Shakespeare's proactivity in publishing is based partly on the fact that there is, undeniably, an order in the sequencing of the sonnets. Some scholars believe that they contain numerical associations, which only the author would have been concerned to incorporate. Other, less conventional enthusiasts perceive coded messages within the sonnets which, they suggest, show that the author must have approved publication (though some think he may not have been Shakespeare).

However, if one accepts that they were originally filed in a substantially coherent fashion, the order of the sonnets can be explained credibly without the author's involvement in their publication. Such order would probably have been largely preserved if they had been filched or if they had been obtained in line with Charlotte Stopes' theory (as described within Part I of this book).

And we need to be cautious as to the existence of numerical associations or hidden codes. A mind, set on extracting patterns, can find such things with surprising ease in a sufficiently large collection of data and/or available associations. This is powerfully illustrated by the so-called Bible Code phenomenon, in which analyses of equidistant letter sequences in the original Hebrew Torah suggest hidden biographies and prophecies of world events, seemingly fulfilled[114]. The writing of Hebrew, which has no vowels, assists this process by greatly multiplying potential associations. However, the scientist, Brendan McKay, and others have shown that similar impressive messages (including fulfilled prophesies) can be extracted in profusion by the same process from the English text of ordinary books such as *Moby Dick[115]*.

Nevertheless, some accomplished and respected Shakespearean experts appear to be persuaded by the Sonnet number correlation theory, which fact invites a closer look at the concept. At its core is an assumption that any correspondence

---

[114] Dr Jeffrey Satinover gives a full account of the phenomenon in his *The Truth behind the Bible Code*

[115] The scientists proclaim "We have performed many independent scientific tests of the Bible Codes claims. All of them failed to detect anything not easily explained by random chance". Their detailed analysis is recorded on the website http://cs.anu.edu.au/~bdm/dilugim/torah.html as of June 2009

between a sonnet sequence number and any part of its content was deliberate.

For example, Sonnet 12 starts with the line "When I do count the clock that tells the time". Under the theory this is regarded as evidence of editorial placement of the sonnet because a clock face is divided into 12 hours.

However, the same argument could be applied to a placing at 24, because the second line goes on to say "And see the brave day sunk in hideous night", which (one could argue if it suited the cause) clarifies that a full day's worth of clock hours is being envisaged. Or one could assign the number 60, this being the number of minutes on a clock face. Or even 78, this being the sum of the hour numerals "counted": such flexibility would be no more extreme than associating Sonnet 20 with the sum of a human's digits, as suggested by one numerologist.

Thus, on a cursory examination only, Sonnet 12 could be placed in at least four different places in the sequence and sonnet numerologists could justify that placing by reference to the concept of a clock, which itself is only one of the many images portrayed by that sonnet. Looked at in reverse, the number twelve can be evoked through many other sonnets not so numbered, such as 7 (with its references to noon), 46 (with its image of an inquest or jury), 104 (with its four seasons in triplicate and a dial, ie clock) and any of at least ten other sonnets which refer to "hours".

The second line of Sonnet 60 contains the phrase "our minutes". Number theorists see a pun on "hour" and a deliberate allocation of the sonnet number to correspond with the number of minutes in an hour. They argue against coincidence by pointing to this sonnet's interruption of a theme of jealousy, which runs though some of the surrounding sonnets. However, they ignore the similar interruption of this jealousy theme by Sonnet 59 (which, incidentally, contains unsung number references in "second", "five", "hundred", "first" and "day") and the existence of stronger available associations with 60 such as the "dial", "minutes" and "time" of Sonnet 77.

The grand climacteric of sixty three (so called because it is a multiple of 9 and 7, each perceived as a significant number) was thought in Elizabethan times to represent an ominous year in the cycles of a human life. Sonnet 63 discusses the ravages of ageing and its remedies through immortal verse[116] and this is pointed to by sonnet numerologists as evidence of why the sonnet was assigned such a meaningful number (though the same theme crops up elsewhere, before and after in the Sonnets).

However, other numbers more significant to Elizabethan human life traditions, 21 and 70, produce no sonnets on the subjects of adulthood and death. Disciples point to Sonnet 71, which does discuss death (as do a number of other sonnets), and suggest that it is allocated this number because it is the first sonnet after the death number of 70. Presumably, if death had instead been discussed in Sonnet 69, it would have been permissible to argue that this placement was because it was foreshadowing the death number.

Sonnet 66 complains of the unfairness of society. One sonnet numerologist has suggested that the sonnet number of 66 is probably deliberate, because it is a multiple of six and such multiples are perceived to have adverse connotations, alluding to the Biblical Beast of *Revelations* (whose number was 666). I have been unable to find any corroboration for this presumed association of lesser multiples of six.

Sonnet 76 deals with the theme of inspiration. So does Sonnet 38, each including variants of the words "argument" and "invention". Number theorists see a numerical significance in the placing of this sonnet, because its number is twice that of Sonnet 38. However, there is no significance attached to the number 38 and in this sequence of 154 sonnets the chances are high that one can find a pair in which one sonnet bears a number equivalent to twice that of another and shares some commonality of topic. For example, Sonnets 35 and 70 each address the flaws of the youth and refer to both "canker" and "bud". In none of these four sonnets is there any reference which could be related to their sequence number.

---

[116] Although, as revealed in commentary on this sonnet in Part II, the real thrust of the poem is a bawdy representation of life's experiences – not old age.

Sonnets 77 and 81 are regarded as special sonnets by some sonnet numerologists, because these numbers are multiples of the two supposedly significant numbers, 7 and 9. Some suggest further that the relevant sonnet themes (keeping a notebook and the victory of poetry over time) interrupt an otherwise continuous theme of poetic rivalry stretching over Sonnets 76-86. Therefore, they argue, these two sonnets must have been inserted as number signifiers, even though there is nothing in the sonnets which is evocative of these numbers.

However, the themes of these sonnets can be readily assimilated within the context of the poetic rivalry and, as brought out in Part I, it is unlikely that 76 really does signify the beginning of the rivalry (and therefore, that the theme is unbroken but for Sonnets 77 and 81). Nor do numerologists explain why 84 is excluded from such special treatment (as are many multiples of 7 and 9 elsewhere in the Sonnets sequence).

In selecting the above sample I had regard only for the least far-fetched of the arguments. Nevertheless, each of the examples displays the following characteristics: (i) a perceived significance of number is plucked from a huge pool of potential numerical associations; (ii) each perceived principle of correlation fails to work consistently; (iii) alternative interpretations, equally if not more plausible, are ignored.

On the face of it, therefore, the evidence for deliberate correlation of numbers in the sequencing of the Sonnets is unconvincing. In turn, this "evidence" fails to support the notion of an author editing the collection with publication in mind.

The Thomas Heywood Letter

Supporters of the author-as-publisher theory have pointed to a number of documented remarks, which they suggest strengthen their case. Some of these can be seen immediately to be too tenuous, but there are three arguments which appear to be advanced or quoted as a matter of course, and which are worth looking at more closely.

The first argument is based on a letter written by Thomas Heywood (an actor, playwright and poet), who appended it to his pamphlet supporting the world of the playhouse against

Puritanism. This pamphlet, *An Apology for Actors*, was published in 1612. However, in order to appreciate the contents of the letter, it is necessary to introduce some background information.

In 1599 a publisher, named William Jaggard, had produced a second edition of a collection of poems entitled *The Passionate Pilgrime by W. Shakespeare*. There is no surviving intact first edition, which is believed to have been published shortly before, triggering the second edition through the high demand it generated. The collection included versions of Sonnets 138 and 144 (which is why it is generally accepted that many or most of the Sonnets were written before 1600), three versions of pieces from *Love's Labour's Lost* and fifteen other poems, many of which are now known to have been composed by other authors.

It seems almost certain that Shakespeare had not authorised publication of any of these pieces, nor the use of his, by then, famous name. However, the law on copyright in those days was very different to now (in essence the owner of a manuscript had copyright), and there is no evidence of an objection at that time by Shakespeare.

In 1609 Jaggard went on to publish a collection of poetry by Heywood, entitled *Troia Britannica*, including two lengthy poems described as Epistles of *Paris to Helen* and *Helen to Paris*. In the same year, as we already know, Thomas Thorpe published the Sonnets.

Then, in 1612, Jaggard produced a third and expanded edition of *The Passionate Pilgrime*. This edition was bulked out with a number of Heywood's poems, including the two Epistles mentioned above, all lifted from *Troia Britannica*. The title page displayed the title, *The Passionate Pilgrime*, with Shakespeare's name printed halfway down the page then, underneath, the narrative: "*Whereto is newly added two Love-Epistles*". Heywood's name was not mentioned and Jaggard clearly intended that prospective buyers should continue to assume that *Pilgrime* was Shakespeare's work and that *Pilgrime 3* contained new poems by Shakespeare.

Heywood was sufficiently upset by this to include it in a letter to his friend, Nicholas Okes, a printer, and it is this letter which he appended to his 1612 pamphlet, *An Apology for Actors*. The letter included complaints as to the quality of printing of *Troia*, followed by the narrative pointed to by proponents of the Shakespeare-as-Sonnets-Publisher theory. This narrative is set out below in bold lettering. My clarifications are set out in parentheses.

"Here likewise, I must necessarily insert a manifest injury done me in that worke [*Troia*], by taking the two Epistles of *Paris to Helen* and *Helen to Paris*, and printing them in a lesse volume [*Pilgrime 3*], under the name of another [Shakespeare], which may put the world in opinion I might steale them [the two Epistles] from him [Shakespeare]; and hee to doe himselfe right, hath since published them [the Epistles] in his owne name [in *Pilgrime 3*]: but as I must acknowledge my lines not worthy his [Shakespeare's] patronage, under whom he [Jaggard] hath publisht them so the Author [Shakespeare] I know much offended with M. Jaggard that (altogether unknowne to him) presumed to make so bold with his name."

What the above shows clearly is that Shakespeare had not authorized use of his name in *Pilgrime 3*. Heywood is publicly countering the possibility that people might think him a plagiarist in his *Troia* (because the Epistles also appeared in a *Pilgrime 3* attributed only to Shakespeare). In addition, he may have forced Jaggard to change tack, because the publisher did produce a second version of the *Pilgrime 3* title sheet without the misleading references.

What Heywood's text does not say, or even hint, however, is that Shakespeare had published the 1609 edition of the Sonnets. Those who interpret the above wording in such a way are assuming that the "hath since published them", in the middle of the script, is referring to the Sonnets. But such an interpretation fits neither the sense of the paragraph (taking account of which publications were under Jaggard's control), nor the reality that the Epistles never appeared in the Sonnets (as they would have to in order to support such an interpretation).

The thoughts of William Drummond

The next argument is based on a supposed entry in the papers of the Scottish poet, William Drummond (1585-1649) couched in the following terms: *"The last we have are Sir William Alexander and Shakespear, who have lately published their Works"*. The theory assumes that the Shakespearean "Works" were the Sonnets and that Drummond, in using this terminology, must have known that Shakespeare was responsible for their publication.

The relevant passage is sourced from a section of a book published in 1711 entitled *"The Works of William Drummond of Hawthornden"*, edited by Bishop Sage and Thomas Ruddiman. The section is entitled *Heads of a Conversation betwixt the Famous Poet Ben Johnson* [sic], *and William Drummond of Hawthornden, January 1619*, and it purports to record matters arising in a single conversation when Jonson (having walked to Scotland in 1618) visited Drummond in his secluded home near Edinburgh.

The section falls into three parts (though these are not identified as such). Part 1 summarises Drummond's record of Ben Jonson's tales from his life, as well as wide-ranging views on various English and Continental poets. Part 2 records Drummond's views on Jonson in rather unflattering terms (hardly likely to have been conveyed to Jonson, notwithstanding that these are recorded under the same "Heads of a Conversation" title). Part 3 is a summary of Drummond's views on English poets who had written on the subject of Love, in which Drummond applies the Renaissance poet, Petrarch, as a benchmark for his assessments.

However, it is unlikely that Part 1 was prepared by Drummond. In a paper entitled *Notes of Ben Jonson's Conversations with Drummond of Hawthornden, in the year 1619* (published by the Shakespeare Society in 1842) the historian, David Laing, demonstrates, from lengthy historical transcripts, that Drummond had prepared much fuller notes of what he had heard from Jonson over the course of a visit lasting several weeks. Part 1 appears to be a precis of those notes. Since Drummond had no reason to abridge notes which he had prepared (or to represent the discourse as occurring in only one conversation), it seems almost certain that this abridgement was effected by the editors of the 1711 Works.

Since Part 2 was almost certainly not the subject of conversation between the two parties, considerable doubt arises as to whether Part 3 was also dealt with in those conversations, particularly as it appears to cover a much narrower range within the topic of poets, as addressed by Jonson. The suspicion must arise that Part 3 may also be a summary and/or agglomeration by the editors of a longer note or notes, expressed in somewhat different terms by Drummond. Nevertheless, it seems that most scholars assume that Part 3 was extracted intact from a note prepared by Drummond at a date in, or after, 1614 (since part of the edited note refers to a publication not available until 1614).

The words relevant to our purposes are included in Part 3, which starts as follows:

> *Mr Drummond gave the following Character of several Authors.*
> *The Authors I have seen (saith he) on the Subject of Love, are the Earl of Surrey, Sir Thomas Wyat, (whom, because of their Antiquity, I will not match with our better Times) Sidney, Daniel, Drayton and Spencer. He who writeth the Art of English Poetry praiseth much Rawleigh and Dyer; but their works are so few that are come to my Hands, I cannot well say anything of them.*
> *The last we have are Sir William Alexander and Shakespear, who have lately published their works.*

The passage goes on to mention briefly Constable and Murray, but only to say that their poetry was excellent by hearsay only, since the latter could not be brought with "others" to publish their works. It then enlarges on Drummond's views on five of the "modern" poets he had "seen" (ie read): Sidney, Daniel, Alexander, Drayton and Spencer – but not the sixth, and last, Shakespeare.

This first section of Part 3, summarised above, forms an internally coherent discussion. It identifies six poets according to the stated criteria and then goes on to assess these poets (except for Shakespeare). It concludes by ranking three of the six poets in first, second and third places against the Petrarchan benchmark. It is self-standing and could, with reasonable probability, have been extracted by the editors from a separate note, which I will refer to as Source A.

However, the next section strays. It starts talking about Donne, Drayton's poem, *Polyolbion* (which was the work published in 1614, as mentioned above), Silvester and Hudson. There is no ranking against Petrarch, and the reference to Drayton appears disjointed in relation to his depiction in the first section. This section could well have been extracted by the editors from a note prepared subsequent to Source A, which I will refer to as Source B.

The reference to the poet bracketed in Source A with Shakespeare, Sir William Alexander, can only relate to Alexander's sonnet sequence published in 1604 under the title *Aurora*. This, therefore, begs the question of what Drummond might have meant by "lately published" in the context of our trying to guess the likely date(s) of his note(s). Shakespeare had published two lengthy poems (albeit on the subject of lust rather than love) in 1593 and 1594. However, there was, of course, *Pilgrime 1 or 2* from 1599 (only five years before *Aurora*) which looked like an anthology of love poetry published by Shakespeare – and the thinness and variability of this work may well explain why Drummond made no amplifying comments on Shakespeare.

I suggest, therefore, that there is a substantial possibility that Source A was prepared around 1605 or 1606 and that Source B was prepared in or after 1614. On this basis, which explains all the above-mentioned peculiarities of Section 3 (including "lately published"), Drummond's words on Shakespeare in this passage have no relevance, whatsoever, to the Sonnets.

At this point it is interesting to look at some detail of Drummond's reading lists. He was apparently a compulsive recorder, for he left behind lists of books he had read in each year from 1606 to 1614. In addition, in 1611 he compiled an inventory of his library. These lists were first published in David Laing's *A Brief Account of the Hawthornden Manuscripts* in *Transactions of the Society of Antiquaries of Scotland (Archaeologia Scotica), IV, 57-116*, and are reproduced in F.R. Fogle's *A Critical Study of William Drummond of Hawthornden*.

The annual reading lists are impressive in the quantity of material and diversity of author. However, the only works of Shakespeare which appear are *Romeo and Julieta, Loves Labors Lost, The Passionat Pilgrime, The Rape of Lucrece* and *A Midsommers Nights Dreame*, all of which appeared in Drummond's list of books read in 1606 (as does the *Aurora* of Alexander – also known as Menstre, after his family home in Menstre, Clackmannanshire). In each of the subsequent years up to, and including, the last listed, 1614, there is no mention of Shakespeare, and the Sonnets remain conspicuous by their absence.

Drummond's 1611 inventory of his library includes only three works by Shakespeare: *Venus and Adonis, The Rape of Lucrece* and *The Tragedie of Romeo and Julieta.*

On the basis of these lists, therefore, Drummond was familiar by 1606 with each of Shakespeare's published long poems and with *Pilgrime 1 or 2* (and Alexander's *Aurora)* but there is no evidence that he ever had any familiarity with the Sonnets, let alone whether Shakespeare was truly responsible for their publication.

This well supports my suggestion of Sources A and B above, but allows a second possibility: that the whole of the edited Part 3 did, indeed, derive from material (or a single note) produced by Drummond in or after 1614, but that he had not at that time read the Sonnets. This would similarly explain why there is no amplification of Drummond's views on Shakespeare (and it would also effectively remove his comments from the context of the Sonnets' publication). But it would not, without some strain, explain the phrase "lately published".

However, let us theorise a third possibility: that Drummond did get around to reading the Sonnets at some time after 1614. In that case, provided the reading occurred before preparation of the note, it would surely have been the Sonnets that he was referring to in that note, as popularly supposed. But this would make even more peculiar the absence of elaboration on Shakespeare, in contrast to the other five poets identified as having been read. Why would Drummond feel unable to comment on the style of a poet whose one hundred and fifty four sonnets he had read relatively recently? And why would

Drummond include *Aurora* (published at least ten years earlier) in the same category of "lately published"? I suggest that this is the least likely by far of the three possibilities.

Even if these issues are glossed over or ignored, the question then would be how tightly constructed was the reference in either the original note or in an abridged version? It would be very easy, in referring to a book entitled *Shakespeare's Sonnets*, to write that Shakespeare had "published" his work (particularly if the author knew that Alexander had indeed published *Aurora*, and couldn't be bothered to complicate a sentence which referred to both poets). Much would depend on the purpose and precision of the original note, and the precision and author of any abbreviation, as well as the extent of Drummond's own knowledge of the process behind the publication of the Sonnets.

Overwhelmingly, therefore, it seems that the Drummond notes are as far away from being a credible factor in the Sonnets publication debate as was Hawthornden from seventeenth century London.

Ben Jonson's offering

A third argument arises from the assumption that the Sonnets' dedication (signed by Thomas Thorpe) was in accordance with Shakespeare's instructions and was addressed to the Earl of Pembroke. If this supposition can be strengthened so, too, will be its precursor, that Shakespeare was instrumental in the publication.

To this end proponents point to a dedication to Pembroke made by Ben Jonson on publication of his *Epigrammes* (as part of his *Workes*) in 1616. The rather tortuous dedication proceeds as follows:

TO THE GREAT EXAMPLE OF HONOR AND VERTUE, THE MOST NOBLE WILLIAM, EARLE OF PEMBROKE, L. CHAMBERLANE, & C.

MY LORD. While you cannot change your merit, I dare not change your title: It was that made it, and not I. Under which name, I here offer to your Lo: the ripest of my studies, my Epigrammes; which though they carry danger in the sound, doe not therefore seeke your shelter: For, when I made them, I had nothing in my conscience, to expressing of which I did need a cipher. But, if I be falne into those times, wherein, for the likeness of vice, and facts, every one thinks another's ill deeds objected to him; and that in their ignorant and guiltie mouthes, the common voice is (for their securitie) Beware the Poet, confessing, therein, so much love to their diseases, as they would rather make a partie for them, than be rid, or told of them: I must expect at your Lo: hand the protection of truth, and libertie, while you are constant to your owne goodnesse. In thankes whereof, I returne you the honor of leading forth so many good, and great names (as my verses mention on the better part) to their remembrance with posteritie.

Supporters of the theory focus on the early words beginning "My Lord" and ending with "cipher". Taken alone, these lines might suggest that Jonson is having a dig at someone who had addressed Pembroke in an inappropriate fashion and whose works contained veiled allusions to shameful or inappropriate deeds: someone who perhaps had addressed him as "Mr WH"?

However, by focusing on only two of the sentences one loses their context. On assessing the dedication more fully, including its addressee headlines which import grandiose personal qualities into Pembroke's title, the message conveyed is along the following lines:

O honourable, virtuous and noble Lord, I must call you this because that is what you are and will remain. I offer you these Epigrammes, in which, though their description may suggest hidden messages, I can assure you there is no encoded scurrilous matter. Nevertheless, I know that you will defend me against any scandal-loving hypocrites who might in future read improprieties into the words and think that I am referring to them, and that you will protect my freedom with the same constancy as you preserve your goodness. In return for which, I have dedicated these, my most productive pieces, to you ahead of all the other great names mentioned in my works.

Jonson's inclination to pontificate on titles in the opening remarks of an address is, incidentally, well illustrated by the following extract from a letter he wrote to William Drummond in May 1619 (as recorded in Fogle's *A Critical Study of William Drummond of Hawthornden*):

"*To my worthy, honoured and beloved Friend, Mr William Drummond, Edinburgh.*

Most loving and beloved Sir,

Against which titles I should most knowingly offend if I made you not at length some accounts of myself, to come even with your friendship.........."

Seen in the above lights, the dedication to Pembroke suggests an author who is most concerned that he should be protected from accusations of libel, or other unacceptable messages. He butters up his patron with references to constancy of virtue in order to strengthen the patron's inclination to provide protection, should it ever become needed. Far from looking at the works of another, his dedication appears to be concerned solely with his own work and safety.

Does such an interpretation fit the facts? Jonson certainly had a track record of falling foul of the authorities. In 1598 he was jailed for three months after the Privy Council deemed his satirical comedy, *The Isle of Dogs* (jointly written with Thomas Nashe), to be lewd, slanderous and seditious. In 1604 he was again hauled before the Privy Council on charges of "Popery" and treason for his play *Sejanus his Fall.* Such charges could have resulted in his execution. In 1605 he was jailed for remarks in a play which were taken to be offensive to the Scots.

As for the situation some ten years later, Martin Butler comments in his article, "*Jonson's Folio and the Politics of Patronage*" (published in the Summer 1993 edition of *Criticism*). Here he explains that, from around 1612, the political and social landscape had been shifting in a way which constrained or punished certain artistic expressions. Poets, such as Chapman, Donne and Campion, had fallen foul of this trend. Jonson, himself, in compiling his *Workes* (a large collection of pieces created separately over the years) was careful to edit this, excluding certain pieces which were no longer in tune with the socio-political scene (one or two epigrams amongst them), and amending previous narrative.

Epigrammes was a substantial collection of pithy verses on a wide range of subjects (including social issues or events), often couched in a satirical way. Given all these circumstances, there are no reasonable grounds for an interpretation of its dedication as a sideswipe at Shakespeare or any other publication.

The negative evidence

There are several significant factors in the background, which work against the theory of an author who was proactive in the publication of the Sonnets. There were no copyright laws to protect him against publication of manuscripts which had been obtained legitimately. The collection lacked the customary author's dedication or introduction (how much effort would this have cost the master wordsmith?). And there were strongly adverse implications for his reputation and his relationships with fair friend, society, daughters and (possibly) wife of publicising sonnets such as 20, 52, 110, 151 and 152. Given this background, we need to see positive credible evidence before accepting that, in all probability, Shakespeare engineered their publication.

However, such evidence has yet to emerge, after more than a century of determined searching by theorists inclined to a Shakespeare who initiated the publication of the Sonnets. It remains a fact that the only two significant works of poetry, known to have been published with Shakespeare's consent, were ones which carried his written endorsement in the form of a dedication (both to the Earl of Southampton). Conversely, two other works issued under his name, but without his endorsement (*Pilgrime*s 2 & 3) were clearly published without his involvement and apparently against his wishes.

Some have suggested that the recurring Sonnet theme of immortalization indicates an intention by Shakespeare to publish, since poems in manuscript were less likely to survive. However, immortalization was a popular conceit of poets, many of whom neither initiated nor expected publication[117]. Shakespeare, a pragmatist, showed no signs elsewhere that he was concerned with the survival of his works beyond their use to him. The image in Sonnet 17 of his ageing yellowed papers in some distant future

---

[117] As pointed out by Lee, Sir Philip Sidney, in his 'Apologie for Poetrie' (1595) wrote that it was the common habit of poets to tell you that they will make you immortal by their verses.

suggests that he did not envisage replication of his sonnets. And, if he had truly wished to ensure his friend's immortality, he would surely have arranged a dedication, or some other device, to identify that friend clearly to future generations.

In contrast to his public plays and publicly dedicated poems, *Shakespeare's Sonnets* was, apparently, not well received at the time. There was no reprint until several decades later (and then the reproduction was in a heavily edited and censored form). Apart from the sensitive nature of the relationship issues (and possible suppressory opposition in 1609 by an aristocratic Fair Friend), the poems contained themes inappropriate to public airing[118]. Their reception was probably well captured by the indignant remark scrawled at the end of an original edition by an early reader of the published sonnets: "What a heap of wretched Infidel Stuff"!

Shakespeare was a master of judgement when it came to assessing what would appeal to his public. How likely is it that he would get this so wrong had he been in a position to control the editing and publication of the Sonnets?

Finally, let us look again at the dedication to Mr WH, argued by some supporters of this theory to be the poet's authorised words, supposedly addressed to a beloved earl:

To the only begetter of these ensuing sonnets Mr WH all happiness and that eternity promised by our ever-living poet wisheth the well-wishing adventurer in setting forth. TT.

Let us compare it to the dedication (undisputedly by Shakespeare) of *The Rape of Lucrece* (genuinely addressed to a beloved earl):

To the RIGHT HONOURABLE HENRY WRIOTHESLEY, Earl of Southampton, and Baron of Titchfield.

The love I dedicate to your Lordship is without end: whereof this Pamphlet without beginning is but a superfluous Moiety [part]. *The warrant I have of your Honourable disposition, not the worth of my untutored Lines*

---

[118] In their portrayals of masturbation, homosexuality and marital infidelity and in the apparent preclusion of the orthodox Christian belief in resurrection of the body.

makes it assured of acceptance. What I have done is yours, what I have to do is yours, being part in all I have, devoted yours. Were my worth greater, my duty would show greater, meantime, as it is, it is bound to your Lordship; To whom I wish long life still lengthened with all happiness.

Your Lordship's in all duty,

WILLIAM SHAKESPEARE.

The contrasts perceptible from this exercise alone must make one doubt the dual proposition that the Sonnets dedication was addressed to an aristocrat and that Shakespeare instigated publication. But, if he was not involved in the dedication, this would weaken the proposition that he was the driver of their publication (and it would weaken to the point of destruction the theory that "Mr WH" was a reference to the Earl of Pembroke).

The primary proposition – that the author was also the architect of publication - has the big advantage of providing the most direct explanation for the publisher's source of material. But, without solid evidence to counteract the awkwardly negative indications against Shakespeare's involvement, it must remain no more than a possibility - to be weighed up in the light of other circumstances more strongly supported.

CROSSING PATHS WITH THOMAS NASHE

Thomas Nashe (1567-1601) was a satirical poet, playwright and author who studied at St John's, Cambridge, leaving around 1587. Here he would have become acquainted with Henry Wriothesley, Earl of Southampton, who attended the same college from age 12, between 1585 and 1589.

After graduation, Nashe became part of the London literary scene. Constantly in need of funds, he was aided by a facile wit, but often afflicted by the reactions to its sarcasm, unleashed with little regard for the consequences[119]. He mocked a number of his contemporaries in print and, famously, he had a literary feud with the scholar and author, Gabriel Harvey (another Cambridge man), which lasted several years.

In the late 1580s and early 1590s he collaborated with Robert Greene (yet another Cambridge man), to whose work *Menaphon*, published in 1589, he provided a lengthy and rather pompous preface addressed "to the gentlemen students of both universities". Early on in this missive Nashe snipes at the misplaced verbosity of common workers who imitate *"vain-glorious tragedians"*. However, he blames this development mainly on the latter's *"idiot art-masters who intrude themselves to our ears as the alchemists of eloquence, who (mounted on the stage of arrogance) think to out-brave better pens with the swelling bombast of bragging blank verse"*. He goes on to typify such authors as *"deep-read schoolmen or grammarians,"* who have *"no more learning in their skull than will serve to take up a commodity, nor art in their brain than was nourished in a serving man's idleness"*. In other words, Nashe was saying, he deplored, even more than vainglorious actors, those playwrights

---

[119] Within an affectionate epitaph (discovered by Professor Duncan-Jones), his friend and collaborator, Ben Jonson, wrote the lines: "Of wit, throughout this land, none left behind: to equal him in his ingenious kind" and "When any wronged him, living, they did feel: his spirit, quick as powder, sharp as steel".

who had not received a university education and who were daring to attempt to emulate their betters.

Greene died in September 1592. Soon after his death a publisher, Henry Chettle, produced a pamphlet entitled (in its modern rendition) *Groatsworth of Wit*, which was attributed to Greene. It comprises a rambling monologue of semi-autobiographical parables and poems, repentance for his own deeds, advice to and castigation of certain acquaintances and a letter of remorse to his wife, all said to have been left by Greene for posthumous publication.

Towards the end of this collection is a section addressed to "fellow scholars about this city", which includes the famous words: "*there is an upstart Crow, beautified with our feathers, that with his tiger's heart wrapt in a player's hide, supposes he is as well able to bombast out a blank verse as the best of you: and being an absolute Johannes factotum* [Johnnie-do-it-all], *is in his own conceit the only Shake-scene in a country*".

Most scholars consider that, with the parody of a line in *Henry VI, Part 3*, the Crow (and Shake-scene) was probably Shakespeare (who never went to university and who was not then accorded the status of gentleman). However, the passage contains attacks on several writers, some, or all, of whom suspected Nashe as being the true author of these words. This is evidenced by Chettle recording their accusation (and denying Nashe's authorship) and by Nashe's need to issue his own denial (in a letter published in the second edition of his work, *Pierce Pennilesse*).

Despite the denials (and the fact that Nashe himself fits the profile of one of the writers taken to task by Greene – albeit as a "sweet boy", dealt with more lightly than the others) a number of scholars down the years have continued to believe that he was the author of the attacks. However, whether or not this was the case, the point here is that people who knew Nashe at the time must have had good reason to believe that he continued to hold the above-mentioned strong views on unqualified actor-authors.

Between 28 April 1593 (when it was registered at the Stationers Company) and 12 June 1593 (when a purchase of a copy was recorded[120]), Shakespeare published his poem, *Venus & Adonis*, which he dedicated to Southampton in the following terms (presented in modern spelling and with slightly modified punctuation).

To the Right Honourable Henry Wriothesley.
Earl of Southampton, and Baron of Titchfield.

Right Honourable,

I know not how I shall offend in dedicating my unpolished lines to your Lordship, nor how the world will censure me for choosing so strong a prop to support so weak a burden, only if your Honour seem but pleased, I account myself highly praised, and vow to take advantage of all idle hours, till I have honoured you with some graver labour. But if the first heir of my invention prove deformed, I shall be sorry it had so noble a godfather: and never after ear [cultivate] *so barren a land, for fear it yield me still so bad a harvest. I leave it to your Honourable survey, and your Honour to your heart's content, which I wish may always answer your own wish, and the world's hopeful expectation.*

Your Honour's in all duty,

William Shakespeare.

Subsequently, in September 1593, Nashe registered at the Stationers Company a novel entitled (in its modern form) *The Unfortunate Traveller*. Shortly thereafter he spent a few weeks in jail before being rescued, then sheltered, by Sir George Carey, the Captain-General of the Isle of Wight[121]. It was February 1594 before the novel was published, though its first edition carried an imprinted date of June 27, 1593, suggesting that Nashe had completed it shortly after *Venus & Adonis* was published.

In this first edition Nashe included the following lengthy dedication (whose spelling I have standardized, with minor

---

[120] By one, Richard Stonley, in his diary, now preserved at the Folger Shakespeare Library, Washington

[121] The circumstances are recorded in a letter from Carey to his wife, written in November 1593 and discovered by Professor Duncan-Jones. Nashe had been jailed for comments offensive to the London authorities in his work *Christe's Teares Over Jerusalem.*

punctuation changes and a split into paragraphs for easier assimilation).

To the Right Honourable Lord Henry Wriothesley
Earl of Southampton and Baron Titchfield.

Ingenuous honourable Lord, I know not what blind custom methodical antiquity has thrust upon us, to dedicate such books as we publish to one great man or another. In which respect (lest any man should challenge these, my papers, as goods uncustomed [unwanted] *and so extend upon them as forfeit to contempt) to the seal of your excellent censure, lo, here I present them to be seen and allowed. Prize them as high or as low as you list* [wish]: *if you set any price on them, I hold my labour well satisfied.*

Long have I desired to approve my wit unto you. My reverent dutiful thoughts (even from their infancy) have been retainers to your glory. Now at last I have enforced an opportunity to plead my devoted mind. All that is in this fantastical Treatise, I can promise, is some reasonable conveyance of history & variety of mirth. By diverse of my good friends have I been dealt with to employ my dull pen in this kind, it being a clean different vein from other my former courses of writing. How well or ill I have done in it I am ignorant (the eye that sees round about itself sees not into itself); only your Honour's applauding encouragement has power to make me arrogant.

Incomprehensible is the height of your spirit both in heroical resolution and matters of conceit. Unreprievably perishes that book whatsoever to wastepaper, which on the diamond rock of your judgement disasterly [disastrously] *chances to be shipwrecked. A dear lover and cherisher you are, as well of the lovers of Poets, as of Poets themselves. Amongst their sacred number I dare not ascribe myself, though now and then I speak English: that small brain I have to no further use I convert, save to be kind to my friends and fatal to my enemies. A new brain, a new wit, a new style, a new soul will I get me, to canonize your name to posterity, if in this my first attempt I be not taxed of presumption.*

Of your gracious favour I despair not, for I am not altogether Fame's outcast. This handful of leaves I offer to your view: to the leaves on trees I compare, which as they cannot grow of themselves except they have some branches or boughs to cleave to, & with whose juice and sap they be evermore recreated & nourished, so except these unpolished leaves of mine have some branch of Nobility whereon to depend and cleave, and with the vigorous nutriment of whose authorized commendation they may be continually fostered and refreshed, never will they grow to the world's good liking, but forthwith fade and die on the first hour of their birth.

Your Lordship is the large spreading branch of renown, from whence these my idle leaves seek to derive their whole nourishing: it rests you either scornfully shake them off, as worm-eaten and worthless, or in pity preserve them and cherish them for some little summer fruit you hope to find amongst them.

Your Honour's in all humble service:

Thos Nashe.

The dedication smacks of exaggerated servility and thinly concealed disdain for Southampton. Also, on comparing it to the *Venus* dedication, just published, it looks - as many have noted - like a deliberate parody of that script. Shakespeare's "unpolished lines" become Nashe's "unpolished leaves". His fear of offending corresponds to Nashe's concern that he "be taxed of presumption". The "first heir of invention", "idle hours" and "bad harvest" become respectively Nashe's "first attempt", producing "idle leaves" and "little summer fruit". Shakespeare's "strong prop" becomes Nashe's "large spreading branch of renown". Shakespeare's vow to work hard in order to honour with a graver labour becomes Nashe's intent to get a new brain, a new style and a new soul, suggesting that this is what Nashe believed Shakespeare to require, rather than hard work. And so on: insults, sarcasm and/or irony are discernible in almost every sentence from the first, which starts off by addressing Southampton as "ingenuous".[122]

The first edition of *Traveller* was followed, later in the year, by a second edition which excluded any dedication to Southampton: a circumstance open to more than one interpretation, but certainly the strong possibility that the original was offensive.

---

[122] Barnaby Barnes' *Parthenophil & Parthenophe* was also registered in May 1593, although it is unclear when it was published. In a supplicatory sonnet to Southampton, Barnes refers to "these worthless leaves ... sprung from a rude and un-manured land" and he respectfully seeks the earl's blessing. It may be that Nashe had seen this address and was mocking both it and the *Venus* dedication. However, in his parody there are no other correspondences with the Barnes sonnet and it is clear that the prime model for his mockery is the *Venus* address.

Such mockery may seem odd, given that many modern commentaries include Nashe in the list of authors to whom the Earl acted as patron. However, on closer inspection, it transpires that there is little to sustain the notion that Nashe was ever properly supported or rewarded by Southampton.

It seems likely that an undated, unprinted pornographic poem in manuscript, *The Choice of Valentines*, respectfully dedicated by Nashe to an unidentified "Lord S" was addressed to Southampton[123]. There is a strong hint of this in the opening verse to the addressee, which hails him (with similarity to the "Rose" connotations of the Sonnets) as a "sweet flower" and "fairest bud the red rose ever bare". However, the poem describes how its hero suffers from a mouthful of pubic hair and premature ejaculation (twice) in an exciting encounter with his lady-turned-prostitute, whereupon she is obliged to resort to the use of a dildo to obtain satisfaction. Moving stuff and very entertaining to the right audience, but hardly the sort of material with which a peer of the realm – however debauched - would wish to be associated. There is no evidence that this dedication was ever accepted.

More pertinently, in his concluding after-address to the reader in *Pierce Pennilesse*, first published around August 1592, Nashe rails at length against an unidentified patron, a Courtier who is avoiding him and who, he implies with a Latin maxim, has failed to deliver on promises of payment[124]. "Easy" says Nashe "for a goodly tall fellow that shines in his silks, to come and outface a poor simple pedant in his threadbare cloak, and tell him his book is pretty, but at this time he is not provided for him". He urges friends to be more careful in their dedications and "not cast away so many months' labour on a clown that knows not how to use a scholar: for what reason have I to bestow any wit on him, that will bestow none of his wealth on me".

---

[123] Others support Ferdinando Stanley, Lord Strange, who became the fifth Earl of Derby in 1593, though his standing (as a married man of rectitude and a serious potential claimant to the succession) is at odds with the poem's theme.

[124] The text may be read or downloaded free at the Internet Archive:
www.archive.org/stream/piercepenniless00nashgoog

The after-word continues in this vein, moving into generalities which angrily bemoan the poor treatment of authors by patrons and the baseness of some vainglorious peacocks of the aristocracy: "buckram giants", whom he contrasts with their more generous peers. Then the fulminations return to the subject of Nashe's private experience (as he puts it). Now, "with a tongue unworthy to name a name of such worthiness", he hails "that wonder, the matchless image of Honor, and magnificent rewarder of virtue, *Jove's Eagle-borne Ganymede*, thrice noble *Amyntas*".

Both Ganymede (a beautiful youth seduced and cosseted by the god, Jove) and Amyntas (a beautiful youth, who, in Virgil's Eclogues, was lusted after by the shepherd, Corydon, and gave himself to the herdsman, Menalcas), had associations with homo-eroticism. The effeminate-looking, youthful Southampton was, in a derisive sense, "thrice noble", having three titles of aristocratic address: Lord, Earl and Baron (used, perhaps pointedly, by Nashe in his address of the *Traveller* dedication, above). He was also by then a Courtier. With these facts we are put on alert that Nashe's words may now be dripping with sarcasm and that, if so, the only realistic candidate for the target of his attack is Southampton[125].

Reading on, we might initially think this notion mistaken, for Nashe says of his Amyntas: "In whose high spirit, such a Deity of wisdom appeareth, that if *Homer* were to write his *Odyssey* new (where under the person of *Ulysses* he describeth a singular man of perfection, in whom all ornaments both of peace and war are assembled in the height of their excellence) he need no other instance to augment his conceit, than the rare carriage of his honourable mind". However, on closer inspection, we can see a

---

[125] This is not an opinion I have seen shared. Other commentators dissociate this passage from the earlier one which complains of a niggardly patron. Rather than sarcasm, they see a eulogy. Sidney Lee believed this to be addressed to Southampton. However, others see praise of some different, beloved patron, commonly guessed to be Ferdinando Stanley, Sir John Hawkins or Lord Henry Compton. The current leader of choice, supported by Malone, is Lord Strange, though the justification is flimsy, being based primarily on a mooted representation of the latter as a recently deceased Amyntas by the poet, Spencer, in a later-dated amendment of his work, *Colin Clouts Come Home Againe*. More persuasive interpretations of the latter point instead to Thomas Watson, composer of works on Amyntas, which had won for him that shepherd-name (used, for example, in the poem, *Narcissus*, by Thomas Edwards).

double edge in the words "high" and "rare" which can be rendered respectively as "haughty" and "infrequent". Thereby appears a derogatory implication: that the perfection of the hero, Ulysses, can be exemplified merely by contrasting him to the character of Nashe's arrogant Amyntas (in whom wisdom and honour are rarely conveyed)[126].

Nashe goes on to remark that many authors praise their patrons and benefactors. However, if he were to contemplate such an exercise he would excoriate those who had been undeservedly beautified with the "periwigs" of poets' praises. He would wish to ensure that all received their just deserts and reputation, and to restore "stolen titles to their true owners", so that "None but thou, most curteous[127] Amyntas, be the second mystical argument of the knight of the Red-cross".

Here he is clearly referring to Spencer's recent part-completed and celebrated work, *The Faerie Queene*. In this poem of allegories one of its heroes, the Red Cross Knight, meets with a series of challenges. In the first he kills the monster, Error, who hates the light of truth. In his second confrontation (the "second mystical argument") Red-Cross fights and kills a renegade knight by the name of *Sansfoy* (meaning Faithless). In effect, then, Nashe is insulting his addressee, Amyntas, by suggesting that the latter should be regarded as the true personification of faithlessness[128]. On this basis, the passage is, indeed, a continuation of the earlier castigation of the niggardly patron.

This is borne out, as Nashe exclaims *"Oh decus atque aeui gloria summa tui"*, before embarking on a mock-reproach of Spencer for not praising that patron. The ambiguous Latin phrase can be rendered as a flattering "Oh distinction and experience: your most great glory" or as a disdainful "Oh plumage and time-

---

[126] Nashe uses similar associations (with height of spirit, measurement of heroism and conceit) in the third paragraph of the *Traveller* dedication, as shown earlier, where he says to Southampton *"Incomprehensible is the height of your spirit both in heroical resolution and in matters of conceit"*. The echo suggests a linkage which Nashe may have wished to emphasise.

[127] Though spelling was then variable, this form may well have been selected here to invoke curtness. Variants of "courtesy" included "courtesie", "cortesie" and "curtesie".

[128] There is an echo here of the opening section of *Pierce Pennilesse*, where the eponymous hero, a poverty-stricken scholar, complains of "promise-breach", the stingy "Mydas-eares" and "men of great calling" who "scarce him give thanks" for works dedicated.

serving: the totality of your reputation". As for Spencer, the latter had appended to *The Faerie Queene* a commendatory sonnet of accomplishments addressed to each of some twenty grandees of the land, including the Earls of Essex, Northumberland, Oxenford and Cumberland – but excluding the Earl of Southampton (and Lord Strange). Nashe twits him that he could "let so special a piller of nobility pass unsaluted". The word "piller" then had a secondary connotation of one who feeds rapaciously on society[129].

Spencer is, however, excused. With sarcastic praise of Amyntas, Nashe goes on to speculate that the very thought of the latter's far-derived (far-fetched[130]) descent and extraordinary parts, which had attracted all kinds of lover, must have driven the poet's creative muse to a renewed frenzy for the impending continuation of *The Faerie Queene*. He suggests that Spencer has refrained from mention of Amyntas in the first part of his work so that he might give the latter all the praise he deserves in the second. Whereupon Nashe offers his own sonnet, "wholly intended to the reverence of this renowned Lord (to whom I owe all the utmost[131] powers of my love and duty)". The sonnet starts by referring to Spencer's commendations, which excluded Amyntas, and concludes with these lines:

> *I read them all, and reverenced their worth,*
> *Yet wondered he left out thy memory.*
>
> *But therefore guessed I he suppressed thy name,*
> *Because few words might not comprise thy fame*

The last line has a sarcastic parallel meaning: it is saying your deeds are too small for even a few words on the subject to be found by Spencer.

---

[129] As reported under "caterpillar" in *A Dictionary of Sexual Language and Imagery in Shakespearean and Stuart Literature* by Gordon Williams

[130] The uncle of Southampton's grandfather (the first Earl of his line) had changed the family name from Writh to the grander sounding Wriothesley, based on a tenuous or wishful association with a personage of that name in the time of King John.

[131] "Utmost", which derives from "outmost", carries a parallel meaning of "most distant".

Nashe continues with the regret that it is too difficult in such a short passage to give most readers a common knowledge of Amyntas's "invaluable" (valueless) virtues and to show himself thankful in some part (perhaps his little toe) for benefits received. He concludes his word games with Latin quotations from Ovid's Love Poems. These, taken in isolation, suggest duty and fidelity by an honest servant and his just reward. The first excerpt, from Amores 1.3, translates along the lines of "Take one who would serve you through long years, one who knows how to love with a pure heart". The second, from Amores 1.10, suggests "Gather fruit from the bountiful fields of Alcinous; let the poor man be esteemed for his duty and fidelity".

In each case, however, the quotation comes from a passage which brings wider meaning. The first excerpt leads into an implied rebuke of an addressee who perceives the supplicator to be of too low a status for preferment. The second is preceded by an observation that it is perfectly appropriate to seek gifts from rich men, since they can afford to pay. Both of these wider scenarios fit the picture earlier painted by Nashe of his encounter with the niggardly patron.

This encounter is further touched upon in Nashe's subsequent exchanges with his great literary enemy, Gabriel Harvey. Harvey, a butt in *Pierce Pennilesse*, responded with his pamphlet, *Four Letters and Certain Sonnets*, registered on 4 December 1592. Within the fourth letter he accuses Nashe, and the recently deceased Greene, of being *"good for nothing... but to cast away themselves, to spoil their adherents, to prey upon their favourers, to dishonour their patrons, to infect the air where they breathe"*. Harvey clearly did not consider that Nashe's homilies on *Amyntas* were respectful of that patron.

Nashe's reply came within his *Strange News*, entered in the Stationers Register on 12 January 1593. Here he rebuts the accusation, saying of Harvey, *"He enviously endeavours, since he cannot revenge himself, to incense men of high calling against me, and would enforce it into their opinions that whatsoever is spoken in Pierce Pennilesse concerning peasants, clowns & hypocritical hotspurs, Midases, buckram giants & the mighty prince of darkness, is meant of them; let him prove it, or bring the man to my face to whom I ever made any undutiful exposition of it"*. Nashe goes on to claim that everything in *Pierce Pennilesse* had its precedent in foreign writings and that he made not "the least allusion to any man set above me in degree".

Now, this seems inconsistent with his after-word to the reader of *Pierce Pennilesse*, in which there is no doubt that Nashe is speaking for himself, and where he bitingly castigates certain men set above him in degree of social standing. Why would he seek to deny this?[132] The answer must lie in the form of his challenge to Harvey: "prove it". Harvey is thereby put in the uncomfortable, potentially dangerous position of being required to out an aristocrat whom he believes is the Amyntas and dishonourable catamite of Nashe's discourse.

Thus forced into playing Nashe's game, Harvey nevertheless responds with some skill within his rejoinder, the voluminous *Pierce's Supererogation*, which carries a prefatory address date of 16 July 1593 and was printed the following October[133]. Here he repeats his accusation, saying of Nashe: he had *"no reverence to his patrons, no respect to his superiors"*[134] and (later on in the pamphlet) that he *"shamefully and odiously misuseth every friend or acquaintance, as he hath served some of his favourablest patrons (whom, for certain respects, I am not to name)"*[135]. In this last clause, Harvey acknowledges that he is in a tricky position with regard to disclosure. However, elsewhere in the pamphlet he provides enough clues that Nashe (and anyone else in the know) will be left in no doubt that he has the ammunition to support his statements.

Within one of many sarcastic and verbose descriptions of Nashe are the following remarks: *"Art did but spring in such as Sir John Cheeke and M. Ascham, and wit bud in such as Sir Phillip Sydney and M. Spencer; which were but the violets of March, or the primroses of May: till the one began to sprout in M. Robert Greene, as in a sweating Imp*

---

[132] Nashe is possibly still playing with words and presenting only the appearance of such denial. The words "set above me in degree" are ambiguous, in that their meaning depends on the attribute or quality whose degree is in mind – such as honour, which Nashe believed Amyntas to lack. However, this possibility does not change the argument which follows.

[133] The text may be read or downloaded free at the Internet Archive:

http://www.archive.org/details/piercessupererog00harvrich

[134] Page 175 of the Internet Archive edition

[135] Page 209 of the Internet Archive edition

of the ever-green laurel; the other to blossom in M. Pierce Pennilesse[136], as in the rich garden of poor Adonis: both to grow to perfection in M. Thomas Nashe; whose prime is a harvest, whose Art a mystery, whose wit a miracle, whose style the only life of the press, and the very heart-blood of the Grape."[137] With his phrase "the rich garden of poor Adonis", Harvey is, I suggest, mocking Nashe's predicament of a rich patron with no cash to spare for his *Pierce Pennilesse*. Southampton was, by July 1593, synonymous with Adonis (being the dedicatee and thinly disguised hero of the recently published *Venus & Adonis*).

Harvey goes further. Later in his tract, he says he could "*here dismask such a rich mummer and record such a hundred wise tales of memorable note with such a smart moral as would undoubtedly make this pamphlet the vendablest book in London and the register one of the famousest authors in England. But I am none of those that utter all their learning at once. And the close man.... may per-case have some secret friends or respective acquaintance that in regard of his calling or some private consideration would be loathe to have his coat blazed or his satchel ransacked.*"[138]. In other words, Harvey is saying, "I have lots of scandalous information concerning a rich actor and a high-ranking person (with a heraldic coat of arms), which would make this pamphlet a best-seller and me famous – but I am too discreet and too loyal to tattle".

Could Harvey here be referring to Shakespeare as the "mummer"? His hints are intriguingly consistent with the story depicted by the Sonnets of an adulterous actor and his dark mistress, both intimately involved with an aristocratic young man. The prosperity of actors relative to that of scholars was a matter deplored by the latter in a number of writings of the time. To them "rich mummer" would be an apt, if derogatory, description. And, of course, Shakespeare was also then strongly associated

---

[136] Here Harvey is clearly referring to Nashe, as the author of *Pierce Pennilesse*. In his third of the *Four Letters* he had spoken of "M. Greene... most woefully faded... and his sworn brother, M. Pierce Pennilesse...his inwardest companion". In the fourth letter, as a preamble to the remark on dishonouring patrons, he refers to the "woeful Greene and beggarly Pierce Pennilesse, (as it were a grasshopper and a cricket, two pretty musicians, but silly creatures)". In *Pierce's Superorogation* he refers to "the young darling of *S. Fame*, Thomas Nash, alias Pierce Penniless"

[137] Page 33 of the Internet Archive edition

[138] Page 202 of the Internet Archive edition

with *Adonis*, for whose characterisation he could be assumed to have been richly rewarded – a point which Harvey would enjoy making to Nashe.

I suggest that Harvey goes on to cement all these associations and to mock Nashe, as he signs off his lengthy discourse with the following, otherwise strange and disconnected, statement: "I write only at idle hours, that I dedicate only to *Idle Hours*; or would not have made so unreasonably bold, in no needfuller discourse, than *the praise or Supererogation of an Ass*"[139]. With these pointed echoes of Shakespeare's *Venus* dedication to Southampton and his second, italic emphasis of "Idle Hours", Harvey puts the finishing touches to a necessarily convoluted series of messages to Nashe, which we can now summarise and paraphrase as follows. "I know, and you know, and he knows that in *Pierce Pennilesse* you were insulting Southampton, whom you depicted as a niggardly ganymede of a patron. And, by the way, not only did you fail to extract money from the young Adonis, but you were beaten to his riches by a lewd actor and part-time author – ha, ha!"

This evidence gleaned from Harvey is circumstantial. Nevertheless, my interpretations explain perfectly why he harks, as he does, on a "rich mummer", his reluctance to name Nashe's misused patron and his remarks on "poor Adonis" and "idle hours": oddities for which I have found no reasonable justification elsewhere[140].

Turning back to Nashe's *Pennilesse* after-word on Amyntas, anyone who (unlike the contemporary Harvey) regards this passage as eulogistic rather than sarcastic, must ask themselves why, in these circumstances, would the postulated benefactor be kept anonymous? When Nashe genuinely has thanks and praise for a patron there is neither anonymity nor scope for double-meaning.

---

[139] Page 214 of the Internet Archive edition

[140] It seems, too, that Shakespeare may have taken note and joined in the fun. In *Love's Labours Lost* he appears to caricature Harvey and Nashe as a comically unlikely couple, the pompous Armado and his page, the imp-like Moth. The evidence is adduced by Charles Nicholls in Chapter 14 of *A Cup of News*.

This can be seen clearly in his treatises *Christ's Teares* and *The Terrors of the Night*, augmented or completed over the winter of 1593/4, when he was given shelter in the Isle of Wight by its self-styled Governor, Sir George Carey. He dedicates these works with unambiguous, heartfelt praise to Carey's wife and daughter respectively and, within *Terrors*, shows great esteem of, and thanks to Carey and his family.

Here he also writes that there is no greater misery on earth than "long depending hope frivolously defeated", and explains that he knows this from a personal experience, which was only alleviated on obtaining Carey's kindness. Hardly consistent with any previous successful patronage.

All the indications, then, are that Southampton was the Amyntas and niggardly patron, who had "frivolously defeated" Nashe's hopes, and that it was this circumstance which triggered the derogatory dedication of *Traveller*.

Many commentators have regarded this dedication as a speculative and clumsy piece of writing, in which Nashe attempted to copy Shakespeare's approach because he believed that this had been successful in securing tangible rewards. Others have suggested that he was merely trying too hard to appear the independent, witty man of letters. Such assessments do not, however, take into account the many contrary indicators associated with *Pierce Pennilesse*, as well as its author's style, irony and forthright waspishness.

With the above background and context let us now focus on these words in the middle of Nashe's *Traveller* dedication: "*A dear lover and cherisher you are, as well of the lovers of Poets, as of Poets themselves. Amongst their sacred number I dare not ascribe myself, though now and then I speak English.*". It is now clear that the first sentence is intended as a mockery of Southampton. Nashe must, therefore, have believed his statement to be both true and unflattering. In turn, this points firmly to the Earl being involved in a situation identical to the triangular relationship depicted in Sonnets 40-42.

Of course, the poet(s) invoked could have been someone like the recently deceased Marlowe (reportedly having a fondness for boys, and another Cambridge man who overlapped with Southampton) – though Nashe is highly unlikely to have disparaged his English. However, the Sonnets aside, there is no evidence that Southampton cherished any poet before 1603, except Shakespeare, whose consecutive and exclusive dedications of *Venus* and *Lucrece* (the latter in remarkably warm terms) do suggest such a relationship. The poets, Barnabe Barnes and Gervase Markham made dedications to Southampton, in 1593 and 1595 respectively, but, in each case, he was just one of several dedicatees and far down in the pecking order. Nor was there any repeat dedication, suggesting that the first and only dedication to Southampton in each case was merely speculative. The reality – as Nashe found out – was that Southampton could not at that time afford to reward a string of poets.

In these circumstances, and with the lampooning of the *Venus* dedication, it becomes highly probable that the jibe on poets and their lovers related to Shakespeare, whether or not Nashe thought him mounted on "the stage of arrogance" and lacking at times in the skills of English.

There is an interesting postscript to these suggestions of disaffection between Nashe on the one hand and Southampton and Shakespeare on the other. An in-house play, *The Returne from Parnassus* (Part 1) was produced c.1600 by an anonymous writer and acted by students at Nashe's old college, St John's.

This play, the second part of a trilogy, is a satire on the trials and tribulations of University men as they make their way in the wider world. The first play introduced a character, *Ingenioso*, depicted as a clever but impoverished university alumnus, who, with allusions to phrases in works of Nashe, was clearly intended to represent the latter (or at least to embody his circumstances).

In the *Returne*, Ingenioso, a literary man, has a niggardly patron by the name of *Gullio*, portrayed as a pompous, gullible popinjay of a Courtier who has an inflated opinion of his abilities as a soldier, lover and man of the arts. Their interaction is presented in three instalments: in Scene 1 of Acts III, IV and V.

Gullio, it transpires, has been involved in several military campaigns, associated respectively with Cals (Cadiz), a Portugal voyage and, "very lately", Ireland. He is a frequenter of playhouses, proud of his "becoming" hair and has a foray to Paris on the agenda. All of the objective part of this portrait fits the

Southampton profile of late 1599 or 1600. It certainly does not fit Ferdinando Stanley, who had died in 1594, some years earlier[141].

Ingenioso is contemptuous of Gullio and makes a number of asides to the audience, dismissing the fop's honour, talents and tastes. However, because of his poverty, he is forced to kowtow to the wealthy patron.

Gullio needs some verse from Ingenioso in order to woo a woman who has caught his eye. He rejects all attempts other than those which are Shakespearean in style. He declaims, using lines recognizable in *Venus & Adonis* and *Romeo & Juliet*, and he extols Shakespeare cloyingly, including the line: "O sweet Master Shakespeare! I'll have his picture in my study at the court!"

When Ingenioso produces lines in the preferred manner Gullio approves: "Marry, sir, these have some life in them! Let this duncified world esteem of Spencer and Chaucer: I'll worship sweet Master Shakespeare and to honour him will lay his Venus and Adonis under my pillow!"

Unfortunately for Ingenioso, his Shakespearean-style contribution (accompanied by a letter and some mangled Latin from Gullio) fails to overcome the lady's antipathy and he is summarily dismissed by his ungrateful patron, to whom he bids good riddance with eloquent vilification.

Let me now recap with a summary of key events:

- In 1585-7 Nashe becomes acquainted with his fellow St John's student, Southampton, then an effeminate boy in his early teens.
- In 1589, in *Menaphon*, Nashe bitingly disparages playwrights who were not educated at university and who dare to write in blank verse.
- In 1592 Nashe completes *Pierce Pennilesse*. He is disappointed by an aristocratic patron who does not pay him for his efforts. Nashe's enemy, Gabriel Harvey, subsequently mocks these efforts "in the rich garden of poor Adonis". The anonymous patron is castigated at length by Nashe and

---

[141] That Gallio is a caricature of Southampton was noted by the Shakespearean scholar, Dr Gregor Sarrazin, in 1895.

described in sarcastic terms suggesting that he is a foppish, dishonourable, under-achieving catamite.

- In late 1592 Nashe is accused by associates of being behind an attack on "Shake-scene", an unqualified actor-author, in terms similar to those he had expressed in *Menaphon*.

- In May or early June 1593 Shakespeare publishes his dedication to Southampton of *Venus & Adonis*. Almost immediately, Nashe produces an offensive parody of that dedication in his own address to Southampton in *The Unfortunate Traveller*. In this parody Nashe mocks Southampton's participation in a triangular relationship involving a poet with an over-rated command of English, and that poet's lover.

- Several years later an anonymous satirist at St John's portrays Nashe and Southampton in a *Parnassus* play. Nashe is depicted as a talented but impoverished writer and Southampton as his despised, niggardly and dishonourable patron, who has a derisible hero-worship of Shakespeare.

Taking all of this into account, it becomes overwhelmingly likely that Shakespeare was the poet in the Southampton love triangle evoked by Nashe, and that the latter was referring to real events, independently portrayed in the Sonnets.

A SEARCH FOR ROSALINE
- EMILIA LANIER -

Over the years several candidates for Shakespeare's dark mistress have been proposed. Most may be eliminated immediately: either because they fall outside the parameters established beyond reasonable doubt in the first section of this book; or because they so badly match the clues provided in the Mistress sonnet sequence. The characteristics we are looking for in Shakespeare's mysterious Rosaline are as follows:

- She is realistically available for a triangular affair with Shakespeare and Southampton around 1592/3 and no later than June 1593 (Appendix B);
- Her hair and eyebrows are jet black (127, 130);
- Her eye colour is dark (127, 130);
- She is probably younger than Shakespeare (138);
- She is probably married (152);
- She is probably a competent musician (128);
- She is promiscuous (135-137, 142) and has been the subject of some previous scandal (131, 150);
- She is probably intelligent and witty (LLL);
- Her beauty is mainly in the heart of her beholder, Shakespeare (131, 141);
- She is no doormat.

The lady concerned may be lost to history. However, there is one candidate of promise, discovered by Rowse in the papers of a quack-astrologer, Simon Forman.

Emilia Bassano, born in 1569, came from a Venetian family of musicians who had served in the English court from the time of Henry VIII. Her mother was apparently English in ancestry. Her father, Baptista, died when she was seven and she later came into the service of Susan, Countess of Kent. She became the mistress of Henry Carey, Lord Hunsdon, who was some forty five years older than her and who, as Lord Chamberlain and first cousin of Queen Elizabeth, was one of the most powerful men in the land.

Hunsdon, according to Forman's notes, had "set her up in great pomp" and maintained her "in great pride" until she came "with child" by him in 1592, whereupon she was married off with a pension to a cousin and musician, Alphonso Lanier, for whom she apparently had little enthusiasm.

Given her family background, Emilia was almost certainly an accomplished musician. She was also a poet: the first Englishwoman to proclaim herself as such. With her artistic interests and court connections, she is likely to have moved in social circles which overlapped with Shakespeare's. Hunsdon, her sugar-daddy until 1592, became the patron of Shakespeare's stage company in 1594.

To date no reliable records of her shade of hair or complexion have emerged, though there are circumstantial indications. According to a modern day descendant of the Bassano family, Peter, two of her cousins, arrested in 1584 for loitering, were described in papers of the offence as "a little black man" and a "tall black man". In the parlance of the time "black" normally meant "black-haired". Her tentatively identified portrait is shown in the Shakespeare section of Peter Bassano's website (http://peterbassano.com/shakespeare) and depicts a woman of pale complexion with a bush of black hair, black brows and dark eyes.

Proponents of Emilia as the dark mistress point to other circumstantial indicators of her identity. A significant number of Shakespeare's plays are set in Italy or have Italian connections, suggesting that he may have been influenced by someone who had projected an Italian background. Also, in *The Merchant of Venice* there is a character named Bassanio; in *Othello, The Moor of Venice*, there is an Emilia; and the father of Katherina, the *Shrew* to be tamed, is Baptista.

Professor Roger Prior has suggested (in an article for the *Financial Times* on 10th October 1987) that Sonnet 150 contains puns on the word "more" (lines 9, 10 and 14) which point to Emilia as the subject. His argument is that the Italian word "moro" indicated both a mulberry bush (which was a heraldic device in the coat of arms of the Bassano family) and Moor, a person of non-European origin.

In his paper, *Emilia Lanier IS the Dark Lady of the Sonnets*, Martin Green draws attention to the more common rendering at that time of her maiden name: Bassany. The latter sounded like the extant French word "basané" meaning swarthy, dark or tanned. Similarly, Bassano sounded like the Italian words, basano and basana meaning dirty or base – or, at a stretch, dark. Green sees either or both associations as part of the reason that the Sonnets make such play with the darkness of the mistress.

This notion is both feasible and attractive, given Shakespeare's fondness for wordplay. Most of the Sonnet allusions to blackness and darkness are not couched in exclusively physical terms, and one only has to envisage a mistress named, instead, Emily Black, in order to appreciate such a possibility.

Green suggests a period of around 1595-7 for composition of most of the Mistress sonnets. However, for his wordplay theory to hold, the Mistress would have needed to be synonymous with "Bassany/Basano" and such characterization for Emilia would have faded after her marriage and change of name to Lanier in 1592. In turn, this points to a prime composition period no later than 1592/3, as established in the first section of this book.

Most of what we know of Emilia comes from her published poems and the casebooks of Forman, whom she consulted from time to time during a period from 1597 to 1600, mainly with regard to the prospects for social advancements.

These sources depict an ambitious, educated woman who had risen from a relatively humble background to the fringes of Court life, dealt with kindly by the Queen, before her entrapment in an unhappy marriage which she saw as below her station.

Forman found her sexually attractive (as he did a number of his female clients) but gives little physical description. He attempted to seduce her and found her willing, in her husband's absence, to entertain him for the night and to allow him to kiss her and fondle all parts of her body. However, she would not then or thereafter permit consummation, a frustration that perhaps led to his later reference to her as a "whore" who "dealt evil" with him.

In those times of unreliable contraception, Forman apparently made little allowance for the threat and difficulties of a pregnancy for which her husband, Alphonso, could not be held responsible. From 1597 the latter spent much time away from Emilia as a gentleman volunteer on military expeditions, apparently in the hope of a knighthood or other advancement in status, as aspired to by his wife. He served on Essex's Azores voyage and Irish campaign, as did Southampton. In fact he was evidently well known to the latter, as illustrated by the following events.

In August 1604, as recorded in the National Archives, Lanier was granted the valuable monopoly of excising London hay and straw imports for twenty years – on the face of it an odd award, given his status as a minor musician and with no record of any noteworthy services to the Crown. However, some light is shed on this matter in a contemporaneous letter to Robert Cecil from Bishop Bancroft, then Bishop of London. In this letter the Bishop promotes the award and says Lanier "was put in good hope of your favour by the Earl of Southampton". Evidently the Earl was supporting Lanier's case and Bancroft had been co-opted by Southampton to add his own endorsement of the grant.

Such benevolence towards a serving musician may have arisen from a friendship forged in shared military campaigns. However, the Earl's motivation might be more realistically explained as a wish to help someone who had been somewhat closer to him in the past: Lanier's wife, Emilia.

Contrary to any other candidates nominated to date, the latter's known attributes fit the profile of Shakespeare's dark mistress without any real strain. Her circumstances can reasonably be projected to encompass the relationships and conduct depicted in the Sonnets (perhaps allowing for some bias or exaggeration from a jealous lover-poet). She moved in circles familiar to Shakespeare, she had similar interests and her reduced station in life was in the reasonable ambit for her wooing by the upwardly mobile showman-poet from Stratford.

What then are the contra-indicators?

The major issue is the timing of events in relation to the triangular affair involving Shakespeare and Southampton, which must have started before Nashe's sarcastic references in June 1593 (Appendix B).

Although Emilia might have been the willing object of worship and attention from the besotted poet before her forced marriage in October 1592, it seems unlikely that there would have been any affair while she was the paramour of Lord Hunsdon. Why would she jeopardize the "great pomp and pride" provided by the Lord Chamberlain for the sake of a comparative yokel whom she did not love?

In addition, her pregnancy by Hunsdon in 1592 which ended their arrangement and forced her marriage to Lanier, would presumably have constrained any inclinations for a consummated affair for a period of some months. Most accounts date the birth of her son, Henry, to "early in 1593" (under modern dating), based, not unreasonably, on a projection of the circumstances and the timing of her marriage in October 1592.

A birth in January 1593 would allow a plausible window of time for the Sonnets' affair to become consummated of, perhaps, two months: March and April (made more feasible if there had been a platonic wooing by Shakespeare over several months before). If, however, the birth was in March or April, the likelihood of such consummation diminishes.

The window of opportunity looks more realistic if, in fact, the initial consummation was with one man only, the Earl of Southampton. The storyline suggested by the Sonnets allows for this possibility: Shakespeare, desperate to advance his prospects with the lady, asks his friend to promote his cause (Sonnet 134). She, seeing a much better prospect in the eligible young lord, seduces him, to the dismay of our hapless poet. Only some time later, probably after she realizes that she is going to get nowhere with the aristocrat, does she relent and allow Shakespeare some limited success.

Nevertheless, the availability of opportunity looks tight, constrained to a greater or lesser extent by the timing of Henry Lanier's birth. I have tried to get better precision for this date with the help of tips from Peter Bassano and a search of the christening records of several prospective churches frequented by the Bassano and Lanier families. However, I was unable to find any relevant record dated within 1592 or 1593.

Henry's absence from likely registers is strange. It occurred to me that, with the support of her aristocratic connections of the time, perhaps Emilia gave birth to Lord Hunsdon's child earlier than convention would have it.

Forman's words, the source for all this reconstruction, are that "being with child she was for colour married to a minstrel [Alphonso Lanier]". These words give little indication as to the timing of the birth: in fact they even allow for Henry to have been born before the marriage to Lanier.

Based on Roger Prior's persuasive analysis of her poems in his paper, *Aemilia Lanyer and Queen Elizabeth at Cookham Prior*, Emilia stayed at, or near, Cookham, Berkshire during the summer of 1592.

Here, it seems, she received great encouragement and support from a number of aristocratic women, including Hunsdon's daughter, Lady Margaret Hoby, and the Queen, herself. Such support was apparently directed in part to her "being with child": not necessarily surprising, given that the father of the child was the Queen's cousin (or, according to some rumours, Elizabeth's illegitimate sibling, born of her mother's sister, but sharing the same father and, hence, grand-parents).

With these thoughts in mind I searched for Henry's christening in the records of churches in the Cookham area. Frustratingly, however, the records of the time for the nearest and most likely church, Holy Trinity, Cookham, have been lost. Nothing emerged from my search of records in other nearby parishes.

If it were to transpire that Henry had been born before Emilia's marriage in October, this would bring forward November 1592 the start of a reasonable window for consummation of the triangular affair. Such timing, in conjunction with the circumstantial evidence and the absence of any other realistic contenders, would point strongly to Emilia as Shakespeare's Rosaline.

Perhaps one day another realistic contender will emerge, or there will be clarification as to the birth date of Henry Lanier. Until then his mother will remain on the short-list of one.

RIVAL OR COLLABORATOR?

Christopher Marlowe, son of a cobbler, was christened in Canterbury on 26 February 1564.

He was educated at King's School, Canterbury and Corpus Christi College, Cambridge, receiving a BA degree in 1584 and his MA in 1587.

His master's degree was awarded only after some unusual intervention by the Queen's Privy Council. The university, apparently disturbed by indications that Marlowe had left permanently for Rheims (location of a Jesuit college which fomented dissidence against the Protestant monarchy in England), were withholding the degree. However, a letter from the Queen's Privy Council, including her chief advisor, William Cecil, Lord Burghley, gave assurance that Marlowe's absence was temporary and in good service of the Queen.

From Cambridge, Marlowe appears to have based himself in London, becoming, for a while, a leading light in the city's exceptional flowering of literary talent at that time. He perfected the art of blank verse, a play-writing style which presents lines in poetic metre (ie with a uniformity of syllable count and regularity of stress) without rhyme.

In the years 1587 through 1593 he wrote several plays, including the hit productions *Tamburlaine the Great, The Famous Tragedy of the Rich Jew of Malta, Edward the Second, Doctor Faustus and The Massacre at Paris.*

Some analysts of style have suggested that he was also a major contributor to some or all of the *Henry VI* plays attributed solely to Shakespeare by the latter's theatrical colleagues. Others, however, explain similarities of style by pointing to the well established phenomenon of "parallelisms" (of which more later).

Marlowe also composed several poems, his two masterpieces being *The Passionate Shepherd to His Love* and *Hero and Leander*. The latter, though not ending in a particularly disjointed fashion, was regarded as unfinished at the time of his death, when it was apparently circulating freely in manuscript form. It was subsequently augmented by George Chapman and printed in its original and extended forms in 1598.

In September 1589, then resident in Shoreditch, London, Marlowe became involved in an argument with an innkeeper, William Bradley. A friend, the poet Thomas Watson, interceding on his behalf, became involved in a sword fight with Bradley, who was killed. Marlowe was cleared by a jury and Watson eventually released on grounds of self-defence.

In January 1592 Marlowe and a goldsmith were arrested in the English garrison town of Flushing in Holland on suspicion of plans to forge counterfeit English coins. Their accuser was an associate, their "chamber fellow", the scholar Richard Baines. It is clear from the surviving letter by the arresting official that he was unconvinced of any crime with regard to the coining and he indicates that Marlowe and Baines, at loggerheads, were accusing each other of the intentions to counterfeit as well as guilt of treason and Catholicism.

Marlowe, Baines and the goldsmith were sent in custody to Lord Burghley, then Lord Treasurer, in England for question, but there is no indication of any consequent punishment. The same letter records that Marlowe claimed to be "very well known" to the Earl of Northumberland and Ferdinando Stanley, Lord Strange.

In May 1592 Marlowe was arrested for "failure to keep the peace" in Shoreditch. The nature of the offence and any consequence are unrecorded.

Robert Greene's posthumous publication, *Groatsworth of Wit* was published in September 1592. In it he urges three unidentified fellow gentlemen playwrights (whom apparently he has known well) to reform their ways. The first of these he addresses as a "famous gracer of tragedians" with "excellent wit", who, he suggests, has followed "Machiavellian policy" (meaning the belief that cruel or immoral deeds are necessary to achieve political goals: interestingly, Marlowe has Machiavelli for his atheistic announcer in his prologue to *The Jew of Malta*). This author, Greene asserts, is an atheist (as once was he) and he urges him to repent of this and to give glory to God. On the basis of his standing at the time and the above clues, most scholars consider the addressee to be Marlowe.

Marlowe was in his family town, Canterbury in September 1592, when he was involved in a dispute with a tailor involving damage to the tailor's property. The case was apparently settled out of court.

His next recorded location was before the Privy Council at Nonsuch Palace, Surrey on 20 May 1593. Here he had been summoned, to account for himself in a matter of unrest against immigrants and possible sedition.

The cause of this was a drive to locate the perpetrators on 5 May of an anonymous, publicly displayed poem and other wall writings (made the previous month), which had attacked and threatened foreign immigrants.

Within the week, and under threatened or actual torture, the poet Thomas Kyd stated that certain manuscript remnants in his possession had been Marlowe's, dating back to a time when the two shared a common writing room.

During this inquisition Kyd declared that Marlowe was an atheist, who thought that the relationship between Jesus and his disciple John was homosexual, and who espoused various other Christian heresies. He also accused him of treason in the form of support for James of Scotland, a pretender at the time to the English throne.

The terms of the Privy Council summons, dated 18 May, required that the arresting officer "repair to the house of Mr Thomas Walsingham in Kent, or any other place where he shall understand where Christopher Marlowe may be remaining, and by virtue hereof to apprehend, and bring him to the Court in his Company".

Thomas Walsingham owned a family estate at Scadbury, near Chislehurst, Kent. His father's cousin, Sir Francis Walsingham, was, until his death in 1590, a member of the Privy Council, Queen Elizabeth's Secretary of State and controller of the government's intelligence network.

There is at least one record suggesting that the younger Walsingham occasionally helped his elder relative in such intelligence matters until the latter's death in 1590. However, subsequently he seems to have confined his activities to local and personal affairs.

According to a dedication in 1598 by Edward Blount (the publisher of the original version of *Hero & Leander*), Walsingham "bestowed many kind favours" on Marlowe in his lifetime, "entertaining the parts of reckoning and worth, which you found in him with good countenance and liberal affection". Walsingham's protégés subsequently included Chapman, who produced an augmented form of *Hero & Leander*.

By 27 May 1593 the Privy Council had obtained evidence from Richard Baines, Marlowe's accuser of the Flushing incident. Baines, in a surviving note in which he claims the support of other honest men, accuses Marlowe of many heresies of opinion on religion, actively communicated in "common speeches" to almost any company. These opinions challenged the authenticity of biblical stories and character depictions, with several denigrations of Jesus, including an assertion that his disciple, John was also his "bed-fellow" and "used" in the manner of the "sinners of Sodom".

Baines also accused Marlowe of converting at least one witness to atheism, of intentions to counterfeit English shillings and of a statement that "all they that love not boys and tobacco are fools".

While on release on bail Marlowe was in Deptford, London on 30 May 1593. Here he was killed, reportedly in self-defence, by Ingram Frizer, an employee of Thomas Walsingham, in the further company of only two other men: Nicholas Skeres and Robert Poley, both previously associated with Sir Francis and Thomas. His killer was exonerated within two days by an inquest of sixteen jurors, chaired by the Coroner of the Queen's Household.

From these facts have emerged many theories. Some do not rely on much in the way of further assumption and are therefore more credible. For example, a good case can be made for Marlowe's death being a deliberate assassination by a government agency he had worked for, instigated by someone unhappy at what he might reveal to the Privy Council under pressure.

However, many conspiracy theories go much further. These hypothesize that Marlowe's death was in fact faked and that he went on to live a life of disguise in which he continued to write the works now attributed to Shakespeare.

These theories are essentially a modern phenomenon. The view in Marlowe's times was that he died in May 1593, though there was a variety of interpretations (mainly associated with his personal habits) as to how exactly his final quarrel arose. The contemporary author(s) of the Parnassus plays (described in the last section of Appendix B) gave the following assessment:

> *"Marlowe was unhappy in his buskined muse.*
> *Alas unhappy in his life and end.*
> *Pity it is that wit so ill should dwell,*
> *Wit lent from heaven, but vices sent from hell."*

In order to assess the credibility of the modern conspiracy theories I sought a reasonable case presentation, readily available to those interested in checking the detail, and settled on Peter Farey's informative and interesting Marlowe website. The latter is a goldmine for anyone interested in Marlowe's works. It also contains helpful detail of original documentation (some of which I have used in arriving at my biographic outline of Marlowe above).

My impression is that Mr Farey is sincere in his pursuit of the truth and has aimed to be objective. I hope, should he ever read this, that he will accept my views below in the same spirit.

In 1955 Calvin Hoffman published his theory of Shakespearean authorship in his book, *The Man Who Was Shakespeare*. An evolved version of this theory, as presented on Farey's website in April 2008, contends that:

- Marlowe's death was faked with the aid of a senior statesman, probably Lord Burghley, for whose secret intelligence service he had worked (Farey shows plausibly how this deception could have been achieved with such aid);
- Marlowe then took on a secret identity and continued intelligence work, probably abroad in the first instance;
- subsequently for a while he adopted an identity in England styled Louis Le Doux, the name of the son of a French

immigrant who grew up at the same time as Marlowe in Canterbury;

- both as Le Doux, working for Anthony Bacon (also involved in intelligence service and the brother of Francis, the philosopher-politician) and under other guises, Marlowe continued to write plays and poems (this aspect of the theory being based on information in Bacon family papers which list articles supposedly associated with Le Doux and pointing to a dual role of spy/author);
- these new literary works of Marlowe were supplied to, and used by Shakespeare under some form of collaboration; stylometric analysis of Shakespeare's works is used in support of this contention;
- the Sonnets were essentially Marlowe's works and can be interpreted to support the theory;
- Marlowe outlived Shakespeare and on the latter's death encoded hints of their collaboration in the wording of Shakespeare's monument.

Arising from the above, however, numerous queries, inconsistencies and/or uncertainties arise. My objective in articulating some of these below is not to deny outright the possibility of the matters theorized; rather it is to give a sense of the likelihood of their occurrence, given the necessity for further assumptions to support the scenario proposed and the availability of simpler alternative explanations.

First then, if it was necessary to fake Marlowe's death then some, at least, of the evidence against him was sufficient to convict Marlowe and/or to endanger his sponsor-statesman. Why would that statesman compound his own risk by both thwarting due process and leaving Marlowe alive? Marlowe, on his history, had a personality associated with provocation of attention, and politicians are not usually altruistic to the point of dismissing personal risk. Farey deals with this by bringing the Queen, herself, into the conspiracy – at which point one has to ask why, if she was content with Marlowe's innocence should such a convoluted charade be necessary?

Farey demonstrates convincingly that that there was unlikely to have been any Louis Le Doux in England other than the one who grew up in the same town as Marlowe. But why would Marlowe (and, by extension, his sponsor statesman) take on the extra risks of unwanted curiosity and discovery through his assumption of such an alter ego rather than a fictitious identity? And what are the odds that the statesman would entertain such risk by allowing the well known Marlowe to come back to England under any identity?

A chest attributed to Le Doux, and its contents at the time of a subsequent listing, are recorded in the Bacon papers. The contents listed can be construed as consistent with intelligence activities as well as literary material of the sort that a Marlowe/Shakespeare would be interested in. For example, they include several works by Francis Bacon. However, such contents would be equally, if not more relevant to the Bacon household and Farey candidly admits in a separate section of his website that there is evidence to suggest that only the chest had belonged to Le Doux.

On literary output, why would Marlowe take, or be allowed to take the risk of public use of his material, especially under the name of someone supposed by conspiracy theorists to have such limited writing ability? How long would such subterfuge deceive contemporaries with a much deeper knowledge of the times and who knew Marlowe and Shakespeare and their writing styles and abilities?

As regards stylometric analysis, Farey starts with a methodology invented by the scientist, Mendenhall at the end of the nineteenth century, as highlighted by Hoffman. This approach establishes the frequency of appearance of different word lengths, as measured by the number of letters per word, to create a distribution profile for selected works from each author's output.

By comparing a selected Shakespearean profile to ones selected for various other authors Farey concludes that the best match by far is that between an early Shakespeare selection and a late Marlowe one. However, as of April 2008 neither his website nor Hoffman's original publication provided sufficient detail to allow proper assessments of the assumptions underlying the selection of authored works or the projection of results into the conclusions drawn.

Nevertheless, it is apparent that the approach contains a bias towards achieving the proclaimed conclusion. Most of the authors identified in Farey's comparison wrote in a different age, in an evolved or devolved form of English, without the constraints of blank or rhyming verse, for a different purpose, in a different medium of communication (for example, novels) and for a different sort of audience. Tellingly, the only selection results disclosed for works by an author who probably had a similar writing environment, Thomas Middleton, produces a profile whose overall correspondence is extremely close to those of the Shakespearean and Marlovian selections.

In a second stylometric approach Farey goes on to examine the use of "function words" (comprising short connector words such as but, by, with, to) under a methodology previously applied by Professor Gary Taylor. Using this approach the latter had concluded that the Marlowe of *Tamburlaine* could not have written the plays of Shakespeare. Farey objects that this conclusion ignores the possibility of a change in authorial style by Marlowe over the years. He suggests that such a change can be discerned in vocabulary trends.

An obvious way of assessing a trend in the usage of function words by a particular author would be to establish the frequency of use of each function word in successive works of that author over a period of years.

However, this data is not offered. Instead Farey uses an approach, whose justification I could not find, in which the number of function words whose frequency declines over a period is divided by the number of function words whose frequency increases. This fraction is calculated for successive works and plotted over a timescale, supposedly to indicate a trend.

The logic for this approach is unclear since the ratio of two such totals gives no information on what is actually happening in the underlying language. Furthermore, because the numerator in the ratio should decline over time (by definition) and the denominator should increase (also by definition), the result should presumably always be a downward sloping line on the graph. However, Farey's graphs contain an upslope in part, suggesting inconsistencies internal to his methodology.

Farey applies a similar approach to an analysis of the frequency of individual letter usage. However, again the data is presented only as a ratio: in this case of numbers of decreasingly used letters to numbers of increasingly used letters. Consequently the same uncertainties apply.

Better information emerges from Farey's analysis of the frequency of use of run-on lines and feminine endings in verse by Marlowe and Shakespeare. The data is presented straightforwardly and shows a low, fluctuating frequency of use by Marlowe and a higher, steadily increasing use by Shakespeare.

Farey sees this as evidence that these characteristics of Shakespeare's style of verse are in line with a projection from a Marlovian base. However, in their works dated to the same period Shakespeare's frequency measures are nearly twice those of Marlowe's, and there is little in the latter's fluctuating frequency measures which would project the significant and sustained increase shown in Shakespeare's measures.

In none of these statistical analyses was there any indication that the methodology had been subject to assessment by experts on linguistics and statistics. Further, one can find other studies which produce contrary conclusions.

For example, there is a paper presented by Ward Elliott and Robert Valenza of Claremont McKenna College, on the website, shakespeareauthorship.com (as of April 2008). This paper records the results from a three year study to see how closely 58 claimed "true authors" matched Shakespeare's style. Amongst these results they conclude that none of Marlowe, Bacon or Oxford came out anywhere near Shakespeare.

Farey concludes his analysis of style by noting the many similarities of phrase in the works of the two men. However, Shakespeare, in a common practice of the time, demonstrably borrowed from other authors. Gibson, in his *The Shakespeare Claimants*, deals comprehensively with this issue of parallelisms, as he terms them, and shows that they were a natural and widespread feature of Elizabethan literature. Indeed, Gibson implies that there are as many parallelisms between Bacon and Shakespeare as there are between Shakespeare and Marlowe. I would add only the thought that if Shakespeare showed a preponderance of imitation of the pre-eminent playwright of the day, this would hardly be surprising.

The latter thought offers another dimension to the question of writing style changes. Why would the style of an established and acclaimed author (such as Marlowe was in 1593) change so markedly? Such changes would be more plausible in an author whose development had lagged (perhaps due to a less congenial apprenticeship) and who had previously been imitating the best in his field in an attempt to survive. The style of such an author would almost certainly evolve significantly as success and self-confidence allowed him to follow his own muse.

Farey's interpretation of the Sonnets to justify the conspiracy theory is unconvincing (as was Hoffman's). Although claimed as a support to Marlowe's biography rather than Shakespeare's, there is little to support this contention. Excerpts from some sonnets are offered without the context of a comprehensive framework (such as described in Parts I and II of this book) and no theories are offered as to the identity of the Rival Poet or to support the triangular relationship involving Fair Friend and Dark Mistress.

The last significant indicator offered by Farey is the wording on the monument to Shakespeare which stands near his grave in Stratford. The monument was commissioned after the poet's burial and paid for from an unidentified source. The wording, on a straightforward reading, appears both clumsy to a modern eye and to make an invitation to the reader to pause a while and think more deeply.

Accordingly many commentators have spent much time analyzing the words and seeking an encoded message hidden therein. Farey has, with some elegance, extracted such a message, to the effect that a surviving Marlowe was the brains behind works which Shakespeare merely polished up.

In essence, Farey assumes a cross-reference in the script to a word in the nearby grave epitaph, a synonym of which he imports into the monument wording. He then substitutes the word "cost" in the monument wording with "ley", an archaic word meaning bill or tax, and searches for an anagram of any of the variants of Marlowe's name, arriving at "Christofer Marley". The ambiguous wording in the remainder of the script is then interpreted to derive the hidden message.

Using some of the same technique, I was able quickly to derive the name "Hal Wriothesley" instead. This anagram is extracted from a whole line of script, rather than the more condensed group of letters used by Farey and in this sense he could reasonably argue that his derivation is more plausible.

However, my anagram is based on equally plausible "clue instructions" within the monument script and does not require any importation of letters or synonyms from the grave epitaph. I can then interpret the remainder of the script as a cry that a part of Southampton, the living inspiration for the poet's works, has died with his friend.

I should say that I am not here promoting a theory that Southampton was involved with the monument. Rather, I am testing the notion that various "hidden meanings" can be extracted from a text, depending on what one is predisposed to find. Supporters of Oxford and Bacon as Shakespeare have also claimed that the monument encodes evidence supporting the primacy of their man.

The content of this appendix is directed at the known facts of Marlowe's life and some of the many uncertainties associated with the theory that he was the author of Shakespeare's works. There is much to suggest that his death was politically contrived. There is, however, no substance to the argument that he composed the Sonnets.

HUES IN ALL THEIR HEWS

In Sonnet 20, line 7 appears a phrase, shown in most modern reproductions as "*A man in hue, all hues in his controlling*": a small line which has triggered a disproportionate number of words in debate as to what Shakespeare meant by it.

Rowse interpreted it as "A man in complexion, all complexions at his command", but I think that this sheds little, if any, further light for most readers. Other conventional interpretations also seem incomplete to me.

In the original 1609 Quarto publication the line was printed: "A man in hew all *Hews* in his controwling (sic)". The second "hew" (or "hue" in the modern spelling) had an upper case first letter and the whole word was italicised. Presumably Shakespeare had indicated (through italicisation or otherwise in his script) that the second "hue" was to be understood as carrying a different or additional meaning to that of the first "hue" and this was the printer's way of indicating this subtlety.

This combination of an initial letter in upper case with overall italicisation occurs in the Sonnets some twenty five times, spread over a variety of words. Some of these are in line with convention for the time for classical character names (such as *Cupid* or *Philomel*) or technical terms imported from Latin (such as *Audite, Quietus and Interim*).

The same convention is extended to *Will*, where clearly a pun on the author's name is intended (Sonnets **135**, **136**, **143**) and to *Rose* (in Sonnet **1**, where a link with the youth's name probably applied). However, it is not immediately clear why the convention has been applied to certain other words: *Hews* (**20**), *Statues* (**55**), *Alien* (**78**), *Satire* (**100**), *Autumn* (**104**), *Heretic* (**124**), *Informer* (**125**).

Perhaps some private double meaning was intended for "*Hews*". Possibly this was a nickname or represented a pun of some sort relevant to the close circle of the sonnet's addressee. Some have speculated that Shakespeare was encoding clues to the addressee's identity and they have produced detailed analyses of the frequency, supposedly unusual, of the letters h, e, w and s throughout the sonnet.

One of the name theories draws on the WH initials of Thorpe's sonnet dedication, the Hews of this sonnet and the Will in many of the Dark Mistress sonnets to postulate that the fair youth was named William Hughes. This theory was initiated by one Thomas Tyrwhitte (1730-86) and has been embellished over the years, notably by Oscar Wilde, whose essay on the subject suggested that William Hughes was a boy actor who played female roles in many of Shakespeare's early plays (only males were allowed to act in Shakespeare's time).

I doubt these name theories. I suggest that the word "hew" was indeed being used in a way equivalent to "complexion", but with the latter's extended sense of "nature" and/or "character".

However, I think that the plural "*Hews*", with its original printing as a proper noun in italics, indicated that men and women were being represented by the word, rather than the plural of an inanimate quality.

Consequently, my interpretation of the line in prose is "A man who has manly attributes and who is able to charm people of each sex and every ilk, and bend them to his will".

I further suggest that this interpretation is reinforced by the poem, *A Lover's Complaint*, published with the Sonnets (as described in the commentary to Sonnet 14). This poem describes a beautiful young effeminate-looking man, who sounds remarkably similar to the fair youth of the Sonnets. In Verse 19 it says:

> *"That he did in the general bosom reign*
> *Of young, of old, and sexes both enchanted,*
> *To dwell with him in thoughts, or to remain*
> *In personal duty, following where he haunted:*
> *Consents bewitch'd, ere he desire, have granted,*
> *And dialogued for him what he would say,*
> *Ask'd their own wills and made their wills obey."*

Some may challenge my extension of the meaning of "hue" to an equivalent of "character" or "nature" on the grounds that this represents a development of the word which had not yet arisen in

Shakespeare's time. According to the Oxford English Dictionary, the word at that time denoted either "form, aspect" or "external appearance of the face". I suggest that the first of these definition sets is actually rather close to my interpretation and that Shakespeare, a master of stretched meanings, would not himself have shrunk from such an application.

Looked at from another angle, however, the word "hew" also meant "carve" or "hack" (as it does today). Shakespeare uses the word in this sense in *Julius Caesar* (II, i, 196). A human can be regarded poetically as a carving of Mother Nature (indeed, I have applied this analogy in my interpretation of the last quatrain of this same Sonnet 20). From here it is but a small jump of shorthand to describing a human who is manly in attributes as being "a man in hew" and humans of every conceivable attribute as being "all *Hews*" (applying the above convention of personalisation).

This reasoning reinforces the probability that the unexplained italicisations appearing in certain other sonnets (as mentioned above) are also indicative of a stretching of conventional meaning, by way of personalisation, pun or otherwise.

In my modernisation of Sonnet 20 I have tried to replicate Shakespeare's poetic shorthand and doubling up of a word in the relevant line, while conveying my above-derived interpretation and retaining the generality of information in the original second quatrain. The constraints of the sonnet format and my own limitations have forced me to shuffle the order of some of the lines.

A further consequence of these limitations was the loss of the so-called feminine format (which includes an extra unstressed syllable at the end of each line) used by Shakespeare (almost certainly deliberately, given the subject) throughout this sonnet. This also happened on my re-jigging of the final quatrain, done mainly to regain rhyme under modern pronunciations. It would have been relatively easy to have kept the feminine format in the opening quatrain, but in the end I opted for a re-working of all three quatrains into conventional ten syllable lines.

WHO THREW HATE AWAY?

Many commentators support the notion that Sonnet 145 refers to the poet's wife, Anne Shakespeare, rather than to his dark mistress, who is the only female lover distinguishable in all the other sonnets.

The theory arises from the words "hate away" in the penultimate line, which, it has been suggested, represents a deliberate play on Anne's maiden surname, Hathaway. The argument is then extended by pointing to the eight syllable format of the sonnet's lines (unique within this collection, though not generally) and a perception of overall poor quality, supposedly consistent with the immature talents of a teenage, unmarried Shakespeare.

The theory of a pre-1583 date of composition is not inconsistent with the route to publication established in Part I of this book. The poem could have been copied to Southampton in response to curiosity aroused from conversation with Shakespeare. It would then have been filed in the secondary sequence, maintained separately by the Earl because its contents had other addressees or were of lesser interest to him.

However, this theory of composition date is weakened by the format of the poem, with its three quatrains and a concluding couplet, all constructed in accordance with Shakespeare's standard sonnet rhyming convention. Shakespeare, for all his talent was not an innovator and this form of poem only became popular in England after the publication in 1591 of Sydney's *Astrophel and Stella*.

Given this doubt, let us assess the probability that a pun on "Hathaway" was intentional and whether there was any real significance to the line structure of eight syllables.

First, what are the chances of the two words "hate" and "away" appearing together, in the absence of an intended pun?

The theme and flow of the poem dictate that the punchline has to end with "not you" and this would have been the foundation stone in Shakespeare's construction of the final couplet. The penultimate line, therefore, has to rhyme with "you", as well as convey the sense that hate has been defused.

Immediately, one is confronted with an acute shortage of amenable end words. Candidates which spring readily to mind include "blew", "threw", "drew", "flew", all of which, however, are strongly associated with "away" in the necessary context of elimination or diffusion.

It is possible to avoid "hate" and/or "away" (as in my modernised version), but only at the cost of poetic resonance lost. In these circumstances it seems to me that the use of these words in close connection becomes highly probable, without any intention of a pun, poor to the ear or otherwise.

Second, how relevant is the non-standard syllable count and supposedly poor quality of the poem?

There are two other sonnets of non-standard construction (99 and 126) and plenty which fall far below Shakespeare's peak, but no evidence to suggest that they go outside the main relationship themes of the Sonnets. Furthermore, Thurio's sonnet in *The Two Gentlemen of Verona (IV, ii)* is composed in seven syllable lines. It is designed to be sung to a tune and this may also have been the intention for Sonnet 145.

On the face of it, then, the internal features of this sonnet are neither definitive nor conducive to identification of its subject.

On the other hand, there is no real problem in construing the poem as a reference to Shakespeare's dark mistress, in line with surrounding sonnets. It shows the kind side of her apparently complex nature, as referred to in a number of the other sonnets (though ultimately disparaged by Shakespeare), and it fits the general picture of a woman who was not in love with the poet, but was disposed at times to accommodate him.

A CLOSER LOOK AT MR. WH

William Hervey (pronounced "Harvey") was born around 1565 in Kidbrooke, Kent. As a young military man he distinguished himself in the defeat of the Spanish Armada in 1588, having boarded one of the enemy galleons and killed its captain in personal combat.

He subsequently served under Robert Devereux, Earl of Essex (as did the latter's acolyte, Henry Wriothesley, Earl of Southampton) when he further distinguished himself as a ship commander in the Cadiz expedition of 1596, for which he was invested as a knight by Essex. The following year he served as a ship commander in the expedition to the Azores also led by Essex.

Hervey became well acquainted with Southampton as, after an affair apparently started in 1596, he finally wed the Earl's mother in January 1599. The Countess Mary was some thirteen years older than Hervey and had been widowed for the second time in 1595. Their nuptials, long expected by at least one social commentator, were probably delayed by resistance from Southampton, whose feelings of 'discomfort and discontentment' at the prospect were conveyed to the Countess by Essex in November 1598.

In 1599 Hervey may have fought in the Irish campaign led by Essex (with Southampton in tow). In 1601, retired from active service, he became for a brief time a Member of Parliament (for Horsham).

Around this time he was apparently a friend, or at least a trusted acquaintance of a neighbour, Brian Annesley, for in 1600 Annesley named him as an executor of his will. Annesley was a gentryman from Kidbrooke in Kent, and had held the posts Master of the Harriers and Warden of the Fleet Prison under Queen Elizabeth's regime.

The bulk of Annesley's estate under his will was left to his youngest daughter, Cordell, who still lived with him (his two older daughters having married). In 1603, with Annesley becoming senile, representatives of his eldest daughter commenced proceedings designed to take control of his assets. These were successfully resisted by Cordell, as was an attempt to contest the will in 1604 after Annesley died. It appears that Hervey, as executor, aided her in these events, which were a matter of some public interest.

In 1604 Hervey became Member of Parliament for Petersfield, a position he held until 1611. In 1607 the Dowager Countess of Southampton died, and under her will, which passed probate in November, he inherited all her chattels and possessions not specifically designated to other legatees. Many of these derived from a brief second marriage of the Countess to a wealthy gentleman, Sir Thomas Heneage who had died in 1596, within two years of their marriage.

Three months after probate, in February 1608, Hervey married Cordell Annesley, by whom he went on to have three sons and three daughters, and through whom he acquired the bulk of the Annesley family estate which he had helped her to secure in 1604.

Ultimately, after further distinguished governmental service and honours in Ireland, he became a peer of England as Baron Hervey of Kidbrooke. He also retained strong links with the navy, serving as rear-admiral in an expedition of 1627 as well as in various high councils or committees. He died in 1642, surviving his wife by six years.

There is an interesting link between Hervey and Shakespeare via Cordell Annesley, as first pointed out by G.M. Young in 1948 and later developed by various commentators, including Katherine Duncan-Jones. In her *Ungentle Shakespeare* she describes in some detail the parallels between Shakespeare's *King Lear* and the Annesley family.

In *Lear*, an old story pre-dating Shakespeare, the king has three daughters. The two eldest are depicted as money-grubbing crawlers who turn on their father after inheriting his wealth; the youngest, Cordelia, loves her father but is disinherited on a misunderstanding of her too-plainly expressed love.

The resemblance of this situation (involving the inheritance of three daughters) to that of the Annesleys was a coincidence. So was the name of the youngest daughter, Cordelia, by which name Cordell Annesley was also known. However, Shakespeare in his re-writing of the Lear story introduced new elements which suggest that he had noticed the parallels and was reinforcing them. The most obvious of these was his depiction of a Lear going mad or senile, an element of the story which had not previously existed.

There are other subtle new parallels within the script, described by Duncan-Jones, who believes that the Annesley case was the immediate trigger for reviving an old work and for Shakespeare's radical re-writing. The play, in its Shakespearean form was first performed in December 1607, just before Cordell's marriage to Hervey.

SOURCES & BIBLIOGRAPHY

Akrigg, G.P.V., *Shakespeare & the Earl of Southampton*. London: Hamish Hamilton, 1968

Anonymous, *The Returne from Parnassus – Part 1*. c 1599. Website: http://ia331302.us.archive.org/0/items/pilgrimagetoparn00macr uoft/pilgrimagetoparn00macruoft.pdf (as of April 2008)

Bate, J., *The Genius of Shakespeare*. London: Picador, 1997

Bryson, B., *Shakespeare*. London: Harper Perennial, 2008

Butler, M., *Jonson's Folio and the Politics of Patronage*. Detroit: Wayne State University Press, Criticism Journal, Summer 1993

Duncan-Jones, K., *Shakespeare's Sonnets*. London: Thomas Nelson and Sons, 1997

Duncan-Jones, K., *Ungentle Shakespeare*, London: Arden Shakespeare, 2001

Edmondson and Wells, *Shakespeare's Sonnets*. 2004

Farey, P., *Marlowe Page*, Website (as of April 2008): www2.prestel.co.uk/rey/index.htm

Fogle, F.R., *A Critical Study of William Drummond of Hawthornden*. New York: Kings Crown Press, 1952

Gibson, H.N., *The Shakespeare Claimants*, London: Methuen & Co, 1962

Green, Martin, *Emilia Lanier IS the Dark Lady of the Sonnets*, English Studies – Amsterdam: Vol 87, No. 5, October 2006, PP 544-576, British Library

Greene, R, *Menaphon*. London: 1589. Website, April 2008: www.oxford-shakespeare.com/new_files_jan_07/Menaphon.pdf

Greene, R., *Groatsworth of Wit*. London, 1592. Website, April 2008: www2.prestel.co.uk/rey/groats.htm

Hamilton, C., *In Search of Shakespeare: A Study of the Poet's Life and Handwriting*. London: Robert Hale, 1986

Harris, F., *The Man Shakespeare*, website (as of April 2008): www.fullbooks.com/The-Man-Shakespeare.html

Hoffman, C., *The Man Who Was Shakespeare*. London: Max Parrish, 1955

Kokeritz, H., *Shakespeare's Pronunciation*. New Haven and London: Yale University Press, 1966

Ledger, G.R., *Shakespeare's Sonnets*, Website, April 2008: www.shakespeares-sonnets.com. Oxford: Oxquarry Books, 2008

McKay, B., *Scientific Refutation of the Bible Codes*. Website, April 2008: cs.anu.edu.au/~bdm/codes/torah.html

Mitchell, J., *Who Wrote Shakespeare?*. London: Thames and Hudson, 1996

Nashe, T., *Pierce Pennilesse*. London: 1592. Website, April 2008: www.uoregon.edu/~rbear/nashe1.html, , University of Oregon

Nashe, T., *The Unfortunate Traveller*. London: 1594. Website, April 2008: www.oxford-shakespeare.com/drk/new_files_nov_29/ The_Unfortunate_Travelle_34.pdf

Nashe, T., *Christ's Teares*. London: 1594. Website, April 2008: www.preteristarchive.com/Books/pdf/1593_nash_christs-tears. pdf

Nashe, T., *The Terrors of the Night*. London: 1594. Website, April 2008: www.oxford-shakespeare.com/drk/new_files_nov_29 /Terrors_of_the_Night_15_30.pdf

Nicholl, C., *The Reckoning*, London, Jonathan Cape, 1992

Nolen, J. with Bate, S., *Shakespeare's Face*. Toronto: A.A. Knopf, 2002

Oxford Dictionary of National Biography

Prior, R., *Aemilia Lanyer and Queen Elizabeth at Cookham Prior, Cahiers Elisabethains 63*, April 2003, British Library

Riggs, D., *The World of Christopher Marlowe*, New York, Henry Holt & Co, 2005

Rowse, A.L., *Shakespeare's Sonnets*. London: Macmillan, 1984

Rowse, A.L., *Discovering Shakespeare*. London: Weidenfeld and Nicolson, 1989

Sage and Ruddiman, *The Works of William Drummond of Hawthornden*. 1711, British Library

Shakespeare, W., *Venus & Adonis*, 1593: from *Shakespeare: The Complete Works*, J.M. Dent & Sons

Shapiro, J., *1599: A Year in the Life of William Shakespeare*, London: Faber and Faber, 2005

Schoenbaum, S., *Shakespeare's Lives*, Oxford University Press, 1970

Stopes, C.C., *The Life of Henry, Earl of Southampton, Shakespeare's Patron*. Cambridge University Press, 1922

Weis, R., *Shakespeare Revealed: A Biography*, London: John Murray, 2007

Wilson, I., *Shakespeare: the Evidence*, London, Headline, 1993

Woods, Susanne, *Lanyer: A Renaissance Woman Poet*, New York & Oxford, Oxford University Press, 1999